D1230229

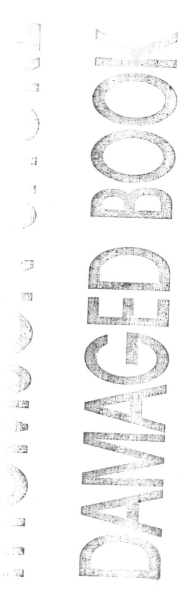

DAMAGED BOOK

Freedom and Tradition in Hegel

Georg Wilhelm Friedrich Hegel ( 1770 – 1831 )

Courtesy of Art and Visual Materials, Special Collections Department,
Harvard Law School Library

# Freedom and Tradition in Hegel

Reconsidering Anthropology, Ethics, and Religion

**THOMAS A. LEWIS**

University of Notre Dame Press

Notre Dame, Indiana

*Library of Congress Cataloging-in-Publication Data*

Lewis, Thomas A.
Freedom and tradition in Hegel : reconsidering anthropology, ethics, and religion /
Thomas A. Lewis.
p.  cm.
Includes bibliographical references (p.      ) and index.
ISBN 0-268-03368-4 (cloth : alk. paper)
1. Hegel, Georg Wilhelm Friedrich, 1770–1831. Vorlesungen über die Philosophie des
Geistes.   2. Liberty.   3. Tradition (Philosophy)   4. Ethics.   5. Religion—Philosophy.
6. Philosophical anthropology.   I. Title.
B2944.V683L49      2005
193—dc22
2005002503

*For my father*

# Contents

# Acknowledgments

I owe an immense debt of gratitude to many more people than I can name here. I first began exploring many of the questions driving this book while working with John P. Reeder, Jr., at Brown University. He continues to be a vital source of critical feedback, support, and wisdom. At Stanford University, Lee Yearley shaped my interest in the significance of philosophical anthropology for ethics. With consistently penetrating comments, he challenged me to explore these issues in a variety of thinkers and to connect them to my work on Hegel. Van Harvey was an irreplaceable source of discerning commentary as well as a superb teacher of nineteenth- and twentieth-century religious thought. Debates with him continue to provide my model of intellectual engagement. I am profoundly grateful to these two individuals, from whom I continue to learn so much. During my time at Stanford, I also profited greatly from courses and conversations with Alice Bach, Rudy Busto, Arnold Eisen, Timothy P. Jackson, Debra Satz, Brent Sockness, and Eckart Förster—in whose course I began to appreciate Hegel.

My understanding of Hegel was profoundly enriched by work with Walter Jaeschke and Michael Theunissen at the Freie Universität zu Berlin. They were generous in meeting with me at length, allowing me to visit their courses, and reading drafts. Professor Jaeschke first directed my attention to the *Vorlesungen über die Philosophie des Geistes*. Most importantly, they have served as exemplars of what it means to study Hegel.

My colleagues at the University of Iowa supported the project with advice and enthusiasm. Diana Cates and David Klemm were not only outstanding conversation partners but also models of excellent scholars who are also good human beings. My students taught me about Hegel and much else; I am extremely grateful to them. An Old Gold Fellowship from the University of Iowa allowed me to spend the summer of 2000 back in Berlin working on the manuscript.

A year as a visiting fellow at the Center for the Study of Religion at Princeton University provided an ideal setting in which to complete substantive revisions to the manuscript. Jeffrey Stout was influential in shaping the project well before then. During that year he provided not only outstanding conversation and feedback but also invaluable counsel. I am deeply grateful for his careful reading of the manuscript. Cornel West provided inspiration as well as insightful responses to drafts of core chapters. Eric Gregory, Rolf-Peter Horstmann, Timothy P. Jackson, John Kelsay, and J. B. Schneewind each made important contributions to the project.

Conversations with new colleagues at Harvard University have played a crucial role in the final shaping of the book. I am particularly indebted to Francis Schüssler Fiorenza, David Hall, and David Lamberth.

I am grateful to Stephen Crites and an anonymous reader for the University of Notre Dame Press, as well as to the Press's editorial staff. David Charles was meticulous and thorough in checking my citations and translations.

Finally, a special thanks to Antonia Kastendiek, James Murdoch, Stephen Wilson, Mark Berkson, Jonathan Schofer, Aaron Stalnaker, and the Hegel *Arbeitsgruppe*, especially Miriam Wildenauer and Olivia Mitscherlich. Without the help of Giles Milhaven and Stanley Wiggs many years ago, this work would have never been started. I feel gratitude of a higher order to my mother and sister. For sound judgment, critical advice, and steady support, I am more grateful than I can express to Despina Stratigakos.

# Primary Texts

In citing Hegel, I have made use of previously published translations when available yet have altered these as I have deemed appropriate. Because these alterations are at points extensive, I have not noted them; I therefore take final responsibility for the translations.

Except as otherwise noted, texts are cited by the page number in the German text followed by a slash and the page number in the English translation if available. Within quotations, italics are Hegel's unless otherwise noted.

*BP*        *The Berlin Phenomenology.* Translated by Michael J. Petry. Bilingual ed. Dordrecht and Boston: Reidel, 1981.

"ERB"    "Über die englische Reformbill." In *Werke 11*, 83–128.

        "The English Reform Bill." In *Hegel's Political Writings*, 295–330. Translated by T. M. Knox. Oxford: Clarendon Press, 1964.

*Enz.*      *Enzyklopädie der philosophischen Wissenschaften (1830). Werke 8–10.* Cited by paragraph (§) number. Remarks are indicated by an "A" [*Anmerkung*] and additions by a "Z" [*Zusatz*].

        *The Encyclopaedia Logic: Part I of the Encyclopaedia of Philosophical Sciences with the Zusätze.* Translated by T. F. Geraets, W. A. Suchting, and H. S. Harris. Indianapolis: Hackett, 1991.

        *Hegel's Philosophy of Nature.* Translated by Michael J. Petry. 3 vols. London; New York: George Allen and Unwin and Humanities Press, 1970.

        *Hegel's Philosophy of Mind: Being Part Three of the Encyclopaedia of Philosophical Sciences (1830).* Translated by William Wallace and A. V. Miller. Oxford: Clarendon Press, 1971.

GW       *Gesammelte Werke.* Rheinisch-Westfälische Akademie der Wissenschaften. Hamburg: Felix Meiner Verlag, 1968–.

PhG      *Phänomenologie des Geistes. Werke 3.*

        *Phenomenology of Spirit.* Translated by A. V. Miller. Oxford: Oxford University Press, 1977.

PR       *Grundlinien der Philosophie des Rechts. Werke 7.* Cited by paragraph (§) number. Remarks are indicated by an "A" [*Anmerkung*], additions by a "Z" [*Zusatz*], and Hegel's marginal notes by an "N."

        *Elements of the Philosophy of Right.* Translated by H. B. Nisbet. Edited by Allen W. Wood. Cambridge: Cambridge University Press, 1991.

PSS      *Hegel's Philosophy of Subjective Spirit.* Translated by Michael J. Petry. 3 vols. Bilingual ed. Dordrecht and Boston: Reidel, 1978.

RphI     *Vorlesungen über Naturrecht und Staatswissenschaft.* Edited by C. Becker et al. Vorlesungen, vol. 1. Hamburg: Felix Meiner Verlag, 1983. Cited by paragraph (§) number.

        *Lectures on Natural Right and Political Science.* Translated by J. Michael Stewart and Peter C. Hodgson. Berkeley and Los Angeles: University of California Press, 1995.

Rph II    *Vorlesungen über Rechtsphilosophie: 1818–1831.* Edited by Karl-Heinz Ilting. Vol. 1. Stuttgart-Bad Cannstatt: Frommann-Holzboog, 1973.

Rph III   *Philosophie des Rechts: Die Vorlesung von 1819/20 in einer Nachschrift.* Edited by Dieter Henrich. Frankfurt am Main: Suhrkamp, 1983.

Rph V    *Vorlesungen über Rechtsphilosophie: 1818–1831.* Edited by Karl-Heinz Ilting. Vol. 3. Stuttgart-Bad Cannstatt: Frommann-Holzboog, 1974.

Rph VI   *Vorlesungen über Rechtsphilosophie: 1818–1831.* Edited by Karl-Heinz Ilting. Vol. 4. Stuttgart-Bad Cannstatt: Frommann-Holzboog, 1974.

VG       *Die Vernunft in der Geschichte.* Vol. 1 of *Vorlesungen über die Philosophie der Weltgeschichte.* Edited by Johannes Hoffmeister. 6th ed. Hamburg: Felix Meiner Verlag, 1994.

*Lectures on the Philosophy of World History: Introduction: Reason in History.* Translated by H. B. Nisbet. Cambridge: Cambridge University Press, 1975.

VGP   *Vorlesungen über die Geschichte der Philosophie. Werke 18–20.*

*Lectures on the History of Philosophy.* Translated by E. S. Haldane and Frances H. Simson. 3 vols. Lincoln and London: University of Nebraska Press, 1995.

VPG   *Vorlesungen über die Philosophie der Geschichte. Werke 12.*

*The Philosophy of History.* Translated by J. Sibree. Revised ed. New York: Willey Book Company, 1944.

VPGst   *Vorlesungen über die Philosophie des Geistes.* Edited by Franz Hespe and Burkhard Tuschling. Vorlesungen, vol. 13. Hamburg: Felix Meiner Verlag, 1994.

VPR   *Vorlesungen über die Philosophie der Religion.* Edited by Walter Jaeschke. Vorlesungen, vols. 3–5. Hamburg: Felix Meiner Verlag, 1983–85.

*Lectures on the Philosophy of Religion.* Translated by R. F. Brown, P. C. Hodgson, and J. M. Stewart. Edited by Peter C. Hodgson. 3 vols. Berkeley and Los Angeles: University of California Press, 1984–87.

Werke   *Werke.* Edited by Eva Moldenhauer and Karl Markus Michel. 20 vols. Frankfurt am Main: Suhrkamp, 1969–71.

WL   *Wissenschaft der Logik. Werke 5–6.*

*Hegel's Science of Logic.* Translated by A. V. Miller. Atlantic Highlands, NJ: Humanities Press, 1969.

# Introduction

For Hegel, "progress in the consciousness of freedom" constitutes the central motif of world history (*VG* 63/54). An emphasis on subjective freedom is, according to him, the hallmark of the modern era, crucial to distinguishing it from the ancient world. Simultaneously, however, he claims that freedom consists in adherence to the reigning mores of the epoch, conceives of education as a process of stripping away particularity, and can appear to call for conformism and to repress or deny individuality. Hegel seeks to weave these multiple elements and concerns together through a conception of freedom that—on one hand—takes seriously the import of historical tradition and stresses our embeddedness within a particular historical situation, while—on the other—prizing autonomy, subjectivity, and reason. His theory therefore unites perspectives that are often viewed as diametrically opposed: modern concerns about individual freedom and attention to the sense of unity and social integration that many believe the modern world has undermined. The result is a conception of freedom that is notoriously difficult to grasp. Though Hegel's conception of freedom differs significantly from those of many thinkers more squarely within the Western liberal tradition, his work remains one of the preeminent confrontations with the issues of freedom, community, and tradition that continue to be central to ethical, political, and religious thought today.

In Hegel's complex conception of freedom—particularly his reconciliation of tendencies that are often viewed as incompatible—his philosophical anthropology plays a fundamental role. Without proper attention to this anthropology, Hegel's claims of reconciliation easily appear as either empty assertions or rhetorical varnish concealing a totalitarian agenda. Addressing these challenges to interpreting Hegel, this book provides a systematic account of his philosophical anthropology and then analyzes its significance for his ethical, political, and religious thought.

This philosophical anthropology consists of Hegel's account of human beings. It considers topics such as the role of habit, consciousness, intelligence, and will, among other elements important to any account of what it means to be a human being. Used in this sense, "anthropology" is a much broader category than what Hegel, within subjective spirit, calls "*Anthropologie*" and a very different category from the contemporary academic discipline of anthropology. Despite these possible sources of confusion, the etymological accuracy of the term suggests it as the most appropriate to refer to the broad category of a theory of what human beings are.

The heart of Hegel's anthropology is located in the section of his system that he labels "subjective spirit." Subjective spirit sets forth an underlying developmental structure fundamental to being human. It is not simply an account of given drives or instincts that seek satisfaction or an account of rational agency. Rather, it traces a development from a naturally determined being, hardly different from the animals treated earlier in Hegel's thought, through a process in which humans come to be what we are in essence: self-determining, free spirit. Not all humans achieve this development. Because this development depends partly on the social world—including the political order, religion, and philosophy—not everyone has the actual possibility of achieving this development. Even though the underlying potential can only be fully realized in appropriate circumstances, however, the anthropology intends to map a universal telos of human development that culminates in self-actualization or freedom.

Within his mature systematic framework, subjective spirit constitutes the first of the three spheres of Hegel's philosophy of spirit. As the first sphere of spirit, it follows Hegel's treatment of nature and precedes the two higher spheres of spirit, objective and absolute. In relation to what comes earlier in the system, the logic and the philosophy of nature, subjective spirit provides the transition from these realms to the higher spheres of spirit and is therefore essential to grasping how these are connected. Because Hegel conceives of his system as unfolding through immanent development, the systematic framework does not call for a simple application of the logic to the domain of the political, treated in objective spirit. Rather, as the first of the spheres of Hegel's system in which we encounter spirit as spirit, subjective spirit constitutes the basis of Hegel's conception of spirit. It thus provides necessary mediation between the logic and the philosophy of nature, on one hand, and objective and absolute spirit, on the other. This intermediate position in Hegel's system means that the logic and philosophy of nature are essential to grasping certain elements of subjective spirit, so that an examination of his anthropology must begin by considering these relationships. At the same time, however, it also means that the "systematic" background of certain central ideas in objective and absolute spirit—which contain Hegel's ethical, political, and religious thought—are more properly found in subjective spirit than in the logic or the philosophy of nature.[1]

Because of the relationship between subjective and objective spirit, Adriaan Peperzak has argued that Hegel's anthropology "*is at the same time a fundamental ethics.*"[2] In relation to objective spirit, the anthropology provides a necessary foundation, establishing limits to what could be a plausible ethic and thereby ruling out some political options; but Hegel's ethical and political thought involves more than a simple "unfolding" of the anthropology. Examining the interconnections between subjective spirit (the core of his anthropology) and objective spirit (the core of his ethics and politics) thus concretely illustrates how anthropologies may shape ethics and politics, and marks out a middle ground between the extremes of viewing anthropology and ethics as unrelated or viewing anthropology as completely determining ethics.[3]

Hegel's anthropology has long been recognized as integral to his thought, especially to his ethical and political thought. While early Left Hegelians may have viewed themselves as demythologizing Hegel in making this point, twentieth-century readers have often seen this point not as a challenge to Hegel's position, but rather as an elucidation of it. In his influential *Hegel*, for instance, Charles Taylor argues that the human subject provides the model for Hegel's conception of *Geist* or spirit.[4] Allen Wood also makes Hegel's anthropology central to his important reading of Hegel's ethics.[5] Despite this acknowledgment, however, a great deal of the secondary literature gives the impression that Hegel's anthropology is both everywhere and nowhere. Though it is claimed to be central to Hegel's ethical and political thought, it seems to be largely deduced and distilled from his ethical and political thought rather than set out on its own terms and then used to illuminate that political thought. It is thus pervasive and yet never straightforwardly there in front of the reader. Specifically, even those treatments that stress the importance of anthropology to Hegel's thought often ignore subjective spirit, which remains one of the least examined elements of Hegel's system. Charles Taylor provides the most striking example of this tendency: He distills an anthropology primarily on the basis of the *Phenomenology of Spirit* and then, in his treatment of Hegel's mature thought, follows the systematic structure of the *Encyclopaedia*, with the noteworthy exception of Hegel's most direct treatment of anthropology, subjective spirit.[6] Hegel's account of subjective spirit has in general received very little discussion among the expanses of writing on Hegel.

An important reason for this absence has been the paucity of material. Hegel's *Encyclopaedia of Philosophical Sciences* presents an overview of his mature philosophical system. Though comprehensive in its scope, the *Encyclopaedia* was written in an outline form meant to be accompanied by Hegel's lectures.[7] Of its three parts, the "Logic," the "Philosophy of Nature," and the "Philosophy of Spirit," the last encompasses anthropology (principally in subjective spirit), ethics and politics (principally in objective spirit), as well as art, religion, and philosophy (principally in absolute spirit). Whereas the latter two sections of the "Philosophy of Spirit" have long been extensively amplified by published material from Hegel's lectures (and in the case of objective spirit by the *Philosophy of Right*), the discussion of subjective spirit—the first section and the core of Hegel's anthropology—has been available only in the outline form of the *Encyclopaedia* and the less reliable *Zusätze* or additions.[8]

With the publication in 1994 of the *Vorlesungen über die Philosophie des Geistes* (Lectures on the philosophy of spirit) (*VPGst*), which consists of transcriptions of Hegel's 1827–28 lectures on subjective spirit, it is now possible to examine Hegel's mature anthropology in substantially greater detail than was previously possible.[9] Based on the compilation of two transcriptions, one by Johann Eduard Erdmann and the other by Ferdinand Walter, they constitute not simply a supplement to the text of the *Encyclopaedia* but an essential component of the intended presentation—of which the *Encyclopaedia* forms only one part. The *Vorlesungen* effectively relate the often abstract language and concepts of the *Encyclopaedia* to concrete human experience, making extremely clear the extent to which subjective spirit is an anthropology. They also provide an extensive account—much more adequate than the one in the *Encyclopaedia*—of the complex relationship between theory and practice, thereby illuminating the centrality of practice to his thought as well as the relationship between political practice and his philosophical system as a whole.

As a result, an examination that draws on both the *Vorlesungen über die Philosophie des Geistes* and the *Encyclopaedia* provides a more nuanced understanding of Hegel's anthropology than is possible by reference to the *Encyclopaedia* alone. The result is a complex, three-tiered anthropology that accounts for both what we inherit from the ethical and religious traditions in which we are raised—through habits—and our ability to criticize and transcend these—through self-consciousness. In setting forth three basic dimensions of the human being that are to be actualized in every individual, this anthropology provides a vital foundation for the interpretation of objective and absolute spirit. For this reason, I provide an extensive analysis of Hegel's anthropology that closely follows the systematic structure of Hegel's presentation.

Beyond the independent philosophical importance of an adequate account of Hegel's anthropology, this approach yields an excellent standpoint for evaluating the legacy of Hegel's ethical and religious thought. Examining his ethics from the perspective of the anthropology grounds the interpretation and immanent criticism of the latter within Hegel's own larger philosophical conception. It thereby provides a foundation—anchored within his systematic approach—for addressing four fundamental difficulties in the interpretation of Hegel's ethics: (1) the question of whether Hegel privileges theory over practice in a manner that neglects the importance of practice; (2) the distinct but interconnected question of the relation of theory and political practice; (3) the possibility of submitting ethical life, based in inherited tradition, to rational critique; and (4) the relation of differentiation and equality within society. While all four topics are important for their own sakes—not simply for the interpretation of Hegel—the third and fourth in particular address problems that remain central to ethical and political discussions today. Finally, approaching Hegel's philosophy of religion from the perspective of his anthropology both reveals the important role of the anthropology within absolute spirit and places in relief the strategy for reconciling tradition and freedom that lies at the heart of Hegel's treatment of religion.

## The Significance of Practice

The first of these problems constitutes an overarching issue in the interpretation of Hegel, though the foundation of Hegel's position is located within subjective spirit. In significant passages, Hegel appears to demonstrate an almost exclusive concern with the theoretical, to the neglect of the practical. Hegel begins the third section of the *Encyclopaedia*, the philosophy of spirit, with the "absolute command," "Know Thyself!" (*Enz.* § 377). In addition, the structure of the system as a whole, which begins with the abstract concepts of the logic and concludes with philosophy itself, easily encourages this reading. Although the sphere of objective spirit deals directly with matters of practice, it concludes not with satisfactory reconciliation but with the unresolved, conflictual plurality of sovereign states in competition through world history. This failure to find unity in an overarching global organization is followed by Hegel's turn to absolute spirit, in which spirit can appear to retreat from the "external," practical world of politics and history to self-contemplation—in art, religion, and philosophy.

To some, this indicates that the only ultimately significant reconciliation of spirit is achieved in the realm of theory—encompassing both the representational thought (*Vorstellung*) characteristic of religion and the purely conceptual thought (*Denken*) that distinguishes philosophy. Practice—including the associated ethical and political realms—is thereby rendered irrelevant to this reconciliation. If this is the case, the goal of spirit's development may be a contemplation of the absolute, withdrawn from the world. In such a vision, political and social issues are ultimately insignificant, functioning primarily to distract one from the absolute. Spirit's highest development is independent of, as well as perhaps invulnerable to, practical realities. Hegel would then stand squarely within a tradition valuing theory or contemplation over practice that extends from Plato, through book ten of Aristotle's *Nicomachean Ethics*, and to much of Christian monasticism—and very much over against Marx.[10] At issue, then, is the value and import of human practice.

Within subjective spirit, this broader topic of the prioritization of the theoretical is situated in the relation between what Hegel calls theoretical and practical spirit, intelligence and will, respectively. Because Hegel here deals directly with these issues, this treatment provides the most adequate grounding for the examination of this issue in his thought as a whole. Even here, however, his position is not easy to discern. Hegel states that "[t]he knowing reason is spirit" and that "reason, which spirit is in and for itself and of which spirit has consciousness that it is, is the concept; and knowledge constitutes the actuality of this reason that exists in and for itself" (*VPGst* 180). Such passages appear to define spirit fundamentally in terms of knowing rather than willing. Further, in the *Encyclopaedia* presentations Hegel provides little indication of the inadequacy of thought—the highest level of theoretical spirit—that drives the transition to practical spirit. At the same time, Hegel consistently argues for the inseparability of intelligence and will, and within the structure of subjective spirit, practical spirit constitutes a later, higher sphere than theoretical spirit. The challenge is to reconcile these various elements of Hegel's thought. Each is important to Hegel, yet it has remained unclear how they can be convincingly brought together.

A number of interpreters have stressed the primacy of theory in Hegel's system. In her analysis of the relationship of intelligence and will, Edith Düsing argues that theoretical spirit constitutes the foundation of the will and that the end of spirit's development is in thought alone. Thus, "The systematic connection of all modes of activity of subjective spirit, its innermost center, in which they possess their uniting middle, is for Hegel . . . thought."[11] Intelligence is the beginning, end, and center of Hegel's conception of spirit, such that the only role of the practical in the development of the theoretical is a minor one. Similarly, Klaus Düsing claims that practical spirit is not integral to subjective spirit, since the concept of the latter is attained "fundamentally already at the conclusion of the examination of 'theoretical spirit' in the concept of thought."[12] Because of the foundational role of subjective spirit in the conception of spirit, this position entails that practice is not integral to the conception of spirit as a whole. Even Adriaan Peperzak, who stresses the relative significance of practice and politics in Hegel, maintains that "the supremacy of the theoretical over the practical is quite obvious in Hegel's philosophy of spirit."[13] Despite their differences, each of these readings fundamentally subordinates practice to theory.

Interpreters such as Taylor, Wood, and Avineri, who by contrast stress Hegel's ethical and political thought, have generally done so without great concern for this aspect of the relation between theory and practice. Hegel's demonstrated concern with ethical and political issues is taken as sufficient, without further worry whether he ultimately subordinates practical to theoretical spirit. As a result, these scholars generally focus their consideration of "theory and practice" on the second of the issues that I discuss.

An investigation of subjective spirit that makes use of the *Vorlesungen über die Philosophie des Geistes*, however, illuminates the multiple relationships that Hegel develops between theory and practice. Because the *Encyclopaedia* presentation is particularly unclear on the inadequacy at the conclusion of theoretical spirit that necessitates the transition to practical spirit, the *Vorlesungen* are essential to an adequate comprehension of Hegel's position. As we will see, the resulting interpretation defends an essential role for the practical yet situates this within a dynamic relationship to the theoretical. The development of practice turns out to be essential to the development of thought. Though Hegel ultimately maintains a degree of priority for theory, what is striking in his treatment is not the superiority of intelligence over will but their interweaving. Most importantly, the culmination of subjective spirit, free spirit, must incorporate both theoretical and practical spirit. While the relationship between theory and practice is most explicit in subjective spirit, its consequences are manifest in the conception of the cultus in the philosophy of religion. A vision of this end that effectively leaves practice behind is inadequate to the fundamental importance Hegel attributes to practice and to spirit's actualization in the world. The present interpretation does not deny that in certain passages Hegel tends to emphasize the theoretical over the practical. Nonetheless, it supports an overall reading of the relationship between the theoretical and the practical that stresses their interrelationship and inseparability and does justice to the enduring significance of the practical within Hegel's thought.

### The Relation between Theory and Practice

A second, related but distinct issue also concerns theory and practice. For this problem, the *locus classicus* is Hegel's much discussed and disputed claim from the preface to the *Philosophy of Right:* "What is rational is actual; and what is actual is rational" (*PR* 24/20). Rather than suggesting a subordination of practice to theory, this passage has been taken to imply that theory has no critical role to play in relation to practice. The issue is a fundamental one concerning the relationship or distance between philosophy and public life. Much of the grandeur of Hegel's system derives from his attempt to connect the abstract logical concepts of the *Science of Logic* and the first part of the *Encyclopaedia* to concrete social issues such as the role of the family and the meaning of war. Simultaneously, he expresses concern about the compatibility of attention to such issues and the study of logic itself, writing of his "doubt whether the noisy clamor of current affairs and the deafening chatter of a conceit which prides itself on confining itself to such matters leave any room for participation in the passionless calm of a knowledge which is in the element of pure thought alone" (*WL* 1:34/42). At stake, then, is the role of philosophy in political life, as well as the role of political life in philosophy.

Hegel provides his most conservative formulation further on in the preface to the *Philosophy of Right:* "A further word on the subject of *issuing instructions* on how the world ought to be: philosophy, at any rate, always comes too late to perform this function. As the *thought* of the world, it appears only at a time when actuality has gone through its formative process and attained its completed state. . . . When philosophy paints its grey in grey, a shape of life has grown old, and it cannot be rejuvenated, but only recognized, by the grey in grey of philosophy; the owl of Minerva begins its flight only with the onset of dusk" (*PR* 27–28/23). This and the two preceding passages have been central to efforts to portray Hegel as a conservative apologist for the Prussian state. In suggesting no critical role for theory, they threaten either to preclude any political significance for Hegel's thought or to define this significance exclusively in terms of a very conservative agenda. Such criticisms came quickly, and Hegel himself was already responding to them in the introduction to the 1827 edition of the *Encyclopaedia* (*Enz.* § 6 A). Yet the criticisms have continued. Jürgen Habermas, for instance, argues that in Hegel's mature thought spirit always advances behind the backs of human beings—as the unintended product of the pursuit of self-interest, not of consciously willed action. Hegel's infamous "cunning of reason" here appears as Adam Smith's invisible hand writ large. In this vision, theory can never become practical.

Major threads in Hegel's thought, however, preclude a reading of theory as simply following practice. Theoretical spirit precedes and is actualized in practical spirit. Free spirit brings together both theoretical and practical spirit. How can these elements of Hegel's thought—which are integral to his system—be reconciled with the assertion that theory cannot "issue instructions" for the world? Pursuing these threads in Hegel's thought, Michael Theunissen provides an alternative to Habermas's view, such that the two together effectively frame the debate on this issue.[14] Theunissen sees in Hegel a unity of theory and practice that is found both at the culmination of historical development, in the final stage of consummate religion, the cultus, as well as in the drive toward a more adequate actualization of reason in the future. The consummate cultus, Theunissen argues, describes a historical moment at which spirit no longer functions behind the backs or without the consciousness of individual human beings. It is distinctly political in import, because this cultus is not limited but rather in principle open to all humanity. The second sense of unity involves the necessary realization of theory in practice. Theory that remains abstract rather than becoming actual in the world falls short of the reconciliation required by its own inward development. Both of these senses call for theory to inform practice in a manner that challenges the adequacy of the preface to the *Philosophy of Right*.

Grounding the analysis of theory and practice in Hegel's fundamental treatment of these issues in subjective spirit yields the account most adequate to his systematic conception of the spheres of spirit. The anthropology provides a sophisticated conception of theory and practice informing one another. Moreover, the relationship itself develops, with each term becoming an increasingly adequate expression of the other. The relationship is therefore neither unidirectional nor static. This reading rejects the adequacy of Hegel's formulations in the preface on the basis of elements integral to his systematic thought. Articulating this relationship between theoretical and practical spirit, with attention to the role of historical development, thus resolves the fundamental issues at stake between Habermas and Theunissen. Each position has a place within a historical process, but either one alone is incomplete. The resulting view undermines ultraconservative interpretations of Hegel's position and provides the account of the relationship between theory and practice most consistent with Hegel's thought as a whole.

### Tradition and Criticism of Ethical Life

A third major problem plaguing the understanding of Hegel's ethical and political thought concerns the conception of ethical life, or *Sittlichkeit*. The content or existing side of ethical life consists of the norms, practices, and institutions that make up the social and political world. In his discussion of this highest sphere of objective spirit, Hegel focuses on the family, civil society, and the state, seeing in these institutions and associated practices the content that he finds lacking in the formalism of Kant's moral thought. The individual, growing up in a particular society, finds mores already in place and internalizes them largely unconsciously. In this sense, their adoption precedes any self-conscious choice by the individual. Although these practices are not chosen, harmony between one's own will and the reigning ethical life of the surrounding society is essential to Hegel's conception of freedom. At the same time, Hegel claims that the ethical life of the modern world—as articulated in his own work—incorporates the need for subjective freedom. This he views as the crucial contribution of modern ethical thought, epitomized by Kant, that distinguishes modern ethical life from that of the ancient Greek polis. It is therefore also what distinguishes Hegel's political vision from certain Romantic strains among his contemporaries who effectively called for a return to medieval or earlier visions of organic communal harmony.

The central issues here are much the same as those raised in recent debates about liberalism and so-called communitarianism.[15] Since the rise of liberalism and the Enlightenment, Western discussions of social justice and political theory have been centrally concerned with the role of religious and philosophical traditions in shaping social and political structures. Emphasizing reason and criticism over against tradition, one line of thinking—in which Kant remains a towering figure—seeks to justify a political vision on the basis of reason alone, without reference to inherited commitments (whether these are explicitly religious or not). Such inheritances are seen as the perpetuators of irrational prejudice and injustice, as well as inevitable sources of conflict within a pluralistic society. Tradition as such is therefore barred as a source of justification for ethics or politics. Overcoming such injustice and prejudice requires a standard of judgment that is independent of particular traditions.[16]

Against this line of thinking, a number of recent critics of liberalism have sought to define an integral role for religious traditions and other "deep" commitments in justifying political visions. The criticisms of liberalism have varied greatly, coming from the right and the left as well as from both religious and secular thinkers, but a common theme has been an emphasis on the ongoing significance of inherited traditions.[17] This concern with tradition has challenged the idea that we can grapple with fundamental questions about justice in a society without bringing our deepest religious and philosophical convictions into play. Rejecting a conception of reason as independent of tradition, reason—at least the reason required to make judgments about what is good for human beings—is seen as generated by traditions rather than an alternative to them. To escape tradition is not simply to escape prejudice but to give up the basis we require to reflect upon profound issues such as how to organize a society; it thus renders ethical discourse incoherent. There is no Archimedean point beyond traditions. If we do not speak a particular language, belonging to a tradition, we can only babble. These claims regarding the role of tradition in our reasoning are generally accompanied by the argument that such traditions make us who we are. Liberalism is accused, by contrast, of presupposing that "rational agency" is more fundamental to humans than is being part of a particular tradition or community, whether religious or secular. Because these traditions are frequently viewed as closely tied to particular communities, the communities in which we live are viewed as playing a constitutive role in defining us.[18] In light of its different understanding of human beings, liberalism is seen as philosophically unsound as well as politically unstable over the long term.

Profoundly influenced by Kant yet committed to the significance of history and community, Hegel is centrally concerned with reconciling tradition and reason. In his treatment of anthropology, as well as his ethical and religious thought, Hegel seeks to do justice both to the situated, historical character of human existence and to our capacity to reflect and be self-critical. However, despite Hegel's claim to incorporate subjective freedom within his conception of modern ethical life, it is not easy to see how he does so. At some points, particularly in the philosophy of history, Hegel seems to call for unreflective adherence to the ethos of the age. Given his account of the role of consciousness in freedom, however, any effective incorporation of subjective freedom must include space not only for individual preferences or expressions of arbitrary will (*Willkür*) on relatively unimportant issues but also for critical, reflective consciousness regarding the institutions that define our social world.

Specifically, an account of ethical life adequate to Hegel's view of the distinctive contributions of modern understandings of subjectivity must involve a critical consciousness regarding reigning mores, not simply an uncritical acceptance of them.

One response to Hegel's claims to do justice to critical consciousness and subjective freedom has been to treat them as mere window dressing. Karl Popper's *The Open Society and Its Enemies* is perhaps the extreme version of this Hegel-as-totalitarian reading. Nonetheless, even Habermas's claim that Hegel's mature thought provides no space for revolutionary consciousness fits into this category. More notably, Allen Wood—who defends the compatibility of Hegel's ethical thought with modern insights on freedom—contends that within Hegel there is a necessary tension between ethical life and critical consciousness. This results in a striking tension within Wood's interpretation. On one hand, Wood stresses that Hegel's vision of a rational society is one in which individuals think of themselves as free, as pursuing their own ends, through their participation in the society: "Hegel's theory . . . proposes that we be self-consciously free (or 'with ourselves') in what we do. Its whole point is to achieve rational self-knowledge and self-transparency in our ethical life."[19] Adherence to the objective ethical life of a society is thus willed by, rather than imposed upon, individuals. This agreement can be either immediate and habitual or reflective.[20] In this mode, Wood maintains that reflection on the norms of a society is not antithetical to agreement with them, but neither will this agreement always be forthcoming, since it "presupposes that reason and reflection confirm the rightness and rationality of ethical norms."[21] Here, Wood sees Hegel powerfully incorporating the modern "reflective principle" into his conception of freedom.

Elsewhere, however, Wood appears to take a different stance on the compatibility of ethical life and reflection. As a nation comes to reflect consciously upon its own ethical practices and institutions, it inevitably undermines them.[22] What Hegel saw happening to the ancient Greek polis as a result of the questioning expressed by Socrates represents an immutable law of history: Critical reflection destabilizes and ultimately undermines a society. Even modernity cannot overcome this antithesis. Although subjective freedom might find limited expression in the freedom of choice offered within civil society, this freedom cannot—despite Hegel's assertions to the contrary—satisfy the demand for rational justification of the existing ethical life. Such strains are clearly present in Hegel. Nonetheless, it is no coincidence that the passages most expressive of this strain come from Hegel's philosophy of history.[23] The decisive question, then, concerns whether the advances in consciousness and subjective freedom that Hegel associates with the modern world in any way transform this earlier situation.

Although other interpreters place greater emphasis on Hegel's claim that modern freedom must incorporate subjective freedom, it easily appears as inherently contradictory—calling for us to choose freely something about which we have no choice—and therefore dangerously ideological.[24] More importantly, such an outcome to the reading of Hegel is difficult to avoid without attention to the philosophical anthropology operative in Hegel's thought. Without distinguishing among habit, consciousness, and free spirit as Hegel does in subjective spirit, one lacks the conceptual apparatus necessary to articulate and ground systematically the crucial difference between our initial, largely unconscious appropriation of ethical life in the form of habit and a critical reappropriation based on rational scrutiny. Only with this structure can we adequately grasp how Hegel's conception of a developed, modern ethical life incorporates the demands for rational justification. Reading objective spirit in relation to the anthropology thus sheds new and essential light on the larger structure of Hegel's ethical thought, particularly on his understanding of the vital role of inherited religious traditions in shaping our ethical judgments, and on our ability to subject these inherited views and practices to criticism. It thereby responds to those critics who see Hegel's championing of *Sittlichkeit*, or ethical life, as the endorsement of any status quo and proposes instead a more complex understanding of the need to take traditional beliefs seriously *and* to critique them rationally, as well as the possibility that we might consciously reappropriate them on the basis of finding them rationally compelling. According to Hegel's anthropology, complete freedom is only achieved in times and places where this third stage is possible.

### Differentiation and Equality

While the first three problems involve issues in Hegel that have led interpreters to conflicting conclusions, the final one more clearly involves reading Hegel against himself. In developing his conception of freedom, Hegel rejects the vision of "negative freedom" that he saw epitomized in the French Revolution as leading inherently to the Terror. Understood in this way, freedom rejects all differentiation as unjust and therefore strives to eliminate all differences and all particularity. The result is pure destructiveness. Hegel rejects a leveling of society that involves equal status for all and argues for the necessity of differentiation or articulation within society. This articulation allows for difference and avoids homogenization while also integrating these differences into a larger whole: the state. Thus, the particular articulations, such as the spheres of family and civil society, produce differences that are complementary rather than conflicting. In order to be complementary, these different elements must each express an integral moment of the concept of spirit. Concretely, this means that each will express principally one element of subjective spirit.

This conception of the state as an integrated whole differentiated into three estates and with very different gender roles raises concerns about how these inequalities can be reconciled with Hegel's claims to make freedom central. This has been one of the fundamental problems in influential recent interpretations that share the goal of rescuing Hegel from the accusations of totalitarianism epitomized by Popper's critique. Amongst such reinterpretations, those of Charles Taylor, Shlomo Avineri, and Allen Wood are themselves distinguished largely by the type of differentiation on which they focus.[25] Taylor concentrates on Hegel's differentiation of society into three estates: a substantial estate, tied to agriculture; the estate of trade and industry; and the universal estate, constituted primarily by civil servants. The estates have different and profoundly unequal roles in society. Taylor views this articulation as central to Hegel's response to what Taylor sees as a defining social problem of modernity: homogenization. While Taylor argues that Hegel's response to the problem fails, he maintains that Hegel identifies the fundamental problem and the need for differentiation to respond to it. Avineri, by contrast, stresses the distinction Hegel maintains between civil society and the state. He considers the autonomy of civil society essential to Hegel's strategy for avoiding a totalitarian state. Hegel holds to this difference even when he demonstrates that civil society, even at its most successful, inevitably produces poverty. The poor, according to Hegel, easily become alienated from society and its institutions to become a "rabble" that—if it becomes too great in number—could threaten to undermine the state. Nonetheless, even though civil society has no means to solve this problem, the state intervenes only in minor ways, leaving the basic institutions of civil society intact—despite the profound problems they create. Finally, Wood—though he notes other forms of inequality—places the greatest emphasis on Hegel's view of women. Women manifest the "substantial principle," which entails an immediate, unreflective identification with one's world. Correspondingly, they live their lives predominantly in the context of the family. Men, however, generally manifest the "reflective principle," which involves reflection and thought. Correspondingly, they live important segments of their lives in the public spheres of civil society and the state. Wood sees this division as in fundamental tension with Hegel's commitment, at other points, to the idea of the equality of all persons.

Grounding the analysis of objective spirit in the anthropology elaborated in subjective spirit powerfully brings together the fundamental issues at the heart of Hegel's treatment of differentiation and the problems with this treatment. In the different levels of the anthropology, subjective spirit elaborates the dimensions of human beings that need to be expressed in a free society. It therefore provides a systematic foundation for the need for differentiation. More importantly, recognizing that this differentiation is grounded in the anthropology, which maps a structure of development universal in human beings, explains why the hierarchical models of differentiation Hegel employs must fail. By contrast, if one skips from Hegel's logic to objective spirit, as Taylor's analysis sometimes does, there is no intrinsic contradiction in the stratification Hegel describes.[26] Particularly in dealing with these issues, subjective spirit, systematically located between the two, plays an essential mediating function. Thus, the anthropological foundation of Hegel's ethical and political thought both provides a standpoint internal to Hegel's own thought for criticizing his models of differentiation and identifies the contradictions built into them.

The fundamental problem—in deep tension with his anthropology—is that each of these aspects of Hegel's solution conceives of differentiation in hierarchical terms. The self-actualization or freedom articulated in the anthropology as the telos of every human existence would therefore be denied to the vast majority of the population. At best, only those on the top will be able to fully realize the potential freedom set out in the anthropology; at worst, the inequality and lack of recognition will undermine even their freedom. With the difference between the estates stressed in Taylor's reading, only members of the universal estate have a chance of realizing the universal potential identified in the anthropology. Similarly, although Avineri acknowledges the threat posed to the state as a whole by civil society's creation of the rabble, he does not deal with the extent to which those whose life is dominated by civil society—i.e., the estate of trade and industry—cannot achieve the level of freedom or self-actualization of those in the universal class. And women, the focus of whose activity Hegel confines to the domestic realm, are in multiple ways denied the opportunity to develop the potential that Hegel identifies as intrinsic to humanity. This hierarchical vision is therefore at odds not only with many contemporary views on equality but also with fundamental elements in Hegel's own conception of human freedom.

While the anthropology does not do away with the need for differentiation, it calls for differentiation to be distributed horizontally throughout society or within each individual, rather than vertically. This is no easy task, particularly since another requirement is that the differences be complementary, not divisive. A solution must provide for differentiation, but not of a sort that condemns certain individuals to a lower level in the development at the core of Hegel's account of subjective spirit. The anthropology cannot on its own produce this solution, but it both articulates the problems and points to resources within Hegel's thought for responding to them.

### Tradition and Freedom in Religion

Turning to the philosophy of religion brings us to the sphere of absolute spirit, in which spirit has itself as an object of cognition. In part because it seeks to cognize spirit itself explicitly, the philosophy of religion provides perhaps the most comprehensive view of Hegel's strategy for reconciling tradition with reason and freedom. The analysis therefore revisits certain issues already considered in the discussion of ethical life but focuses specifically on the attitude toward tradition.

Hegel stands at a remarkable juncture in the history of modern Christianity. The early-nineteenth-century world in which he lived witnessed an unprecedented convergence of challenges to the authority of inherited traditions. In philosophical and religious thought, Kant provided for Hegel the paradigmatic formulation of a critical approach. The Romantics frequently stressed individual experience over religious doctrine. The French Revolution pressed this challenge to tradition and the demand for rational justification in politics. At about the same time, reports had begun pouring into Europe from missionaries and colonizers describing other lands and cultures, implicitly forcing the question, "Which tradition?" Because Hegel saw these challenges as intrinsically interrelated, he sought a unified response, and because, for Hegel, religion and philosophy have the same object and content, this response was necessarily central to his philosophy of religion.

The enduring dilemma is that inherited traditions cannot be taken for granted. Alternatives as well as critical questions are all too apparent. Yet the attempt, often identified with the Enlightenment, to defend religious views on the basis of a "pure" reason that ignores tradition and seeks to "start from scratch" faces inevitable difficulties. Hegel has little respect for attempts to develop a "natural religion" that discards the positive elements he sees as necessary in religion.[27] At the political level, the degeneration of the French Revolution into the Terror represents, according to Hegel, the inevitable outcome of this strategy. Despite the tremendous historical and intellectual developments of the past two centuries, Hegel's diagnosis of the challenge of modernity remains apt. Alasdair MacIntyre's *After Virtue*, for instance, provides a contemporary restatement of a great deal of Hegel's diagnosis—despite MacIntyre's very different response to these challenges.

Hegel's response to these challenges reveals the fundamental significance of the anthropology even within the sphere of absolute spirit. Tracing the manifestation of the anthropology there places Hegel's response in relief and generates a novel framework for examining his philosophy of religion. His strategy rejects any juxtaposing of faith and thought, tradition and reason, or tradition and freedom. It attributes to tradition an essential role in a developmental process that occurs both within individuals and at a social level. We initially take on a religious tradition through a largely unconscious process in which we learn its practices and basic teachings. Here, tradition exists simply as authority, with no need of justification. This process provides a starting point for an ascent that moves through critical reflection to—when possible—self-conscious and rationally justified acceptance. Adequate justification for the journey, however, can only be provided at the summit of the development, from the standpoint of the thinking that characterizes philosophy. The authority of tradition as such has both proven necessary to initiate the process and been undermined by the process. The resulting culmination in philosophy justifies the doctrines and practices that could not be justified within the sphere of religion itself. The tradition is vindicated and the demands of rationality satisfied. This outcome is only possible, however, when the religious tradition is implicitly rational. While Hegel claims that Lutheran Protestantism is rational in just this sense, this claim is not necessitated by the larger strategy.[28]

In order to explore the full significance of Hegel's anthropology, then, my project includes two closely related tasks: a treatment of Hegel's mature anthropology and an examination of the consequences for ethical, political, and religious thought. The former elaborates an anthropology responsive to contemporary concerns about the significance of inherited traditions as well as the need for criticism. The latter develops the normative consequences of this anthropology by exploring its significance for Hegel's account of objective and absolute spirit.

To establish the context—within Hegel's own system—for the examination of his anthropology, chapter 1 examines the systematic supports of subjective spirit, addressing the relationship between Hegel's anthropology and what Hegel saw as the foundations for his system. I focus on elucidating those elements of Hegel's logic and philosophy of nature that are important to grasping the starting point of subjective spirit and the process through which the sphere of subjective spirit develops. Having arrived at the level of subjective spirit, the chapter concludes with an analysis of the type of anthropology Hegel articulates in subjective spirit.

Chapters 2 through 4 provide the core of my interpretation of Hegel's anthropology. Because this issue has been so little discussed within the scholarship, I focus closely on explicating Hegel's works, aiming for a much more systematic interpretation of this area of his corpus than most interpreters provide. I believe that precisely because his thought remains of vital importance to contemporary issues, it merits not simply selective appropriation but careful examination with adequate attention to the systematic structure. The developmental character of Hegel's anthropology makes such an approach necessary if we are to avoid locating concepts at the wrong level of the developmental process. Without such an approach, it is particularly easy to take passages from Hegel out of context and quickly do great damage to the interpretation of his thought. As Michael Theunissen writes, "[i]n this respect, Betty Heimann's pronouncement remains valid: 'To cite Hegel is to misunderstand and misuse him.' One is guilty of misuse when one bases an interpretation on quotations torn from the context of dialectically developing thought." [29] For this reason, a comprehensive grasp of Hegel's anthropology requires a careful tracing of each stage of Hegel's elaboration of subjective spirit. At the same time, my discussion, with its particular concern for the emerging conception of freedom, is more thematically focused than the paragraph-by-paragraph interpretations in either Iring Fetscher's *Hegels Lehre vom Menschen: Kommentar zu den §§ 387 bis 482 der "Enzyklopädie der philosophischen Wissenschaften"* (1970) or Adriaan Peperzak's *Hegels praktische Philosophie: Ein Kommentar zur enzyklopädischen Darstellung der menschlichen Freiheit und ihrer objektiven Verwirklichung* (1991). [30] It thereby more clearly illuminates Hegel's contemporary relevance and addresses a broader audience than these works.

This analysis reveals three levels to Hegel's conception of human beings: habit, in which we subordinate particular sensations and impulses to largely unconscious patterns of behavior (chapter 2); self-consciousness, in which we reflect upon ourselves and become aware of ourselves as subjects (chapter 3); and the level of spirit, in which we comprehend ourselves as free through acting freely, thereby actualizing ourselves in the world (chapter 4). The last of these discussions directly addresses the importance of practice in relation to theory.

With this interpretation of Hegel's anthropology established, chapters 5 through 8 examine the implications for ethics, politics, and religion, employing the anthropology to address the issues raised here in the introduction. In light of this purpose, these chapters are structured thematically rather than by Hegel's own systematic structure, though—mindful of Theunissen's admonition—I have sought to provide the systematic context necessary for the interpretation of each point.

Chapter 5 focuses on a preliminary but essential issue for any attempt to argue that Hegel's anthropology has normative consequences: the possibility of philosophy's criticizing the existing world, the second of the problems examined above. Here I argue that Hegel's anthropology undergirds his most consistent and coherent position on this issue and requires a very different conception than that suggested if Hegel's own most explicit—yet least systematic—statements are read in isolation. Chapter 6 considers another aspect of the foundational connection between anthropology and ethics by analyzing the development or manifestation of the three moments of the anthropology in Hegel's conception of the social and political world. I distinguish the prereflective appropriation of ethical and religious traditions in habits, the overcoming of this immediate identification through the self-consciousness that characterizes morality, and the unity of the two brought about by a conscious recognition of the rationality of the existing ethical life. Although the final stage is possible only in a certain type of society, we are only fully free in such a society.

Chapter 7 investigates the tensions between Hegel's anthropology, which describes a universal human telos toward self-realization or freedom, and the various forms of social stratification built into his political vision. Hegel's anthropology produces an immanent critique of much of his account of the institutions he sees constituting the modern state: the family, civil society, and the estates. Only his conception of the universal estate and its relation to the state appears to satisfy the drive toward freedom at the heart of his anthropology. Rather than seeking to rewrite objective spirit to address these criticisms, I conclude by suggesting that even before providing such a systematic reworking of this sphere, we might construe the ethical and political consequences of Hegel's anthropology in terms of mid-level norms that are more general than concrete policy statements yet more concrete than abstract principles such as Kant's categorical imperative.

The final chapter examines the role of the anthropology within the philosophy of religion.[31] Hegel clearly identifies the preconscious process of taking on a tradition and views this cultivation as one of the principal responsibilities of the church. The second moment of the anthropology, self-consciousness, is not manifest in a distinct stage (like morality in objective spirit) but appears in Hegel's emphasis on the "witness of spirit" as essential to the most developed form of religion. The development culminates in the knowledge of God as spirit, where this is actualized in ethical life. The conclusion encompasses the theoretical and the practical and reconciles, for Hegel, the authority of tradition with the self-determining freedom of reason.

# 1 Developing toward Spirit
## *Logic, Nature, and Human Beings*

Hegel was not simply a theoretical philosopher concerned with the problems of the logic who—as an afterthought—tried to draw out implications for political and religious questions. Nor was he basically an ethical and political thinker for whom the logic functioned as a mere background to justify his views on the social and political issues that *really* concerned him. An adequate approach to Hegel must keep all of these foci—and his understanding of their interconnection—in view. His entire corpus responds to what he saw as the complex, multidimensional crisis of his day. Representing for Hegel a turning point in world history, this crisis was at once social, political, cultural, religious, and philosophical. While the French Revolution and Napoleon shattered the European political and social orders, the Enlightenment and its aftermath called for new understandings of religious traditions. In philosophy, Immanuel Kant's critical philosophy was agreed by many to have brought about a Copernican revolution in thought that undermined metaphysics as it had previously been understood. External authority—whether in ethics, politics, or religion—was highly suspect. In each of these spheres, inherited traditions were challenged by calls for freedom.[1]

Hegel saw the many facets of this crisis as deeply interrelated. For instance, since concerns about the limits and possibilities of reason and faith were inseparable from concerns about human freedom and its limits, an adequate social and political vision would need to confront Kant's claims about the limits of theoretical reason. In Hegel's view, the need for a unified response to these various crises called for a system, for a philosophy conceived as a science made up of spheres that together constitute a whole. Hegel provides the most comprehensive statement of his system in his *Encyclopaedia of the Philosophical Sciences in Outline*, three editions of which were published in 1817, 1827, and 1830. The logic, the philosophy of nature, and the philosophy of spirit constitute the three parts of the *Encyclopaedia*. More than a merely formal logic, Hegel's logic—both in the *Science of Logic* and in the shorter version presented in the first part of the *Encyclopaedia*—treats the self-development of the concept "in the abstract element of *thinking*" (*Enz.* § 19), and in particular the "determinations of thought" [*Denkbestimmungen*] that constitute the structure of reality. The philosophy of nature seeks to provide not a comprehensive account of nature but rather a *philosophical* analysis of the elementary concepts or structures of nature. Finally, the philosophy of spirit provides Hegel's treatment of philosophical anthropology, ethics, politics, history, art, religion, and philosophy.

The relationship among the different aspects of Hegel's thought is much debated. Hegel himself claimed that his analysis of the distinctly human spheres treated in the philosophy of spirit depends upon his logic; the proof of the former cannot do without the latter. Others, however, have argued that most if not all of Hegel's ethical, social, and political thought can be maintained without adopting the metaphysics that they see as central to his logic; for them, it is in the former realms that his greatest contribution lies. Allen Wood writes, "The Hegel who still lives and speaks to us is not a speculative logician and idealist metaphysician but a philosophical historian, a political and social theorist, a philosopher of our ethical concerns and cultural identity crises."[2] Both in separating these aspects of his thought and in focusing on the enduring relevance of Hegel's social and political thought, Wood follows Charles Taylor.[3] Both suggest that Hegel's driving insight was his "vision of human agency and its products."[4] As Wood writes,

> This is not necessarily to contradict the assertion that we cannot understand Hegel's social and political concerns without reference to his speculative metaphysics. But we are likely to miss the connection between the two if (with Hegel) we suppose that Hegelian thought is *grounded* in Hegelian metaphysics, and conclude that speculative logic is a propaedeutic to Hegel's theory of modern society. In fact, the relation between the two may be very nearly the reverse of this; often Hegel's treatment of metaphysical issues is best viewed as an attempt to interpret these issues as an expression of cultural and existential concerns.[5]

In recent debates over the relationship between the logic and Hegel's social and political thought, however, the logic whose relationship to Hegel's political thought is being investigated has appeared as something of a moving target.

That is, while interpreters such as Robert Pippin and David Kolb have rejected Taylor's claim to be able to separate the logic and politics as he does, they simultaneously reject Taylor's understanding of Hegel's logic. Pippin is one of the most prominent of a number of recent interpreters who have rejected interpretations of Hegel as developing a metaphysical spirit monism.[6] For Pippin, Taylor's interpretation of Hegel's logic as thoroughly metaphysical produces a dilemma: "The metaphysical Hegel looks like some premodern anachronism (or totalitarian bogeyman in some versions), and accounts of Hegel's political and social theory cannot be said, finally, to be genuinely Hegelian without some reliance on the speculative system." The way out of this dilemma is to interpret Hegel's logic "in a way that is not committed to a philosophically problematic theological metaphysics."[7] This line of interpretation has become extremely influential—particularly in the English-language secondary literature—in recent years.[8] By challenging the spirit-monist interpretation, Pippin and others have demonstrated that using central elements of the logic to interpret Hegel's social and political thought does not commit one to the strong metaphysical claims that many people claim to find in Hegel and see as a basis for rejecting him.

This development in Hegel scholarship reinforces the point that even a concern with Hegel's contemporary relevance should not induce us to dismiss Hegel's logic too quickly. In the course of the logic, Hegel analyzes and develops precise conceptions of elementary terms—"thought determinations," to use Hegel's language. Consequently, the meaning of terms such as "object," "reason," and "actuality" [Wirklichkeit] cannot simply be assumed or taken from daily usage when they are encountered later in the system. Moreover, the logic contains Hegel's most explicit treatment of the notion of immanent development that is central to the structure of his argument and analysis in the higher spheres.

Because of the central role of immanent development, articulating the logical background most essential to interpreting Hegel's philosophy of spirit requires two basic tasks: tracing the development of Hegel's system up to the beginning of subjective spirit and providing an account of the method of development (articulated in the logic) that should continue to operate throughout the higher spheres of the system. My concern here is with the project, structure, and goals of the logic. Thus, where particular concepts from the logic are important for interpreting a particular point later in the system, I return to the logic at that point rather than attempting to set out such terms in my overview of the logic. Finally, Hegel's actual method does not always correspond to his avowed method. Consequently, while the logic is important for understanding the metaphysical status of claims Hegel is making in the philosophy of spirit, one cannot take for granted that the method set forth in the logic will always determine the structure of the higher spheres. This difference suggests that there is no general solution to the question of the relation between the logic and the higher spheres.[9] While we cannot ignore the logical background, neither can we view it as a straitjacket in the interpretation of other elements of his system.

To complete the background necessary to frame the analysis of subjective spirit in chapters 2 through 4, the discussion of the logic will be followed by an analysis of the conception of the philosophy of nature and the "Concept of Spirit" that Hegel provides as an introduction to the third part of the *Encyclopaedia*, the philosophy of spirit. The final section of this chapter will introduce subjective spirit as a whole by discussing it as a type of philosophical anthropology.

## Logic

Providing an overview or sketch of Hegel's logic is intrinsically problematic. The *Science of Logic* is one of the most difficult works in the history of philosophy. Central to its argument is the claim that the argument itself progresses through immanent development that resolves the emerging contradictions. Any summary necessarily passes over the details of this development. An overview of the central concepts and terms necessarily treats them externally, providing stipulative definitions, rather than analyzing how they emerge from the other terms. Yet Hegel's goal is not simply to provide definitions of terms but to show their necessity and necessary interrelationship. In light of this situation, I focus here on identifying the task of the logic—what Hegel sees it as accomplishing and the kinds of claims that are being made. Moreover, because one of the principal results of the logic is the articulation of the developmental structure that permeates his system, this structure merits particular scrutiny.

In the *Encyclopaedia*, Hegel introduces the logic as "the science of *the pure Idea*, that is, of the Idea in the abstract element of *thinking*" (*Enz.* § 19).[10] The logic deals with "pure abstractions," because it considers the movement of thought, of the concept, as it is in itself rather than manifest in actuality (as do the spheres of nature and spirit). The logic therefore consists, Hegel claims, of a systematic analysis of the determinations of thought [*Denkbestimmungen*] necessary for thinking: "the system of pure reason, as the realm of pure thought" (*WL* 1:44/50). These include abstractions such as being, nothing, becoming, quantity, quality, and so forth. These distinct determinations do not simply coexist, indifferent to each other. Rather, the analysis begins with what initially seems to be the simplest, least presupposing concept: being. "Being" reveals itself to be unstable, to proceed to reveal another determination, nothing. Then being and nothing yield becoming. The advance is not produced by the application of a pregiven, external method but by transitions produced by the determinations themselves (*Enz.* 11–12/1). This development continues throughout the logic. As Hegel describes it, "[f]irst of all, this advance is determined as beginning from simple determinatenesses, the succeeding ones becoming ever *richer and more concrete*" (WL 2:569/840). This immanent development continues until it comes to have itself as an object and grasps its own beginning.

While these determinations are necessary for thinking, they are more than subjectively necessary for human thought. They are more than arbitrary forms that human thought must assume. For this reason, Hegel's logic is more than a purely formal logic. To the contrary, the Idea constitutes the truth of the actual:

> [E]verything actual *is* only in so far as it possesses the Idea and expresses it. It is not merely that the object, the objective and subjective world in general, *ought to be congruous* with the Idea, but they are themselves the congruence of concept and reality; the reality that does not correspond to the concept is mere *appearance*, the subjective, contingent, capricious element that is not the truth.... [W]hat anything actual is supposed in truth *to be*, if its concept is not in it and if its objectivity does not correspond to its concept at all, it is impossible to say; for it would be nothing. (*WL* 2:464/756)[11]

This and similar passages easily appear to make a boldly metaphysical claim that entirely rejects Kant's claims about the limits of theoretical reason. That interpretation generally yields an onto-theological reading of Hegel as a spirit monist. This strongly metaphysical reading need not claim a traditional Christian theism, but may bear more similarity to an Aristotelian conception of God.[12] For this line of interpretation, Hegel's claim that "[t]he objective logic [the first two parts of the logic], then, takes the place rather of former *metaphysics*" entails that Hegel resurrects a pre-Kantian, pre-critical metaphysics (*WL* 1:61/63).

Such claims about the relation between the concept and reality, however, need not—and should not—be interpreted in this manner.[13] Rather, in passages such as the lengthy one quoted above, Hegel seeks to articulate the "conditions necessary for objects to be objects at all . . . ."[14] In this sense, the logic is neither metaphysics—as this term was understood before Kant—nor merely an analysis of our own thought games. It is an account of the determinations that make objects, existence, actuality, and so forth possible. Central to Hegel's project, then, is undermining the presupposition of some "spectral *thing-in-itself*" behind or beyond phenomena—not claiming knowledge thereof (*WL* 1:41/47).[15] His claim is not that we can overleap the chasm and limits to reason highlighted by Kant but that this chasm and the so-called "thing-in-itself" are themselves presuppositions that collapse upon further analysis. Hegel states the result concisely at the end of the passage above: "[W]hat anything actual is supposed in truth *to be*, if its concept is not in it and if its objectivity does not correspond to its concept at all, it is impossible to say; for it would be nothing" (*WL* 2:464/756). Similarly, "The object [*Gegenstand*], kept apart from thinking and the concept, is an image [*Vorstellung*] or even a name; it is in the determinations of thought and the concept that it *is* what it *is*. Therefore these determinations are in fact the sole thing that matters; they are the true object and content of reason, and anything else that one understands by object and content in distinction from them has value only through them and in them" (*WL* 2:560/833). In such passages, Hegel articulates the role of thinking in constituting the object without claiming that these objects are metaphysical substances or that they are created by some supersensible being, God. Kant's shortcoming, for Hegel, is to assume there is some residue, some metaphysical substance, left outside of or only approached by thinking; to do so is to posit a chimera, which itself is generated by metaphysical presuppositions. To read Hegel as claiming more than this—specifically, to read him as claiming knowledge of metaphysical substances—is to underrate dramatically the extent of Kant's influence. Hegel sees Kant's theoretical philosophy as "incomplete," not having gone far enough (because he kept the thing-in-itself) rather than too far (because he undermined traditional metaphysical claims) (*WL* 1:45/51; see also 1:59/61 note). As Pippin writes, "Hegel's rhetorical bark is worse than his appropriating bite when it comes to Kant."[16]

Understanding Hegel in this light stresses the importance of the precise meaning that he develops for particular terms. Although the resonance with everyday language is important to Hegel, he criticizes metaphysics for taking concepts such as "soul," "world," and "God" from representation [*Vorstellung*] as "*ready-made or given subjects*" (*Enz.* § 30). While such terms "seem at first to provide thinking with a *firm hold*," they reveal themselves to be anything but stable; consequently, "what they need all the more is to receive firm determination only through thinking" (*Enz.* § 31). The same must be said of terms such as "object," "objectivity," and "actuality" (all of which are central to the interpretation of the status of Hegel's logic), as well as for Hegel's use of traditional theological language.[17] Many misreadings of Hegel are grounded in interpretations of terms in precisely the manner that Hegel has undermined. This recasting of central terms enables Hegel to reappropriate much from the broader tradition of Western metaphysics, particularly the work of Aristotle, within a distinctly post-Kantian frame. To read him as post-Kantian, therefore, is not to see him as intellectually indebted only to Kant and Fichte.

The development of logic culminates in the stage at which it has itself as an object. For this reason, the method driving the logic, which Hegel also claims to be the method driving the development in the other spheres of philosophy, is here treated explicitly. In the introduction to the *Science of Logic*, Hegel offers a provisional account of this method, which can only be preliminary precisely because the method is understood to be developed through the process, not something pregiven and somehow applied or added to material. There, Hegel begins his discussion of the "General Concept of Logic":

> In no science is the need to begin with the subject matter itself, without preliminary reflections, felt more strongly than in the science of logic. In every other science the object and the scientific method are distinguished from each other; also the content does not make an absolute beginning but is dependent on other concepts and is connected on all sides with other material. These other sciences are, therefore, permitted to speak of their ground and its context and also of their method, only as premises taken for granted . . . .
>
> Logic, on the contrary, cannot presuppose any of these forms of reflection and laws of thinking, for these constitute part of its own content and have first to be established within the science. (*WL* 1:35/43)

Because the method cannot be presupposed or brought to bear from without, the only method possible is one that is contained in the object itself, "for the method is the consciousness of the form of the inner self-movement of the content of logic. In the *Phenomenology of Spirit* I have expounded an example of this method in application to a more concrete object, namely to *consciousness*. Here, we are dealing with forms of consciousness each of which in realizing itself at the same time resolves itself, has for its result its own negation—and so passes into a higher form" (*WL* 1:49/53–54). This "inner self-movement" is central to the logic as well as to Hegel's system as a whole. This unfolding, immanently developing system of concepts "has to complete itself in a continuous, pure course in which nothing extraneous is introduced" (*WL* 1:49/54). The method must emerge from the content, not be applied to it.

In the treatment of method that comes at the end of the logic, where Hegel now has the systematic basis for articulating the method as a result and not simply in the form of an introductory preview, he provides a schematic account of the basic movements that characterize the method. Here, in "The Absolute Idea," the logic has itself for its object, which is to say that it considers the concept in-and-for-itself. Up to now, through the course of the development, the objects of analysis—the particular determinations of thought—have proven themselves to be unstable and self-dissolving and, in this sense, untrue. Insofar as these determinations are not the concept, the concept itself has not been the object of study until these final stages of the logic. From another perspective, however, insofar as the logic's object throughout its development has been thinking about the object, and precisely because each of these earlier determinations is a determination *of the concept*, in that sense the concept (in its determinations) has been the object all along. Consequently, at the end of the development—when the concept itself is the object—we are back to the beginning in the sense that we now see that all along we have been examining the determinations of thinking, which is now our explicit object. The movement now made explicit, the method, is precisely that which has driven the entire development and has thus been operative from the beginning. Expressing the standpoint here attained, Hegel writes,

> [The science of logic's] entire course, in which all possible shapes of a given content and of objects came up for consideration, has demonstrated their transition and untruth; also that not merely was it impossible for a given object to be the foundation to which the absolute form stood in a merely external and contingent relationship but that, on the contrary, the absolute form has proved itself to be the absolute foundation and ultimate truth. From this course the method has emerged as *the self-knowing concept that has itself*, as the absolute, both subjective and

objective, *for its subject matter*, consequently as the pure correspondence of the concept and its reality, as a concrete existence that is the concept itself. (*WL* 2:551/826)

Having traversed these many determinations through the course of the work, the concept is revealed as self-moving and self-knowing. What remains at this point, then, is the elucidation of this self-moving form: "Therefore what remains to be considered here is not a content as such, but the universal aspect of its form—that is, the *method*" (*WL* 2:550/825).

While the proof of Hegel's system rests in the details of the particular movements and transitions, the general form of the movement constitutes the method and can be outlined. This method is simply the movement of the concept itself (*WL* 2:551/826), so that "what constitutes the method are the determinations of the concept itself and their relations" (*WL* 2:553/827). The explication of the method therefore simultaneously constitutes a definition of the concept. The beginning is simply the immediate, an abstract universality apparently without determination. It does not begin with an object given by sensuous intuition or representation but with a product of thought itself, "a supersensuous *inner intuition*" (*WL* 2:553/827–28). Already, within this immediacy, lies a deficiency: "Even the abstract universal as such, considered in its concept, that is in its truth, is not merely the *simple*, but as *abstract* is already *posited* as infected with a *negation*" (*WL* 2:555/829). To be abstract is to be not determinate; an abstraction is posited as devoid of particularity and thus negating particularity. Because this difference is already implicit within the beginning, the concept has satisfied the requirement for self-movement, that "the immediate of the beginning must be *in its own self* deficient and endowed with the *drive* to carry itself further" (*WL* 2:555/829). Otherwise, the method would be externally applied in a manner inadequate to a science of logic.

This urge or drive within the first moment of the concept results in the second moment, associated with "the emergence of *real difference* [*Differenz*], judgment, the *process of determining* [*das Bestimmen*] in general" (*WL* 2:556/830), as well as the negative, the determinate, and relationship. Here, the determinacy and difference implicit but concealed in the first moment becomes explicit: "Taken quite generally, this determination can be taken to mean that what is at first *immediate* now appears as *mediated, related* to an other, or that the universal appears as a particular. Hence the *second* term that has thereby come into being is the *negative* of the first, and if we anticipate the subsequent progress, the *first negative*" (*WL* 2:561, 834). This negative introduces difference, overcoming the simplicity of the first moment. Although it negates the first moment, the outcome is not nothing. To the contrary, the determinacy and negation that define the second moment as "*the other of the first*, the *negative of the immediate*," yield a positive advance beyond the first moment, while containing and retaining that moment within itself (*WL* 2:561/834). This negativity constitutes the movement of the concept. Hegel describes it as "the *simple point of the negative relation* to self, the innermost source of all activity, of all animate and spiritual self-movement, the dialectical soul that everything true possesses and through which it alone is true; for on this subjectivity alone rests the sublating of the opposition between concept and reality, and the unity that is truth" (*WL* 2:563/835). This negativity, implicit within the concept and not introduced or imposed from without, generates the determinacy and particularity of the second moment.

The third moment, the individual or singular [*das Einzelne*], arises in the second negation, the negation of the negation, through which the immediate is recovered. Uniting and containing within itself the previous moments, this third moment moves beyond them: "Now more precisely the *third* is the immediate, but the immediate *resulting from sublation of mediation*, the simple resulting from *sublation of difference*, the positive resulting from sublation of the negative, the concept that has realized itself by means of its otherness and by the sublation of this reality has become unity with itself . . ." (*WL* 2:565/837). The virtual neologism "sublation" and its related forms have traditionally been used in Hegel translations and scholarship to render *Aufhebung*, which Hegel uses as a term of art to convey a simultaneous canceling and preserving. This final movement restores the universal, but no longer in the abstract form of the first moment. It is therefore the universal that is also identical with its determinations and consequently the truth into which the first two "untrue" moments pass over (*WL* 2:566/837).

Not only does the third moment contain the first two, but in the absolute Idea, which comes at the end of the entire development of the logic, nothing is excluded. No possible thought determinations lie outside the circle created, and in this sense the moments of the method together constitute a system (*WL* 2:567/838). This system constitutes a totality in the sense that it is a system of all possible objects, where objects are understood in the only way they meaningfully can be according to Hegel: not as metaphysical substances but as determinations of thought. Yet while the rejection of such strong metaphysical claims makes Hegel appear less outlandish to many contemporary readers, his claims to a system of thinking are by no means trivial. Although he acknowledges the need to improve on particular points in the argument, at points he makes a strong claim that all the determinations of thought can be set forth in their necessary interrelationships to form a complete, exhaustive system: "The Idea is thinking, not as formal thinking, but as the self-developing totality of its own peculiar determinations and laws" (*Enz.* § 19 A). Revealing this self-development has been the task of the logic. These determinations of thought are not the accidental arbitrary whim of a particular subject; for this reason, it is not a subjective idealism. To the contrary, they are the necessary determinations of thinking itself. Finally, to make this claim does not imply thinking by some superhuman subject. While thinking cannot be reduced to particular instances of thinking by particular human beings, only human beings think, as is revealed in the account of subjective spirit.

In the *Encyclopaedia*'s presentation of the system, the conclusion of the logic is followed by the philosophy of nature. While the development of the logic has included objectivity as well as its own realization, as logic, it has remained within thinking. Nonetheless, "Because the pure Idea of cognition is so far confined within subjectivity, it is the *drive* [*Trieb*] to sublate this, and pure truth as the last result becomes also the *beginning of another sphere and science*" (WL 2:572–73/843). While this movement proceeds from a "drive," Hegel claims that it is not a "transition" like the transitions necessitated above. Where those involve the sublation of the prior moments as a result of a contradiction, the movement to the sphere of nature is not driven by contradiction but results from the Idea freely moving beyond the abstraction of thought. The Idea thus posits itself in the external form known as nature. While religious representation [*Vorstellung*] expresses this development in terms of God's act of creation, its philosophical formulation in terms of the Idea positing this externality presupposes neither a theistically conceived divine being nor a cosmic spirit that creates nature as its manifestation. To the contrary, thinking itself is the agent that brings about the sphere of nature—in which the concept is implicit but not explicit, not an object for itself but only to thinking—through its own positing.

## Philosophy of Nature

A brief discussion of the philosophy of nature, particularly its beginning and end, not only outlines the developments in the system between the logic and the philosophy of spirit but also provides an account of contingency and empirical research fundamental to both the philosophy of nature and of spirit. Hegel concisely introduces the defining characteristics of nature in "The Concept of Nature." He begins with the point already indicated at the end of the logic, that the sphere of nature is defined by its externality in relation to the Idea: "Nature has yielded itself as the Idea in the form of *otherness*" (*Enz.* § 247). The *philosophy* of nature is not an inventory of all that is found in nature but thinking comprehension of the Idea as it appears in nature. It thus provides the philosophical foundation for, rather than replacing, particular natural sciences, such as zoology or chemistry. In the logic the determinations of the concept emerge from each other, while here, because nature is the Idea in externality, the determinations "have the appearance of an *indifferent subsistence* and *isolation* with regard to one another"; not being self-moving in the manner of the logic, nature appears as determined not by itself but by "*necessity* and *contingency*, not freedom" (*Enz.* § 248).

Because the determinate forms of nature appear as external to each other, the development within the sphere of nature takes place on the basis of the concept implicit in nature, not in the external forms of nature themselves: "Nature is to be regarded as a *system of stages*, the one proceeding of necessity out of the other.... This is not to be thought of as a *natural* engendering of one out of the other, however, but as an engendering within the inner Idea which constitutes the ground of nature" (*Enz.* § 249). The movement is driven not by contradictions within the externally existing objects, such as the plant, but in the concept that constitutes the object. Hegel here explicitly rejects the type of metamorphosis that evolution represents, though one could argue that his own conception of development might have anticipated rather than rejected evolutionary theory (see *Enz.* § 249 and A). For the present purposes, however, what matters most is that the method elaborated at the end of the logic continues to operate in this sphere.

Paragraph 248 also introduces an essential role for contingency. While the *philosophy* of nature develops through a necessary movement, the sphere of nature itself is constituted to a significant degree by contingency: "The *contradiction* of the Idea, in being external to itself as nature, is more precisely the contradiction of, on one hand, the conceptually generated *necessity* of its formations and their rational determination within the organic totality, and on the other, their indifferent contingency and indeterminable irregularity" (*Enz.* § 250). The concept does not and cannot determine the number of species of parrot that exist, for instance (see *WL* 2:524/804). While what it is to be a plant or a species is determined by the concept, much regarding particular, individual plants and species is contingently determined. While the point appears obvious, caricatures of Hegel make it worth stressing. Moreover, despite the differences between the spheres of nature and of spirit, contingency continues to play an important role in the latter as well.

This role for contingency also raises the issue of the relation between this philosophical science and experience.[18] While "the *origin* and *cultivation* of philosophical science have empirical physics as a presupposition and condition," experience cannot constitute its foundation, which must be constituted by the concept (*Enz.* § 246 A). Though empirically based natural sciences arise and make tremendous progress without sound philosophical grounding, such grounding itself cannot come from experience but only from philosophy. Philosophical science cannot appeal to experience as something given. Within Hegel's work, the logic (and the *Phenomenology of Spirit* before that) has already undermined any appeal to immediacy; as we have seen above, the immediate gives way to the mediated, and the concept is on the move, seeking stable determinations of thought. Nonetheless, experience is not to be disregarded or ignored. The results of the conceptual development must be shown to correspond to experience, and while experience cannot determine the philosophy of nature, it will be essential in grasping nature's contingent aspects—as in the counting of species of parrots.

In the final paragraph of the "Concept of Nature," Hegel determines nature with respect to the end toward which it advances: "[M]ore closely considered, the movement through its [nature's] series of stages consists of the Idea *positing* itself as what it is *implicitly*, that is, the Idea passes *into itself* by proceeding out of its immediacy and externality, which is *death*. It does this . . . to bring itself forth into the existence of spirit, which constitutes the truth and ultimate purpose of nature, and the true actuality of the Idea" (*Enz.* § 251). The purpose and end of nature is its own overcoming: the overcoming of the Idea's externality or otherness to itself. As foreshadowed here and developed in the final paragraphs of the philosophy of nature, this transition to spirit is brought about—conceptually—through the death of the individual. Through death the Idea moves beyond its identification with something merely external, in which the Idea can never exist for itself: "[T]hrough this sublation of the *immediacy* of its reality, subjectivity has coincided with itself. The last *self-externality* of nature is sublated, so that the concept, which in nature merely has *implicit* being, has become for itself.—With this, nature has passed over into its truth, into the subjectivity of the concept, whose *objectivity* is itself the sublated immediacy of singularity, i.e., *concrete universality*. Consequently, the concept is posited as having the reality which corresponds to it, i.e., the concept, as its *determinate being*. This is *spirit*" (*Enz.* § 376).

## The Concept of Spirit

Only in the realm of spirit are the limitation to the realm of pure thinking and the mere externality that characterized the logic and the philosophy of nature, respectively, overcome. Here we find Hegel's explicit treatment of human realms. The systematic location of Hegel's philosophical anthropology, subjective spirit, has therefore almost been reached. All that remains in Hegel's analysis is to complete the framing of the background of subjective spirit with a preliminary overview of the conception of spirit. Focusing on the process of development at its core, my discussion here will draw extensively on §§ 381–84 of the *Encyclopaedia*, which Hegel titles "The Concept of Spirit" and which make up much of the transition from the philosophy of nature to the philosophy of spirit. Hegel's analysis at this point can only be formal and abstract, however, "since what spirit is, is precisely the object of our science" (*VPGst* 12). Spirit can only be fully comprehended in the course of the development of the philosophy of spirit. This introductory treatment, then, necessarily deals only with the abstract structure of spirit, not with its actual, concrete existence.

Emerging from nature, spirit consists in the negation of the apparent givenness and externality of nature. Whereas in nature the Idea was outside of itself, or an other to itself, in spirit the Idea returns to itself: "Nature has vanished in this truth, and spirit has yielded itself as the Idea which has attained to its being-for-self, the *object* of which, to the same extent as its *subject*, is the *concept*" (*Enz.* § 381). The subject and object of the development are once again united, as they were in the logic. In the bifurcation of the philosophy of nature, the concept had its other for an object; in the realm of spirit, the concept (as subject) is comprehending itself (as object). Here, however, the concept is manifest as spirit, not simply remaining in the realm of pure thinking in which the logic was set. This return to itself is therefore not a regression to the logic but the attainment of a negative identity mediated by externality. Spirit, as will be demonstrated, achieves identity with itself in its external forms. The concept only achieves this identity (as subject and object) in spirit "as return out of nature" (*Enz.* § 381).

Though negation takes different forms at different stages of the process, this ability to abstract from any particular determinacy provides the basis for spirit's freedom: "The *essence* of spirit is therefore formally *freedom*, the absolute negativity of the concept as self-identity" (*Enz.* § 382). This process of negation, of a surpassing of all particular posits or externalizations, is essential to being spirit: "On account of this formal determination, spirit *can* abstract from all that is external and even from its own externality, its own determinate being . . ." (*Enz.* § 382). Consequently, though spirit exists only in particular manifestations, it cannot be identified with any one of these. This infinite capacity for negation is precisely what differentiates spirit from nature; it is in this sense the "essence" of spirit, even though this capacity to abstract constitutes only the formal element of freedom. Spirit, in its abstract universality, can maintain itself in the face of the negation of all particular externality.

As in the logic, however, negation does not result in nothing but is a determinate negation, with a positive result. In the realm of spirit, the process of liberation from a particular externality contributes to the positing of a higher one. Consequently, "The whole development of the concept of spirit simply portrays spirit's making itself free [*das Sichfreimachen des Geistes*] from all forms of its determinate existence [*seines Daseins*] that do not correspond to its concept . . ." (*Enz.* § 382 Z). Spirit's entire development is its liberating itself through negation from inadequate externalities; and each act of negation drives the development of a further, higher revelation of spirit, which is in turn negated as also not being fully adequate.

The process or activity that defines spirit consists therefore not only in negation but also in manifestation. Such manifestations constitute the moments of spirit's development, spirit's positing of itself as an other: "As being for itself, the universal *particularizes* itself and in this particularity is identical with itself. The determination of spirit is therefore *manifestation*" (*Enz.* § 383). As Hegel expresses it in the *Lectures on the Philosophy of Religion*, "spirit's essential [character] is to be altogether active. More exactly, it is the activity of self-manifesting. Spirit that does not manifest or reveal itself is something dead" (*VPR* 1:85). Initially an abstract universal, spirit manifests itself in determinate existences— i.e., concrete historical forms. As explained in the addition,

> This determination belongs to spirit as such and therefore holds good of it not only insofar as it is simply self-relating, is the I that has itself as an object, but also insofar as it comes forth from the abstract being-for-self of its universality by positing within itself a determinate distinction, something other than itself. For spirit does not lose itself in this other but maintains and actualizes itself there, expressing its internality, making

the other into an existence corresponding to it [spirit], comes therefore—through this sublation of the other, of the particular actual difference—to concrete being-for-self, to determinate self-revelation.
(*Enz.* § 383 Z)

The abstract universal, in a process of diremption, posits itself as something
other, though this otherness ultimately reveals itself to be not other at all. Spirit
advances through negating the externality that it has posited but which constitutes an inadequate manifestation. As examined through the course of the philosophy of spirit, the positing takes many different forms. Some posits are
theoretical, in that they concern cognition of the world, while others involve
the practical transformation of the world, as in the formation of political institutions. As the system develops, spirit's expressions become increasingly adequate reflections of spirit's essence. The movement is spiraling in that each
manifestation is in some sense higher than the last, but viewed from another
perspective, as a formal process of self-externalization and return to self, it is
the circular process that lies at the center of much of Hegel's thought.

Spirit's self-revelation, however, is not simply the "translation" of its content,
what spirit *is*, into another format. Rather, spirit is this *process* of self-revelation:
"The self-revelation is therefore itself the content of spirit, and not somehow
merely a form added externally to the content of spirit. Consequently, through
its revelation spirit reveals not a content differing from its form, but rather its
form—which expresses the entire content of spirit—i.e. its self-revelation"
(*Enz.* § 383 Z). Spirit is not a something which is then revealed, as though
something external made it perceptible. Spirit itself is the agent of the revelation; moreover, this revealing is what it is to be spirit. *Spirit reveals itself as
self-revealing*, as positing itself as other. Spirit is thus a process defined by negation and self-positing, not simply a thing or substance. Describing spirit is
made more difficult because it is not some static "thing" that can simply be
defined and counted on to remain the same through the elaboration of Hegel's thought.[19] Spirit is engaged in a constant process of becoming what it is.
Or rather, it *is* this process itself; spirit's "end is not the finished product but the
activity of production" (*VG* 36/33).

This activity of negation and manifestation, resulting in more adequate self-
externalizations of spirit, aims toward one final end: spirit's self-knowledge.
Initially, spirit exists only implicitly or in itself (*an sich*). Hegel's entire *Encyclopaedia* traces the process of spirit's developing self-knowledge, its becoming spirit for itself (*für sich*) and then in-and-for-itself (*anundfürsich*).

The goal of spirit's development, then, is "to make itself into and become *explicitly* [*für sich*] that which it is *implicitly*" (*Enz.* § 387 A). The struggle toward this self-knowledge constitutes the driving force behind and ultimate meaning of spirit's entire development—not only in art, religion, and philosophy but also in world history itself: "It may be said that the discovery of this definition [of the absolute as spirit] and the grasping of its meaning and content was the ultimate purpose of all education and philosophy. All religion and science has driven toward this point, and world history is to be grasped solely from this drive" (*Enz.* § 384 A). Through the identity achieved between spirit and that manifestation which initially appears as its other, the alterity is overcome; spirit becomes conscious that what appeared as its other is spirit's own. It returns to itself in that it becomes conscious that "in self-knowing spirit, that which is produced and that which produces it are one and the same" (*Enz.* § 379 Z). For this reason, spirit does not lose itself but rather comes to itself, returns to itself, through knowing itself in this manifestation. Through overcoming this otherness, sublating or canceling it, spirit completes its return to itself. It comes to be "at home," or *bei sich*, in its manifestations, thereby actualizing the freedom that was only formal or abstract in the moment of negation. In the process, spirit has also transformed itself; it has become self-knowing, becoming for itself what it is implicitly from the beginning. Thus, the "know thyself" to which Hegel refers in the second sentence of the "Philosophy of Spirit" concerns not only philosophical anthropology; it stands at the heart of his entire philosophical project.[20]

What makes this path to spirit's self-knowledge of more than theoretical interest, the reason it underlies world history as well as the history of philosophy and the reason that Hegel has something interesting to contribute to our understanding of the role of the external world in human self-realization, is that this process or activity is far from exclusively cognitive. In positing nature, thinking spirit projects a realm beyond itself; yet spirit does not create nature in the sense that a God or gods do in creation stories taken literally. In manifesting itself as spirit, however, spirit acts in the world, creating social and political institutions, history, art, religion, and philosophy. Concretely, humans transform the world—through work—such that it more clearly expresses spirit; we transform it into an expression of spirit. In this sense, the positing of the realm of nature—examined in the philosophy of nature—is crucially different from many of the manifestations that take place in the realm of spirit. Spirit actively creates its (our) world. Spirit's path toward self-knowledge is a very long one, consisting of many moments or levels of development. Spirit comes to know itself through manifesting or revealing itself.[21]

The four paragraphs of the "Concept of Spirit" set forth the essential elements of spirit: Spirit emerges from the sublation of the externality of nature (*Enz.* § 381), which then leads into the account of the essence of spirit as formally freedom (§ 382). But the negation of a particular manifestation also results in another manifestation, or self-determination, which Hegel proceeds to discuss (§ 383). Through this process of self-revelation, spirit returns to itself and comes to know itself as spirit (§ 384).

One further point regarding spirit's freedom merits particular attention. We have already seen the essential role of negation in providing the basis for freedom, as well as the way that this merely abstract freedom is actualized when spirit finds itself "at home" in its manifestations. Both of these elements reflect the centrality of self-determination to Hegel's conception of freedom. Hegel's concept of spirit draws heavily on an Aristotelian conception of the realization, development, or unfolding of an implicit potential; in this sense, spirit's entire development is a matter of making explicit what it already implicitly is.[22] At the same time, Hegel distinguishes teleological development as it occurs at the level of nature from its appearance in spirit. In nature—as in the case of an acorn that develops into an oak tree—this development is regulated by an external force. The acorn does not dictate its own development and is therefore not free; its telos is given rather than self-determined.[23] In the case of spirit, however, development is not dictated externally but by spirit itself. This emphasis on self-determination strongly reflects the impact of "modern" conceptions of freedom as developed in Rousseau, Kant, and Fichte.[24] For Hegel, action can be free only when it is determined by the agent's essence. Spirit thus determines its development in accord with its own essence. Because spirit *is* self-revealing activity, in revealing itself to itself it is only being itself. Since this "essence" is a process rather than simply a substance, it is neither dependent upon nor identical with any particular manifestation; this makes the abstract freedom of negation a foundational element of Hegel's more comprehensive conception of freedom. Freedom as self-determination also precludes random or arbitrary action, precisely because such action is not determined by the self. Hegel's view of freedom, like Kant's, excludes *Willkür* (arbitrary acts of will) just as much as other forms of heteronomy.[25] Because spirit's development is an unfolding of what it implicitly is, this development is necessary. Consequently, Hegel can say that "just as the seed bears within it the whole nature of the tree and the taste and form of its fruits, so also do the first glimmerings of spirit contain virtually the whole of history" (*VG* 61/53). Because what spirit implicitly is is free, however, this development is also free. Here freedom and necessity coincide.

Freedom is only fully actualized when spirit has entirely determined itself, or become what it (implicitly) is. Since this end entails spirit's self-knowledge, spirit is only fully free when it has attained self-knowledge. In so doing, spirit recognizes itself in its determinations, knows them as its self-manifestations, and thereby comes to be at home, or *bei sich*, in them. The complete actualization of freedom can thus be summed up as self-conscious self-determination.[26]

Finally, it is important to stress that spirit's freedom is, like spirit as a whole, initially present only implicitly. It too must become, must manifest itself and become known to itself so as to be truly self-conscious and free: "actual freedom is therefore not something existing immediately in spirit, but rather something to be brought about through spirit's activity" (*Enz.* § 382 Z; see also *Rph II*, 231). In freeing itself from particular, inadequate manifestations, spirit comes to know itself as free; in so doing it first *becomes* actually free in that it becomes explicitly (*für sich*) what it initially was only implicitly (*an sich*).

## Subjective Spirit

Whereas these introductory paragraphs of the third part of the *Encyclopaedia* provide a provisional, highly abstract account of spirit as a whole, the determinate developments of spirit are divided into three spheres: subjective, objective, and absolute spirit. The first, subjective spirit, concerns spirit as manifest in individual human beings, largely in abstraction from their social context; this forms the core of Hegel's anthropology. The second, objective spirit, treats spirit's manifestation in the external, social world as an existing reality, such as economic and political systems. In the third and final sphere, absolute spirit, spirit reflects upon itself, seeks to comprehend itself, through art, religion, and philosophy.

At the first level, subjective spirit, spirit is "in the form of *relationship to itself*," i.e., in abstraction from its concrete manifestation in the world (*Enz.* § 385). Formulated in the most abstract terms, Hegel here examines the further immanent development of the concept as it returns out of nature to itself as spirit. In subjective spirit, spirit is considered not in its determinate form but in its abstract universality, as the first moment of the sphere of spirit. It begins where the sphere of nature left off and, as in the other spheres, advances through the movement or development of the object itself.

In tracing these further developments of the concept or Idea, Hegel discusses topics generally considered part of an account of human beings, such as

the distinction between humans and nature, sensation, consciousness, imagination, memory, thought, and action. Moreover, the *Vorlesungen über die
Philosophie des Geistes* (Lectures on the philosophy of spirit)—which amplifies
the *Encyclopaedia*'s treatment of subjective spirit—makes particularly clear that
Hegel is here discussing human beings. In the introduction, for instance, he
criticizes empirical psychology and pneumatology—both of which constitute
approaches to the understanding of individual human beings and therefore
what I am calling anthropology—as these represent competing notions of how
to address the topic. In the *Encyclopaedia*, however, the discussion of empirical
psychology and pneumatology occurs in the second paragraph (*Enz.* § 378),
placing it within the overall introduction to the philosophy of spirit, not within
the discussion of subjective spirit. This should emphasize for us that Hegel's
conception of human beings is not given in the philosophy of subjective spirit
alone, but is revealed throughout the philosophy of spirit. Nonetheless, it is in
the philosophy of subjective spirit—and in the lectures which correspond to
it—that Hegel analyzes the underlying structure of spirit considered in itself. It
is precisely this analysis which, as will become clear in chapters 2 through 4,
deals directly with Hegel's fundamental understanding of human beings.

Subjective spirit therefore simultaneously considers both philosophical
anthropology and the immanent development of spirit—which results from
the development of the concept through the logic and the philosophy of
nature—in relation to itself. These are not two separate treatments but two
ways of describing the same treatment. Grasping why it can and must be both
of these depends upon an adequate understanding of the logic's relation to the
sphere of spirit. The logic does not simply provide a structure or framework
into which the content or material relevant to the sphere of subjective spirit (or
the other higher spheres) must be fit (*PR* § 31). Nor does it produce a method
that can be mechanically, externally "applied" to given material in the higher
spheres. To the contrary, Hegel consistently stresses immanent development, a
process of unfolding driven by contradictions that propel the analysis forward,
and the logic has undermined any notion of a "given" material. To conceive of
the method as applied would make the structure or form distinctly external to
the content of the sphere itself. It would be comparable, within a Kantian
framework, to maintaining that we have experiences, which we secondarily
structure in terms of time and space. For Hegel, it would reopen a divide
between phenomena and things-in-themselves, because it would entail that
there is a reality somehow "behind" these phenomena, rather than construing
them as constituted as what they are only by thinking.[27]

Instead, subjective spirit consists of the further immanent development of the system. Whereas in the logic the object was the concept in the element of pure thinking, here the object is spirit, whose conception and emergence has resulted from the previous two spheres. While what spirit is is determined by the system, spirit is actualized only in human beings and the human world. For this reason, the articulation of the further development of the system at this point simultaneously provides Hegel's account of human beings. This convergence is not stipulated in advance by the system, but when one considers spirit, it becomes apparent that one is considering what we generally refer to as human beings. Because spirit achieves determinate existence in human beings, there is no other possibility.

This convergence, however, does not mean that subjective spirit is based upon empirical investigation. As we saw in the discussion of the philosophy of nature—and as Hegel already argues in the introductory material of the *Encyclopaedia*—appeals to an apparently immediate experience are inadequate to science and cannot justify their own claims. The account should agree with experience, but it cannot be based upon experience. To the contrary, Hegel must demonstrate that this dynamic, immanent development is intrinsic to habit, self-consciousness, intelligence, and will, when the latter are properly understood. Consequently, the conception of immanent development is the most important contribution of the logic to the understanding of Hegel's account of subjective spirit. The movement must be found within the objects themselves.

The anthropology that results considers human beings in abstraction from history and experience. Such an anthropology is plausible only on the basis of some degree of underlying stability or structure integral to what it means to be a human being, such that at least some things can be said about humans that do not change with history. Because of the significance of history to spirit's development, Hegel's account of this "universal" anthropology must be in some sense formal—to be "filled" with the content that the individual appropriates from the world in which she lives. As Peperzak argues in discussing the account of practical spirit within the sphere of subjective spirit,

> Although the will must be defined as spirit which gives itself its content, its particular content cannot yet be derived in the chapter on subjective spirit. In this respect its concept here remains "formal": Only the form of the will or the *how* of willing is specified here, not *what* it must will. This "*formalism*" characterizes the entire theory of subjective spirit, thus the different levels of theoretical spirit as well . . . .[28]

Hegel expresses this position clearly in a crucial passage in the introduction to the *Vorlesungen über die Philosophie des Geistes*:

> When it is asked what spirit is, the actual meaning of the question is "What is the truth of spirit?", and that is equivalent to "What is the determination [or definition, *Bestimmung*] of human beings?"—Determination expresses a difference, an aim, a purpose, that ought to be achieved[.] [I]nto what ought the human being make himself, what *ought* he be, what ought he produce in himself through his freedom? Determination, however, also means just as much, on the other hand, originally, what the human being implicitly is. The human being ought to produce himself, but he can make himself into nothing other than, can have no other purpose than, what he originally, implicitly is. That which he implicitly is is what one calls an endowment [*Anlage*]. The nature of spirit is to produce what it is, to bring what it is to manifestation, revelation, to consciousness. Thus, its determination is to make itself what it implicitly is. (*VPGst* 6–7)[29]

First, the passage should put to rest any doubts about subjective spirit providing an anthropology.[30] Beyond this, Hegel here provides a key term for understanding the type of anthropology he provides. He refers to that which human beings implicitly (*an sich*) are as an *Anlage*. The term *Anlage* has a range of relevant meanings: in relation to human beings, it generally refers to talent or ability, usually something given by nature rather than developed. Accordingly, Michael Petry, in his translation of the *Philosophy of Subjective Spirit*, renders the term "endowment."[31] Yet in *Enz.* § 410 A Hegel explicitly relates *Anlage* to what is in us implicitly (*an sich*). And the term can also refer to a design or plan as well as a rudimentary form or germ, suggesting that what can be said about human beings in general, what we implicitly are, constitutes a sort of abstract plan which has its realization as its purpose, much as the acorn has as its goal the developed oak tree.

This potential is intrinsic to being human and is to be thought of largely in terms of the Aristotelian conception of the realization of potential. Not all human beings will realize this potential. This realization is deeply affected by "external" circumstances beyond the individual's control, and Hegel thinks that only a fraction of the population can ever fully realize this potential. The particular possibilities actually available in any given historical context will vary significantly. Moreover, in contrast to an Aristotelian conception that sees human development and flourishing principally in terms of the development of virtuous dispositions, the significance Hegel gives history means that human flour-ishing cannot be spelled out in terms of the development of universal virtues.[32]

Nonetheless, uniting the very different human beings who emerge in differ-ent times and places is an underlying, implicit structure—one that aims toward becoming free, self-conscious spirit. Although it is abstract or formal rather than concrete, this underlying structure is universal. Abstractly all human beings have the potential to overcome their givenness and manifest spirit, even if not all individuals are given this opportunity. It is helpful to distinguish here between an abstract *potential* and a concrete *possibility*. To say that someone had the potential (innate ability) to become a great writer, for instance, does not entail that she had the actual opportunities (the additional training) neces-sary to develop this potential; there may have been potential but no possibility of realizing the potential. What or how advanced a manifestation of spirit is possible for a given individual depends a great deal on the society in which the person lives—considerations which become more concrete in objective and absolute spirit.[33]

To develop this potential is for Hegel the fundamental ethical imperative. "Know thyself"—which I have already discussed as being at the heart of He-gel's project—is identified at the beginning of the "Philosophy of Spirit" as an "absolute commandment [*Gebot*]" (*Enz.* § 377). Spirit's commandment to know itself, and therefore to develop, is specifically normative for Hegel. Further, this command—which he applies to concrete human beings in the long passage cited above "is not to be taken as one command among many others, but as the command of the knowing God, in relation to which all else is dependent and subordinate" (*VPGst* 5). Spirit's further development is the highest priority and not something that can be looked upon as a matter of indifference. As much as Hegel criticizes the "mere ought" that stands over against actuality,[34] his use of the term "ought" (*sollen*) in this context indicates the distinctly normative dimension of his point, though it is not to be con-ceived in opposition to spirit's "actual" unfolding.[35] This "commandment," then, is "*at the same time* a task and a necessity. For human beings, as finite and not necessarily good spirit, the task appears . . . as an *ought*, which one could formulate as '*Become what you are* (namely, spirit)!'"[36] It is for this reason that "*Hegel's psychology is at the same time a fundamental ethics*."[37]

In this conception of ethics in terms of the command to become what one is, Hegel sits within an Aristotelian tradition of teleological thought, despite the transformations he imposes on this thought through his emphasis on self-consciousness and freedom. From this perspective, ethics consists in conforming to and developing in light of a purpose or function that is inherent in the subject from the beginning. Aristotle pursues an understanding of the highest good through seeking the function or characteristic activity (*ergon*) of human beings.[38] For him, the good (human) life is to be determined in accord with the characteristic function of human beings; an understanding of human beings will reveal what it means to be a good human being. For both Aristotle and Hegel, identifying the human end requires comprehending an activity that constitutes what it means to be human.[39] For Hegel, this understanding cannot be derived from experience or observation but only through tracing the immanent unfolding of the concept of spirit that emerges from the system's previous developments. Thus, both Hegel's and Aristotle's visions involve the realization of human potential, a process of becoming explicitly what we implicitly already are. This means that for both Aristotle and Hegel ethics cannot be derived solely from what it means to be a rational agent, but follows from a philosophical anthropology.

As compared to anthropologies with a highly elaborated account of human *nature*, where certain drives, such as those for food and sex, are seen as fixed and universal in all human beings, Hegel's account conceives of what is implicit as a structure rather than a set of tendencies or dispositions. Activity and actualization are once again central to this conception, and the account at this level is abstract in the sense of always being "filled in" or actualized in a particular human being. Human beings never exist simply as the abstract structure that Hegel develops as "subjective spirit." We are not this and then, *later*, socialized and involved in a particular culture. Rather, whenever we are considering actual, existing human beings, we are not dealing simply with the abstract structures laid out in subjective spirit. How potentials are realized is crucial, not just the underlying structure.

The first step in setting out Hegel's anthropology, then, must be an exploration of this underlying structure or *Anlage* in itself. This level considers the totality of spirit's development, but only as an "ideal" or abstract development, i.e., only within the subject, not externally in the world. Here, spirit "is in the form of *relation to itself*, the *ideal* totality of the Idea being within it, i.e., that which constitutes its concept becomes for it, and its being is that it is with itself, i.e., free—*subjective spirit*" (*Enz.* § 385). Yet spirit already develops at this stage; spirit's foundation is an active one, not a static substance. While spirit does not attain existence in this abstract form, it is this structure that underlies the whole of spirit's development. It is to Hegel's account of spirit in this abstract form, as discussed in his philosophy of subjective spirit, that we now turn.

## The Basic Structure of the Anthropology

In the philosophy of subjective spirit, Hegel describes spirit's emergence out of nature as it occurs in human beings: the transformation from a naturally determined being that is only implicitly spirit to manifested, free spirit. By the end, it has completed the task, "to make itself into, and to become *for itself* [*für sich*], what it is implicitly [*an sich*]" (*Enz.* § 387 A). The overall movement through subjective spirit is a process of overcoming what is merely given to proceed toward a freedom in which we are self-determining. It is a development from external determination to self-determination, from heteronomy to autonomous freedom. It is here that we see Hegel's understanding of *being* human as a process of auto-poiesis or self-production. Where we "find" ourselves having arms, we learn to control them and how to use them to express ourselves or transform our world; where we "find" ourselves having certain values that we have inherited from the society in which we live, we examine or reflect upon these values and then perhaps appropriate them, making them ours in a way that they were not when we accepted them unquestioningly from the world around us. The process begins with spirit still submerged in nature (in the "Anthropology"[40]), proceeds through the dichotomy of a consciousness that reflects upon itself (in the "Phenomenology of Spirit"), and concludes with the overcoming of this posited difference and the emergence of free spirit (in the "Psychology").

Spirit's development out of its self-alienation in natural determinacy proceeds through a series of moments. Whereas in the sphere of nature these moments each have an independent, external existence, in spirit they rarely appear in their pure form. Certain moments of development, for instance, only become externally apparent in mental illnesses; when these moments are incorporated into a developed spirit, they are not easily identifiable. This means that in daily life we do not encounter people who perfectly represent one moment of this development; in most of our activities and experiences, many of these moments are in play and cannot be separated from others, which hinders our understanding of Hegel's references at points. In some cases, Hegel brings in later stages of development to explain earlier stages, simply because the abstract account alone is so difficult to follow.[41] Moreover, moments are not simply passed through never to be returned to, either by individuals or cultures. We do not cease to feel once we have attained the level of thought; nor is it clear that as soon as we have "thought" once we never again feel in an "unsublated" manner. Thus, while there is clearly development, it is not a simple process, and the larger dynamic of overcoming the "given" determination in which we find ourselves is repeated at many levels.

Central to my interpretation of Hegel's anthropology is that this development consists of and is brought about by both cognitive and practical activity. Although Hegel often emphasizes the transformations in consciousness, the changes in consciousness can only come about as a result of practical activity in the world, and the free spirit in which this development culminates constitutes a synthesis of both theoretical and practical spirit. It is only "through its activity" that spirit is liberated to objectivity and full consciousness of its concept (*Enz.* § 387). Consequently, understanding the relation between theoretical and practical spirit as well as their role in free spirit will provide the essential background for understanding Hegel's analysis of objective spirit and the realm of the philosophy of right.[42]

In discussing the philosophy of subjective spirit, my goal is to focus on those parts that I deem central to Hegel's conception of human beings as this relates to the concerns outlined in the introduction. Nonetheless, I do follow the systematic structure of Hegel's treatment because the fundamentally developmental structure necessitates a systematic approach to his thought. A comprehensive grasp of Hegel's anthropology requires attention to virtually every stage of Hegel's elaboration of the subjective spirit.

The present chapter has prepared for this task by setting forth the systematic background of subjective spirit. We have drawn upon the logic as providing Hegel's most explicit treatment of the method of development that characterizes his system, and have sketched an overview of the spheres of logic and nature, which generate the starting point of subjective spirit. With the starting point and the method of development in hand, we have the essential systematic background. Finally, we have discussed this anthropology as an account of an underlying structure or endowment that must be developed or actualized in particular human beings in order for us to become what we are—free. With this larger framework for the examination of Hegel's anthropology in place, we turn now to his account of this structure—to "what we implicitly already are."

# 2 Habit

*The First Overcoming of Natural Determination*

In his systematic account of subjective spirit as well as in his understanding of the experience of particular human beings, Hegel begins with our being determined by forces beyond our control: first by natural influences—such as the particular character traits we happen to be born with and immediate responses to physical stimuli—and second by the habits, customs, and beliefs we unconsciously take on from the society around us. These impulses—both those that are immediate, or natural, and those that are habituated—initially appear as given and fixed rather than as subject to transformation by spirit. In the analysis of the process through which natural determination is superseded by unconsciously appropriated habits, Hegel seeks to do justice to what we inherit from the communities and traditions in which we find ourselves. Because the more advanced and complex instances of habit—such as the mores we absorb from our culture— make use of later developments in the anthropology, Hegel's initial analysis of habit addresses only its most basic forms. Ethical and religious attitudes, however, are also first acquired through a process of habituation. Consequently, his analysis of habit develops a fundamental building block of his anthropology, which ultimately provides the foundation of his account of the appropriation of tradition.

"Anthropology," the first section of the philosophy of subjective spirit, constitutes one moment of human development. It begins with spirit as immediate being, what Hegel calls the "soul." Within this sphere, the subject moves through two basic stages, from determination by natural forces to determination by habit. In the first, the person's activity is determined by natural, external forces and influences. In the second, this natural determination is overcome by habit; our activity is no longer determined by immediate impulses but rather shaped by habits that have become "second nature." Natural impulses still inform our action, but they are no longer the ultimate determinants. This movement from natural to habitual determination constitutes the first stage of spirit's liberation, but in neither stage is the subject reflecting on itself, i.e., self-conscious.

The "Anthropology" considers prereflective aspects of human existence that precede the development of self-consciousness. Whether we act on natural impulses or subordinate these in habit—such as by ignoring cold in order to focus on the task at hand or typing without focusing on the keys in order to concentrate on what we are trying to express—we are not acting reflectively or consciously and thus are not self-determining or free; we are still at the level of mere existence, rather than acting as conscious beings or as spirit in itself. In this sense, we are here only implicitly spirit.

Although this stage will be surpassed in the later segments of subjective spirit, it describes the aspect of human existence that dominates our daily activities. Even the most self-conscious individuals live most of their lives acting on natural impulses or out of habit or custom rather than consciously choosing every action; it is only in quite circumscribed contexts that we are conscious of our habits. For this reason, Hegel argues that the tendencies, drives, habits, and customs that make up this level of existence are in an important sense who and what we are. They are what we refer to when we say, "I'm the kind of person who . . . ." Our own particular habits provide the content to the formal structure Hegel here lays out. In doing so, they provide a content to who we are. At the same time, our identity is not ultimately identical with this "existence." Hegel's anthropology—like his thought as a whole—is an account of progressively emerging freedom, of liberation from that which is merely given. Insofar as we are in truth spirit, we are activity, and spirit's full development involves overcoming this nonreflective identification with particular existence. Nonetheless, although this stage is sublated in consciousness and in becoming spirit, this aspect of our existence retains an important role even in spirit's higher stages of development. My drives and habits constitute a content to my being that must be considered together with the power to abstract, to distance myself from myself, which is represented in consciousness.

## The Natural Soul

Following upon the realm of nature (part two of the *Encyclopaedia*), the "Anthropology" must begin by considering spirit at the level of existence characterizing nature. Spirit is here "in the form of *otherness*" (*Enz.* § 247), immersed in and determined by nature. At this level, the subject *is* its natural impulses, feelings, and body—not something that *has* these impulses, feelings, and body (even though it is implicitly already more). It is so sunk in this immediacy that not only does it not know that it has a consciousness, it simply does not have this consciousness. We are dealing here with spirit that is merely implicit, not yet explicit. Immersed in immediacy, the soul is a slave to natural impulses and immediate desires—driven by inborn traits and characteristics rather than an educated, cultivated rational will. In this context, Hegel describes such factors as the influence of seasons, inborn temperament or characteristic tendencies, and physical stimulation.

While this starting point is justified within the development of Hegel's system, it also responds to basic challenges confronting any anthropology with a telos of freedom. Some of the most obvious obstacles to such a conception of human beings are forces and influences that appear to be simply given from without and entirely beyond our control. Hegel's anthropology begins by examining how this initial external determination is overcome by habit and then, in later moments, analyzes how habit is overcome by self-determination.

Although such external factors appear to be "natural" and "given," Hegel is not suggesting that human beings are ever born into some "pure nature." This beginning of spirit in its immediacy "is the most untrue mode of its being; the immediacy is also an abstraction and determines itself essentially as posited. (The parents are mediated by an other in exactly the same way as the children, although we could view them as immediate.) . . . We begin therefore with the immediate, but we also know that spirit as soul presupposes itself, a game of spirit, in order to come to itself" (*VPGst* 31). This "immediate" beginning too is posited or mediated. The world we are born into, which—to anticipate—means as well the significance for our lives of such "natural" factors as seasons and times of day, is largely determined by the particular human society into which we are born. In some cases, for instance, because of human technological developments the seasons of the year do not have a tremendous effect, whereas in other times and cultures they may play a central role in regulating life. The impact of these natural factors is thus mediated by spirit, through its work in transforming the world.

In accord with the method of immanent development, the object of analysis advances from this starting point through self-differentiation. The first level of differentiation or determination that reveals itself is the most general level of natural determination—"The Natural Soul," the first subdivision of the "Anthropology." Within or presupposed by the seemingly immediate starting point are several levels of distinction—encountered within the natural soul itself, not imposed or applied from without. The first, "natural life," concerns such factors as seasons, climate, and times of day, which can have an impact on human beings. Hegel thinks that such natural factors can influence human behavior, and highly "undeveloped" spirits are greatly affected by them, having much of their lives determined by them. At the same time, factors such as the position of the planets do not, according to Hegel, influence human behavior (*VPGst* 35); not all the differences to be found in the universe relate to differences in the development of spirit. In its most immediate form, the soul is captive to these factors. Their influence, however, is not fixed; through the development of our spiritual potential, we overcome their influence upon us: "In the human being these connections increasingly lose significance the more cultivated [*gebildeter*] he is and the more his whole condition is thereby set upon a free, spiritual foundation" (*Enz.* § 392 A). Concretely, whereas people "naturally" seem to be active during the day and to rest at night, we also have the potential to reverse this arrangement, particularly as a result of the technological advances that humanity has produced.

At the next level of differentiation or determination, "[t]he universal planetary life of the natural spirit . . . particularizes itself into the concrete differences of the earth and is divided into the *particular natural spirits*, which on the whole express the nature of the geographical continents and constitute *racial diversity* [*Rassenverschiedenheit*]" (*Enz.* § 393). Although Hegel says little on this point in the text of the *Encyclopaedia* itself, both the addition and the *Vorlesungen über die Philosophie des Geistes* elaborate extensively on the significance of race.[1] The placement of race before the discussion of the concept of a people [*Volk*] entails an even more immediate or "natural" conception of the former than the latter (see *Enz.* § 394 Z). Hegel's views here are profoundly unconvincing. However, not only are they not integral to his anthropology, they stand in deep tension with the underlying motif of the freedom of spirit in relation to nature. Analyzing them therefore places the more fundamental structure of the anthropology—which undermines his claims about race—in relief.

Hegel sees both physiological and spiritual differences among Africans, Asians, and Europeans and contends that these two levels of difference are interrelated: "What concerns us more is to what extent this [skeletal difference] is connected with reference to the spiritual. This is not to be denied. . . .

Thus the physiological has a spiritual significance. If racial differences are regarded in this manner, they are not just externally but essentially connected with the spiritual" (*VPGst* 42).[2] Here, physiological, i.e., natural, characteristics determine spiritual ones.

Pursued to its conclusion, Hegel's discussion of race entails spirit's being not only initially but also ultimately determined by nature.[3] On this analysis, spirit would remain subordinate to nature. Such a relationship, however, would stand in stark contrast to the central conception of spirit as being in essence free or self-determining and to the specific movement of the anthropology, which is spirit's emerging from its captivity to nature.[4] If a fixed, natural characteristic such as race were the ultimate determinant for—not just an influence upon—spirit, that would mean that spirit is not entirely free of nature. Hegel raises this issue in the addition just before his discussion of race: "The human being is implicitly rational; therein lies the possibility of the equality of rights of all human beings—the nullity of a rigid differentiation of humanity into genera with and without rights" (*Enz.* § 393 Z). Unfortunately, he does not adequately pursue the implications of this point. Hegel's most alarming claims regarding race would imply either that not all human beings are implicitly spirit or that spirit is not in every case in itself free—neither of which is consistent with fundamental contentions of Hegel's anthropology. Thus, not only *can* we reject Hegel's views on race without rejecting basic motifs of his anthropology, we *must* reject them (as Hegel should have) in order to be compatible with these central themes.

Perhaps most illuminating in this context is the point quoted above from the lectures: While from one perspective the soul—i.e., this level of development—is immediate, from another it too is posited or mediated.[5] In this case, the difference that Hegel describes as natural and given reveals itself to be posited by Hegel himself (along with many of his contemporaries); that which human beings have created is made to appear given and fixed.[6]

Following his treatment of race, Hegel discusses the further differentiation of spirit into local spirit (*Enz.* § 394), roughly corresponding to nations or peoples (*Völker*), and then individuals (*Enz.* § 395). Here again, the discussion raises questions regarding inborn qualities which may pose significant limits to freedom for particular spirits, but in these cases Hegel does not emphasize so strongly the connection between (unchangeable) physical characteristics and levels of spiritual development.[7]

If Hegel's discussion of individuality in this context leaves open the possibility of throwing off one's innate tendencies in order to become free spirit, it also excludes one possible basis for a conception of individuality. The individuality in question at this level is based on natural determination; that is, it is a particularity given by nature rather than something acquired or self-determined (*Enz.* § 395). Thus, "Its *mode* of being is the special temperament, talent, character, physiognomy and other dispositions and idiosyncrasies, of families or singular individuals" (*Enz.* § 395). While these traits may constitute what is unique to us—empirically speaking—Hegel does not think that they constitute what is essential to us. They are externally, not autonomously, determined; and it is the role of education, or *Bildung,* to overcome these differences, to root out this particularity that stands against the universal. *Bildung,* for Hegel, refers to education in the comprehensive sense of forming the individual through acculturation, through taking on the mores and habits of one's culture. It is closely connected to Greek notions of *paideia.*[8] Thus, in our schooling, "spirit must be brought to abandon its irregularities for the knowledge of and desire for the universal, to assimilate the general culture [*Bildung*] about it. This reshaping of the soul, and this alone, constitutes education [*Erziehung*]. The more educated [*gebildeter*] a person is, the less will his behavior exhibit anything contingent and simply peculiar to him" (*Enz.* § 395 Z). Precisely because these particularities are accidental, not determined by reason, they must be overcome for the further development of spirit. Even in the case of character, which Hegel discusses in the addition as maintaining its importance even for actualized spirit, the will must take on a universal content, not simply be the expression of private interests. We are not defined by our particularities or uniqueness: "These irregularities do not concern what is essential in human beings; religion, reason, science, etc. are not affected by them . . . . What is essential is that the human is human, and all humans have an equal right to that which makes him that" (*VPGst* 49).[9] What is essential to us is that we are implicitly spirit, that we are free, not that we have certain given qualities. The latter must be overcome in order to actualize ourselves as spirit. If spirit's development entails rooting out what is particular in it so that it actualizes a universal essence, a recurring question will be what basis Hegel gives for a conception of the individual as something other or more than simply a member of a collective. Hegel's response to this question emerges in later developments in the anthropology.

After the specification into individual subjects, Hegel turns to "natural changes," which are the most general form of difference or differentiation in the single subject: "In the soul determined as *individual,* differences occur as *changes* in the individual, which is the *one* subject persisting within them, and as *moments* in the development of this subject" (*Enz.* § 396). The changes include (1) the stages of life (*Enz.* § 396), (2) "[t]he moment in which the individual's opposition to itself is real, so that it seeks and finds *itself* in *another* individual;—the *sex-relationship* . . ." (*Enz.* § 397), and (3) sleeping and waking (*Enz.* § 398).

Hegel's account of gender roles is another instance in which he seems to "naturalize" phenomena that have a large cultural component. Like his discussion of race, the discussion of gender points to tensions within Hegel's thought. One notable difference between the discussions of race and of gender is that gender differences have a more important role to play later in the system than do racial differences. Hegel's conception of the family in the *Philosophy of Right* depends on differentiated roles for men and women. At that point, the existence of a subordinate gender seems essential to the further development of the system.[10]

We cannot deny and should not conceal that Hegel held objectionable views about women. Moreover, these views cannot simply be attributed to Hegel's cultural milieu: Seyla Benhabib has pointed out that Hegel was well aware of alternative possibilities for gender relations, both as presented by other cultures (Egypt and China, for instance) and—more importantly—by his own contemporaries. He was not simply unaware that things could be different. With regard to gender relations, "Hegel saw the future, and he did not like it."[11]

Without denying that Hegel held such beliefs, however, a careful reading of the anthropology provides important tools for rejecting precisely these views, because such vertical differentiation is incompatible with fundamental aspects of Hegel's anthropology. If women are human beings, they are spirit; if they are spirit, they are implicitly free of natural determination. To make biology destiny would be to subordinate spirit to nature and thereby undermine the basic movement of spirit's freedom. Focusing on this anthropology, which reveals basic problems with hierarchical differentiation, allows us to make use of important aspects of Hegel's thought without being apologists for certain problematic—and offensive—aspects of Hegel's own beliefs.

The final differentiation within "The Natural Soul" is sensation (*Empfindung*). This includes both those sensations with an external origin (as in the sensation of heat caused by touching a burner) and those that originate internally (as in the sensation of anger) (*Enz.* § 401). We are naturally determined insofar as we act in immediate response to such stimuli.

These particular sensations, however, are transient and in their changing reveal a posited "substantiality of the soul" that *has* these particular sensations (*Enz.* § 402). This development therefore yields "The Feeling Soul," the second subdivision of the "Anthropology," which concerns the soul in relation to the totality of these sensations. Prior to this development, the soul is "sunk" in these sensations, not yet an independent subject to which they belong. If that moment is dominant, or completely determines the subject's existence, we witness psychic disturbances, which are a matter of an inadequate relation between the subject and particular sensations, e.g., allowing one particular sensation to dominate the subject's existence.[12] In the developments of the feeling soul, however, the soul emerges as an "inner individuality" distinct from its given, natural determinations (*Enz.* § 403).

### The Feeling Soul

Habit (*Gewohnheit*) is the final stage of "The Feeling Soul," in which the subject overcomes this sunkenness in particular sensations. More significantly, it marks the transition from natural determination to a "second nature" determined by habit. It is the central step toward liberation taken in this sphere. Habits encompass much of our daily existence, including activities ranging from standing upright to using language. They guide the majority of our lives, constituting so much of who we are that Hegel can say that "what I am is the totality of my habits" (*VPGst* 124). The account of habit in the first moment of subjective spirit establishes the basic structure that characterizes it here as well as in the more complex forms it attains later in the system.

Hegel's discussion of habit deals initially with sensations or feelings—such as feeling cold or warm—and with becoming sufficiently used to such states that our attention is no longer directed toward them. Habit abstracts from particular feelings and subordinates these to more general patterns. We learn to tolerate cold and to stand upright without thinking about it, often in order to focus on something else. Hegel delineates three types of habit: The first is "*hardening* against external sensations such as cold, heat, weariness of limb, etc., taste, etc." (*Enz.* § 410 A); my attention is no longer focused on the feel of the chair I am sitting in or the desk I am leaning on. The second is "indifference to *satisfaction;* desires and drives are blunted by the *habit* of satisfaction, which is the rational way of liberating oneself from them" (*Enz.* § 410 A); here I learn to subordinate and ignore my immediate desire for ice cream so that I can continue working. The third kind of habit is that involved in skills: "In habit as *skill,* the abstract being of the soul should not only be maintained for itself but also made effective as a subjective purpose *in* corporeality, which it subjects and completely permeates" (*Enz.* § 410 A). The body is made to act in a certain way to execute the subject's goals, such as riding a bicycle or speaking a language.[13] While the first two kinds of habit focus specifically on the overcoming of natural sensations and drives, the final deals with the replacement of "natural" motivators by acquired motivators, such that we are no longer simply guided by our immediate impulses. In all of these cases, we are no longer sunk in particular sensations, such that "I am affected first by this and then by that and . . . the soul is immersed in its content," but rather stand over and above these determinations (*Enz.* § 410 Z).

As a result, the soul is no longer immediately identical with these particular sensations—as it was in the early stages of subjective spirit—but a subject distinct from them which possesses them as its determinations: "In this way the soul has the content *in possession* and contains it within itself, so that it is not sentient in such determinations but possesses and moves within them without sensation or consciousness,—standing in relationship to them, but neither distinguishing itself from nor being immersed within them" (*Enz.* § 410). This possession comes about by getting used to something, accustomed to it such that one is not distracted by it. The soul is at this point more than its corporeality; it is a subject, distinguished from its sensations at any given instant. Further, it is more than the "ideal" abstraction from given sensations that it was at the beginning of "The Feeling Soul." I *am* no longer this or that physical sensation but a subject with certain habits: "Here [in habit] it is not only individual, a momentary satisfaction, etc., but rather I am this, it is my general [*allgemeine*] way—what I am is the totality of my habits, I can do nothing else, I am just that way" (*VPGst* 124). In this sense, my habits, including my customs, make me who I am. They replace raw sensations as the content of the soul.

The ability to abstract from particular sensations, which is at the heart of habituation, constitutes a critical step in the development of spirit's freedom. Because the soul is no longer absorbed in these sensations, the soul has achieved its freedom from these (natural) determinations: "In habit the human being is in the mode of natural existence and for that reason unfree, yet free, insofar as the natural determination of sensation has been reduced by habit to *his* mere being and he is no longer in a state of differentiation with respect to it, i.e., interested in, occupied with, and dependent upon it" (*Enz.* § 410 A). In relation to the immediate drives and sensations that we receive from nature, habit is freedom or liberation: "The essential determination is liberation, which the human being wins from sensations . . . through habit" (*Enz.* § 410 A).[14] Through habit, we become master rather than slave to our feelings; we train ourselves (or are trained by others) to direct our attention in one direction rather than another. And because the object of our attention is no longer determined simply by the sensations we experience, we are free from these sensations.

While Hegel's claim raises questions regarding just how far we can go in this habituation—for instance, how much one can do to ignore hunger or cold past a certain point—it is important to emphasize how mundane Hegel's point is for the most part, and how essential such processes are to our daily lives. The kind of habituation Hegel has in mind is involved every time we walk without concentrating on it, lose awareness of the feeling of our clothing against our skin, or focus on one sound rather than another. It is only because of this usually unconscious ability to direct our attention in this manner that we are able to accomplish life's most basic tasks—or more complex ones.

Yet while habit entails freedom insofar as it consists in freedom from immediate sensation, insofar as the particular content of habits is not reflected upon, mediated through consciousness, and freely willed, it is still unfree. While certain habits, particularly skills, such as riding a bicycle, involve a conscious decision to develop them, most do not. Hegel's discussion of habit precedes consciousness in his systematic development, and one of his primary examples is that of standing upright, something of which we are rarely conscious. Habit is unfree precisely because it is automatic, thoughtless: "What one does out of habit, one does without thought, mechanically, it proceeds on its own as compared to our conscious will, like a necessity" (VPGst 130). This is the dual character of habit with regard to freedom: "That is the determination of habit in contrast to natural determinacies; it is like a natural quality, but posited. This is the side toward natural qualities. Habit then also has a side against the will as such, and in this respect it appears as a necessity over against freedom. According to the first, in relation to the natural, the individual sensations, it is a liberation; in relation to the will, a necessity" (VPGst 125). Because of this double relationship, the term "second nature" is particularly appropriate. Habits are not natural in that they are not inborn and are abstractions from immediate, natural sensations—therefore entailing the subordination of these sensations. Habit is thus distinguished from the natural determination with which Hegel's "Anthropology" began. But the more internalized or natural a habit is to us, the more it is something given, necessary, and not fully free.

Although habit itself is only partially free, its role in spirit's development is not only in overcoming our initial subordination to nature but also in providing a basis for freedom's further development. While habit must be surpassed for genuine freedom to emerge, it must also be maintained for this same freedom. Spirit can reach its highest, freest levels of thought and activity only by focusing its attention, something which requires habituation. As Hegel states in *Enz.* § 410 A: "When one is not in the habit, sustained thinking causes headaches." Only through practice do we become able to engage in the difficult philosophizing Hegel thinks necessary to reach the highest levels of freedom.

And while Hegel's initial account of habit focuses on the most immediately physical sensations, the process is not limited to this basic physical level but is repeated at higher levels: "The form of habit includes all kinds and levels of the activity of spirit" (*Enz.* § 410 A). Consequently, the process of internalization or appropriation so as to constitute a second nature or content of the soul has a role in the realms of ethical life and religion as well, and it is at this level that we can better understand why Hegel says we are "the totality of [our] habits" (*VPGst* 124). Habit is "what is most essential to the *existence* of all spirituality within the individual subject. It enables the subject to be a *concrete* immediacy, an ideality of *soul*, so that the religious, moral, etc. content *belongs* to him as *this self*, *this* soul, and is in him neither merely *implicitly* (as an endowment [*Anlage*]), nor as a transient sensation or idea [*Vorstellung*], nor as an abstract inwardness cut off from action and actuality, but in his being" (*Enz.* § 410 A). In making up our being, habit—which is here conceived broadly, to include religious and ethical aspects of our way of life—constitutes our concrete existence in the world. Hegel's point is that our habits, our ways of doing things, and our background beliefs make up much of our identity and determine the vast majority of our activity in the world. These are acquired habits, but they have become part of us; they are no longer external or opposed to the self.[15] Hegel's account of habituation, then, is an explanation of the process by which we come to be constituted by our context. Traditions that we unconsciously appropriate as habits therefore do a great deal to make us who we are.

At the same time, for Hegel, spirit cannot be identified with or reduced to this existence. His emphasizing of the word "existence" [*Existenz*] in the passage cited above stresses that the "being" under consideration here is a lower level of existence, in the form of a thing (we are still dealing with "Anthropology," as Hegel uses the term); it is not the underlying essence of spirit or human beings, which is a process that cannot be captured in any merely existing "thing." Through its further development, spirit can abstract from and reflect upon any of its particular habits. And, if spirit is fully free, it can change these habits as well—in order to will in accord with reason, not just to choose out of habit. For this reason, it is significant that habit comes early in the philosophy of subjective spirit; although it endures in some form, habit can be overcome and, like natural determination, reveals its apparently given or fixed status to be an illusion.

## The Actual Soul

The final subdivision of Hegel's "Anthropology," which initiates the transition to the next level, is "The Actual Soul." At the level of habit, the subject has overcome natural determination with a determination directly mediated by spirit. We are not driven by natural impulses but subordinate these to the modes or norms of behavior that we have adopted. The body has been subordinated to spirit; it has become the instrument of spiritual activity.

Developed to a new level of the soul, habit develops into the actual soul, which Hegel describes as the "entirety of habit as accustomed [*Ganzes der Gewohnheit, als eingewohnt*]" (*VPGst* 132). The actual soul is the soul thoroughly penetrated and constituted by habit. Its body has become idealized, a sign of the subject rather than the subject itself: "The soul is in its thoroughly cultivated and appropriated corporeality as an *individual* subject for itself, and the corporeality is thus the *externality* as predicate, in which the subject relates only to itself. This externality represents not itself, but the soul and is its *sign*" (*Enz.* § 411). The soul thus maintains its universality in its determinacy. The face and the hand express the soul or subject, not simply themselves; they are thus subordinate to the soul (*Enz.* § 411 A, *VPGst* 132). Consequently, we show ourselves through our deeds: "That through which the individual makes himself known are his actions; the side of deeds shows what the human is; he *is* that. There is not something other in him besides his deeds; he shows what he is through them" (*VPGst* 135). The soul is in unity with the body, but this unity is mediated, not the immediate unity with which the "Anthropology" began. Actual soul represents the completion of the process whereby the inner (soul) comes to determine the outer (body). "As this identity of the inner with the outer, the latter subject to the former, the soul is *actual*" (*Enz.* § 411). While Hegel's conception does subordinate the body to the soul, the outer to the inner, he neither dissociates them nor renders the former insignificant. Hegel takes the outer seriously, as well, precisely because he conceives the inner as attaining concrete existence and expression only through the outer. This relationship will experience further modifications in the later developments within subjective spirit, but it emerges as an issue early on in Hegel's anthropology.

In distinguishing itself from this body, the soul has overcome the immediacy it had before it differentiated itself from its corporeal existence: "The soul which has posited its being over against itself, sublated it, and determined it as its own has lost the significance of *soul*, the *immediacy* of spirit" (*Enz.* § 412). Distinguishing itself from its corporeal existence, the soul has transcended the sphere of the soul. It is no longer spirit in its naturally determined form but rather something which is more than matter, than body.

Whereas at this stage the actual soul "is indifferent toward this immediacy" (*VPGst* 136), in the transition to the next stage this indifference turns to opposition: "Insofar as it [the soul] has made itself free through the sublation of the immediate, it releases the immediacy out of itself, but as infinite negativity, so that it *excludes* the immediate and is not simply indifferent toward it" (*VPGst* 137). The exclusion of the immediate goes from a mere distinction to an opposition. Precisely in this transition, the soul awakens to itself as an I (*Ich*) and thereby effects the transition to the sphere of consciousness; the soul has ceased to be soul and become the I. In so doing, it has concluded the "Anthropology" and brought us to the second section of Hegel's philosophy of subjective spirit, "The Phenomenology of Spirit: Consciousness."

# 3 The I and the Individual

While the first moment of Hegel's anthropology examines a prereflective dimension of human existence, the second focuses on the process of reflection. Through this process we overcome the apparent fixedness or givenness of the sensations and customs to which we initially relate through habit. Here we first see the distinctly spiritual potential of human beings, which both provides the possibility of and necessitates the movement toward freedom. Whereas the first moment deals with the substantial content of the individual, the second addresses the individual's freedom from this content, though not yet—as in the third moment—the individual's ability to transform this content. Most basically, it is the level at which the subject comes to relate to and eventually reflect upon itself. In Hegel's language, the subject posits a difference within itself, such that it is both the subject and the object. The self has itself as an object, which is what it means to be an "I."[1] While this process initially involves making its own sensations—such as a sensation of light—into this object, at the higher levels of development it entails a more abstract consciousness of itself as a self-consciousness, not simply as having particular sensations. In these later stages, Hegel provides the foundations of his account of individuality as well as human freedom.

From one perspective, this self-consciousness represents the extreme of individual subjectivity, yet its pure formality eventually reveals it to be the key to the transition to universality as well as the basis of universal recognition among human beings. Although the third and final section of subjective spirit sublates the level of consciousness, many aspects of consciousness are retained in this higher development. Integrated into a more complete human self-understanding, the I represents a necessary dimension or aspect of developed human beings. Close attention to what is retained through this sublation will

be essential to realizing how Hegel does justice to some of the insights fundamental to contemporary Western conceptions of the individual. At the level
of objective spirit, the discussion of consciousness corresponds principally
to the discussion of morality, in which the subject reflects critically, not
simply accepting mores because they are mores but seeking to act as a rational
agent.

In both the *Encyclopaedia* and the *Vorlesungen über die Philosophie des
Geistes*, Hegel begins the second section with an overview of consciousness.
Whereas the subject in the "Anthropology" was the soul, the subject in the
"Phenomenology of Spirit" is the I (*Ich*); consequently, this overview of consciousness focuses primarily on the I. The I signifies precisely the process of
consciousness.[2] The developments within the sphere of consciousness trace the
I's attempts to know itself as an I, which requires giving itself external, recog-
nizable existence in order "to raise *its certainty of itself to truth*" (*Enz.* § 416).
This movement develops through three stages: consciousness as such, dealing
largely with the subject's relation to external objects of knowledge; self-
consciousness, in which spirit comes to know itself as an I through encounter
with other similar subjects (here the master-slave dialectic finds its place in the
*Encyclopaedia*); and reason, in which the I implicitly overcomes the apparent
duality between itself and the world (including its own body), thereby necessi-
tating the transition to the "Psychology," which considers spirit as such.

For the purpose of grasping Hegel's anthropology, the most significant sections of the text are the introductory overview of the I and the second moment
of the development, self-consciousness. Although the first of these is framed as
an introduction, it provides the most extensive treatment of the conception of
the I, which is fundamental to all three levels of the "Phenomenology." The first
and third sections are more relevant to the subject's relationship to the material
world, addressing Kant's epistemology in particular and revisiting topics
addressed in the logic.[3] While I discuss these sections because they are important to seeing how Hegel sets out his argument, they are in certain respects less
central to his anthropology, so I treat them briefly.

## Overview of the I

The conception of the I with which Hegel begins the "Phenomenology" is fundamental to the entire sphere, underlying the various developments that tran-
spire. At the same time, the I is a matter of consciousness, not simply a given; it

is constituted by consciousness of itself. It is "created" by the subject's excluding relation to the content or material that constitutes the soul. Thus, the I is not an underlying something that remains constant throughout the developments but a process that transforms from an implicit self-awareness to a more adequate self-knowledge. From the beginning, the I is this having itself as an object, but through its development it comes to a more adequate awareness of this object, i.e., itself. Because the subject is also this object, however, this transformation also entails a transformation of the subject-object, the I. It is this transformation that eventually sublates the I, bringing about spirit as such. As in the "Anthropology," the developments within the sphere overcome the principle that defines the sphere: in this case, the duality constitutive of the I as such.

Following upon the actual soul with which the "Anthropology" ended, the I is the abstraction from all the particularity of the soul. It is the movement in which the self differentiates itself from itself and has itself as its object. Initially, this means a consciousness of one's sensation of objects. In the development toward self-consciousness, the consciousness becomes a consciousness of itself as a self-conscious I. The I both is this object and is not; it is "a difference which is not one [*ein Unterschied, der keiner ist*]" as Hegel repeatedly states.[4] In this movement of stepping back, the subject effects a division within itself, creating a subject that is reflecting and the object that is reflected upon: "I am the universal; but when I say 'I,' I have myself as an object, I am this movement in myself, the being-for-self, I relate myself to myself . . ." (*VPGst* 138). The self creates a relation within itself, overcoming the unmediated identity that characterized it at the level of soul. Reflecting upon itself, the I is "*one* side of the relationship and the *entire* relationship" (*Enz.* § 413). The reflecting I relates itself to itself by viewing its object as something other: "[T]he immediate identity of the natural soul is raised to this pure ideal identity with itself; the content of the former is an *object* for this reflection which is for itself" (*Enz.* § 413).

Although the content of the soul constitutes the object of reflection, the reflecting I is itself without content. In making all the soul's particularity other, the I abstracts from particularity and becomes ideal, universal: "[The] I is the entirely pure and empty, completely simple sameness to itself [*sich selbst Gleiche*], the entirely indeterminate" (*VPGst* 138). The content is provided by the I's other, its object; as Hösle states, "the I *relates* at the same time to what it *excludes* . . . ."[5] Although the object itself is something particular—the given, immediate soul—the process through which this soul becomes an object for the self rises above this particularity. It is not any particular content but this movement and relation to this content—a relation of abstraction—such that it is other than this particularity. In making this content something other than itself, the I negates this content, frees itself from it.

This abstraction or purity from particularity is the dimension of ourselves we exhibit in hypothetical questioning of the sort, "What if I had been born a peasant in eighteenth-century France?" One answer to this question is that, "Born into such a situation, I would not be I." That is, we can take "I" to refer to a more particular, concrete identity (much more than what Hegel uses "I" to denote). Such a response is in one sense a very Hegelian one, pointing toward the necessity of moving beyond the abstraction of the "Phenomenology" to the "Psychology," where the abstract I becomes concrete as spirit and is consequently no longer simply an "I" in the sense Hegel uses the term here. At the same time, even this response would more likely be expressed as "I would not be who I am." This formulation distinguishes between the universal, formal I and the more concrete, specific "who" that this I is (for which Hegel does not use the term "I"), suggesting that Hegel's quite abstract point is also revealed in our everyday language. His argument at this level or layer in the development of his anthropology points to the sense of being a subject that goes beyond particularities (such as my gender, upbringing, and language). That such "what-if-I-had-been" questions make sense at all points to precisely this universality and indeterminacy that Hegel attributes to the I.

This moment of the anthropology, the I, cannot be concretely manifest in its purity; it appears only together with other moments, not as an independent existence in the world. Spirit exists only in concrete form. Consequently, Hegel is not advocating the existence of some radically ideal, disembodied subject— as it seems if his account of the I is removed from its larger context in his conception of human beings and not seen to be a *moment* thereof. Rather, his treatment of the I reveals and accounts for the possibility of reflecting upon— making into an object—any given content. It is the process of questioning involved in critical thinking, the not taking for granted of what appears to be fixed and given. The I represents this process in relation to oneself. This does not necessarily entail calling into radical question everything at once, only the possibility of questioning any given particularity. We can stand on one part of the raft while we examine other parts. What is essential is the possibility of examining, of making into an object of reflection, any given part and thereby overcoming particularity.

Although Hegel's claim here involves a significant capacity for transcending one's own situation, his conception simultaneously emphasizes the social embeddedness of even this possibility. This capacity for abstraction, this use of

I, is not something simply given to human beings. Rather, it is only possible as a result of significant developments of consciousness—developments that would not have occurred without certain changes in the world. In the context of the "Phenomenology" (as well as in the 1807 *Phenomenology of Spirit*), one of the essential steps in this development is the struggle for recognition carried out in the master-slave dialectic. Perhaps more pertinently, Hegel argues that in modern states such recognition is built into the structure of the society and into its culture—specifically, its members' self-understanding (*VPGst* 175).[6] Without living in such a society or going through a process of recognition such as Hegel describes, however, humans do not develop this power of abstraction.[7] Like much of the universality achieved in spirit's development, this freedom from particularity comes about only on the basis of a process that leads through particularity. It is dependent upon a certain cultural context not available to all people at all times.[8]

This potential to become an I thus belongs to the underlying conception of human beings, the *Anlage*, or endowment, discussed at the end of chapter 1. It pertains to all human beings and is part of the implicit structure making up what it is to be a human being. But whether this potential is actualized depends to a great extent upon the context in which a human being lives. Without the necessary cultural context for developing this potential, it remains merely a potential, lacking the necessary conditions for it to become actual. In this sense, it is not a concrete possibility for people in certain cultures, even though it is still an abstract potential for them.[9] It thus belongs to the abstract structure of human beings that Hegel sets out in the philosophy of subjective spirit, though it is not necessarily empirically universal in human beings.

Finally, this "origin" of the I in the particularity of the soul brings us back to the second aspect of Hegel's point regarding "a difference which is not one." The abstracting I is a subject relating to its own self as an object. While it can abstract from this object, it still is this object and not some separable, radical other. As Willem deVries states, "That the I can be abstracted from its embodiment no more implies their separability than the abstractability of shape from color or equilaterality from equiangularity implies their separability."[10] This subject and object will therefore reveal themselves to be in truth identical. The difference is not a difference, only a posited, internal self-relation. Thus, the difference between the soul and the I is only a matter of a new self-relation, not a new content. Precisely emphasizing the connection to existentialism, Fetscher argues: "What is added in the transition from the Anthropology to the Phenomenology is actually nothing, that Heideggerian nothing, . . . which existentialists since Kierkegaard have wanted to hold onto in opposition to the 'great Reconciler.'"[11] Nothing has been added; the content is still the same, but it now relates itself to itself through a negation that maintains this content. It is the full consciousness of this identity that transforms the abstract I into concrete spirit: "[The] I, as this absolute negativity, is implicitly identity within the otherness" (*Enz.* § 413); making this implicit identity explicit is the function of the further development. The unmediated identity of the soul passes through the division of consciousness to the mediated identity of spirit. Although the full meaning of this identity will only be revealed in the "Psychology," the identity is already implicitly present in that the I's object is itself; it is a self-relation.

### Consciousness as Such

This underlying conception of the I just discussed is located in Hegel's introduction to the "Phenomenology." The first moment within the sphere itself is consciousness as such, which begins where actual soul ended. The first level of consciousness, sensuous consciousness, begins with the I related to an apparently external object. The contents of this consciousness are the sensations, the determinations of the soul, which have been excluded from the I and which the I reflects upon as objects rather than as itself. This content initially appears to be the richest, because it is made up of the myriad concrete details of physical experience, but it is the poorest at the level of thought. These immediate sensations (hard, smooth, brown) seem to refer to some "other," some thing (a desk?) external to the I. But the attempt to grasp this "other" leads beyond the level of sensuous consciousness to the attempt to grasp the object's truth in perception (*Wahrnehmen*). Here consciousness seeks to get behind the immediate appearance of sensations to distinguish an object from mere appearance. This is the level of everyday consciousness. It is a mixture of the particularity of individual sensations and the universality of laws that seek to order the sensations.

Out of this mixture emerges the consciousness "that the object is rather *appearance*, and its reflection-in-itself is, in contrast *something inward*, which is for itself, and a universal" (*Enz.* § 422).[12] At this point, the subject is conscious of the object both as a unity and as having a multiplicity of predicates (a single desk with multiple properties, such as height, width, color, and texture). It is a differentiated identity, a "difference which is not one." Yet insofar as the I is conscious of an object that exists as an apparently unified object (a desk, not simply a bundle of physical sensations I experience or even just a strangely shaped piece of wood) only by virtue of the I's understanding (*Verstand*), the I has come to have itself as an object.[13] Consequently, the apparent object's otherness has already been implicitly overcome: "In this determination of form in general, there is an *implicit* disappearance of that which maintains the mutual *independence* of the subject and object, i.e., of consciousness as such. [The] I, as judging [*urteilend*], has an object that is not differentiated from it,—*itself*;—*self-consciousness*" (*Enz.* § 423). In regarding its object with understanding, grasping at its mediated self-identity, the I has an I as its object. Without realizing it, the I comes to have itself as an object, passing from consciousness as such to self-consciousness.

While the principal significance of consciousness for the anthropology lies in its describing a path to self-consciousness, it is also important for its contribution to understanding the abstraction at the core of the I. Specifically, the account of consciousness emphasizes that the determinations of the soul that are "excluded" by the I are not only the physical body "belonging to" that subject but also the entire world as that world exists in the subject's sensations. The soul from which the I abstracts is not merely what we commonly think of as just the individual person but the entire world of this subject.

### Self-Consciousness

Together with the introductory discussion of the I, the section on self-consciousness constitutes the central anthropological dimension of the "Phenomenology." It examines the process by which we come to know ourselves and other human beings as I's—the manner in which we comprehend ourselves as transcending the particularity central to the first sphere of subjective spirit. It is here that Hegel deals most directly with our being more than simple products of our physical and social environment. Though we often take for granted that we are I's—that we can reflect upon and question external influences—Hegel does not. He sees such self-understanding as a great accomplishment achieved only as the result of a difficult struggle and relatively easy for us only because the fruits of this struggle have been incorporated into the structures, mores, and institutions of our society.

The sphere begins with the I attempting to demonstrate what it is through the satisfaction of desire. Such a proof disappears as soon as it is achieved, however, so the I must seek something that testifies to the I's superiority over immediacy without disappearing. This brings about the struggle for recognition in the master-slave conflict. As a result of this struggle, the slave eventually achieves the independence of givenness, the subordination of natural desire, necessary for the universal recognition of what it means to be a self-conscious I.

Throughout the level of self-consciousness, the I is driven by its need to know itself by giving itself objective existence. It seeks to show itself what it is by demonstrating that it is more than a mere thing, more than the immediately given. A demonstration is required because it is only through objectifying itself in the world that the I attains knowledge of what it is and thereby becomes more fully itself: "I am not satisfied simply to be [an] I; human actuality is to go beyond this substance [the abstract I], to realize it" (VPGst 161). Self-consciousness, then, is not simply some thing but a process, in which the I "gives itself this objectivity, makes itself actual" (VPGst 163).

The I begins this process, in the form of desire, by showing its superiority over an immediately given object. By consuming or otherwise appropriating objects such as food, the I demonstrates that what initially appeared to be an independent object affords no resistance and therefore shows itself to have no "truth" as something existing over against me. Desire at this level is not principally about the satisfaction of needs, such as hunger, but about demonstrating one's own existence and that one is more than a mere given thing. Once the object is consumed, however, it has also ceased to provide evidence of my own being. Because the object is immediate, it is completely annihilated by the negation it undergoes. It therefore provides no standing demonstration; as soon as desire is satisfied, it is recreated.[14] The proof is ephemeral (Enz. § 428 Z). While this point is often emphasized, however, there is also another reason for the inadequacy of this first attempt: In this attempt, self-consciousness remains negatively determined by its relation to an object that is only immediate (Enz. § 428). It knows itself as not that immediate object; it has shown what it is not but not what it is.

What the I requires is a negation of the immediate that remains, which is not destroyed by the negation—what Hegel calls a standing negation. In order not to be destroyed by the negation, such an object must also be more than immediate. Simple objects cannot provide such enduring witness to the I, because they are destroyed in the process. Hegel believes that the only object that can is one that is also a subject, i.e., another self-consciousness that can also negate itself through overcoming particularity. This is the source of the need for recognition by other human beings. Despite the differences between this level and the previous one, the central issue is still the I's overcoming of immediacy. The development is driven by the I's need for the "negation of immediacy; with this there enters the differentiation of my freedom from my life, from the particularity which is in me generally, immersion in the sensory, selfishness" (*VPGst* 167–68).[15]

One can ask, however, why an object that has been transformed through labor would not provide this lasting testament to the I. Why, for instance, would using materials to construct a work of art not constitute the enduring proof that the I requires? It would involve the negation of the materials in their immediacy and thereby demonstrate the I's power over the given, yet it would not be destroyed by this process. Hegel does not address the question, and—although the transformation of the world through labor plays an important role in the later stages of the master-slave dialectic—he does not raise the possibility of desire's being satisfied by something other than the total consumption or negation of the object. Although material construction on the part of the I would produce a lasting testament to its existence, it still would not provide knowledge of what the I is, only of what it is not. Here again, the inadequacy of the satisfaction achieved at the level of desire stems not only from its ephemerality but also from its defining the I negatively and in relation to some mere thing rather than affirmatively in relation to another I. Even with lasting evidence of the I's ability to overcome nature or immediacy, it would still not achieve knowledge of what it is.

Consequently, "The foundation is that this unity realizes itself and that this can only realize itself in the self-consciousness of other individuals. The material in which [the] I, freedom, can realize itself is exclusively another self-consciousness, this [is] its reality, objectivity, externality" (*VPGst* 170).[16] Self-consciousness can only adequately realize itself in another self-consciousness. Only by recognizing another I can the I grasp itself. Knowledge requires that the I know itself not simply negatively—in terms of what it is not—but also positively through a consciousness of the kind of being I am: "[F]or me it is necessary, in order to be self-consciousness, to know myself in another, and to this extent I *lose* my self-consciousness in another; but precisely in the other I know myself affirmatively, because the limit, which previously lay in desire and selfishness, has been sublated" (*VPGst* 174). In having another self-consciousness, another I, as the object of consciousness, the I knows itself for what it is, and is now positively, not just negatively, determined.

The perception of another I, however, is initially contradictory. I see something that seems, on one hand, totally other than me and, on the other, a self-consciousness, which seems to be I: "Within it [the other human being] I have an immediate intuition of myself, and at the same time of something other than I am, so that this externality is still a wholly distinct unyieldingness" (*PSS* 3:330–31/*BP* 72–73). The other's body is not under my control and therefore seems other, in a way that even inanimate matter was not. But it also seems exactly the same as me, such that I cannot distinguish myself from it; it seems to be me.

This contradiction means that in this initial form contact with the other cannot provide knowledge of the self. Achieving this requires demonstrating the I's superiority to the immediate, such that self-consciousness itself is clearly revealed and known. This contradiction drives it into struggle with the other, in which it wages the entirety of its given existence. Because the conception of the I involves a total negation of the immediate, the particular, this struggle must be a struggle to the death in which everything is at stake. The I must show its superiority to the immediate by subordinating all physical, material needs to the drive for its own self-consciousness; the natural existence of the soul (from the "Anthropology") must be subordinated to the more spiritual existence of the I.

One potential outcome to a life-and-death struggle is that one of the parties is killed. In dying, the loser has demonstrated the ability to subordinate the soul to the I and therefore his or her freedom: "He who dies in battle dies a free man. Indifference toward vitality [*Lebendigkeit*] would be proven; the elevation of freedom over life would be realized; but the fundamental determination, which pursues recognition, would be lost" (*VPGst* 169). The I has given existence to its freedom, but it has been completely destroyed in the process, which means that it cannot be a lasting freedom. It, too, is ephemeral. At the same time, being destroyed, the loser does not provide a lasting proof of the winner's self-consciousness either. The winner has effected a destroying negation rather than a standing negation.

The other possible resolution to the struggle is that before dying one party concedes and becomes the slave of the other. The slave then mediates between the master's needs and desires and the material world. By giving in, the slave has specifically not subordinated physical existence to existence as a free self-consciousness, but the slave nonetheless provides the path along which consciousness develops (*Enz.* § 435, *VPGst* 172).

Although the master has the slave to work for her, the slave is not respected as a self-consciousness precisely because she has given in, has valued physical life more than freedom. The master therefore does not have an object in which she sees herself, through which she comes to know what she is. Moreover, in directing the slave's labor, the master simply tries to satisfy immediate needs and desires. Thus, her will is still determined by the particular, not by anything beyond her natural existence.

The slave, on the other hand, although initially more determined by subservience to the physical (which is why she conceded) and to the master, is on the more viable trajectory toward freedom. In working to fulfill the master's desires, the slave has to postpone her own wishes and subordinate her own will to the master's. Thereby, "the slave, however, works off the singularity and egoism of his will in the service of the master, sublates the inner immediacy of desire, and through this renunciation and fear of the master makes the beginning of wisdom . . ." (*Enz.* § 435). This overcoming of particularity and of immersion in the immediacy of need and desire is the path toward freedom.

Although the master has subordinated natural existence by risking her life, she has not "inwardly" negated immediate desire; it continues to determine her action after the struggle has ended (*VPGst* 172). While the master uses the slave precisely for the satisfaction of desires, it is the slave who becomes truly free of such desires: "This sublation of the self-interestedness of particularity of wanting moves forward in the slave . . ." (*VPGst* 172). By obeying the master, the slave gains control of her own desires, and it is only through such control that the I becomes truly free of such desire. This freedom does not entail the annihilation of desires but rather their subordination. The process of liberation from natural determination that began in habituation here takes another major step forward. This overcoming of one's own immediate will and mediation of this will with that of another makes this next level of abstraction from particularity possible. Through obeying, the slave comes to know herself "as one in whom the determination of sensuous particularity and selfishness is negated" (*VPGst* 173).

Hegel's claim that freedom develops through slavery does not imply that the slave is or can be genuinely free in slavery. As becomes apparent in the next level of the anthropology, Hegel's conception of freedom also requires an ability to express one's own will that is denied slaves. Modern society is more free than a society incorporating slavery in part because its structures and institutions generally provide the recognition sought after by the master and slave (*VPGst* 175). As a result, the life-and-death struggle and ensuing slavery need not be repeated, and a higher level of freedom can be achieved. As much as Hegel sees obedience as a necessary stage on the path toward freedom, it must also be overcome; this negative, obedient side is only the beginning of freedom (*Enz.* § 435 Z).

The slave's elevation above the level of immediacy constitutes the transition to the third and final level of self-consciousness, universal self-consciousness.

Through the negation of its desires, the I overcomes its particularity, its imme-diate, given character. As a result, in relating to another self-consciousness that has also overcome this particularity, I see myself.

It is precisely particularity that has separated the two subjects up until this point. The I or self-consciousness is the process of abstraction, and its univer-sality comes from its ability to consider itself a subject distinct from its given impulses and desires. Now, however, "we have the mighty diremption of spirit into various selves, which in and for themselves and for one another are com-pletely free, independent, absolutely rigid, resistant,—but which are at the same time identical with one another, and hence not independent, not impenetrable, but confluent" (*Enz.* § 436 Z). This development entails that spirit exists at least implicitly within all self-conscious, or potentially self-conscious, beings. Spirit cannot be conceived as limited to only a portion of humanity. By overcoming particularity as the slave does, she finally becomes conscious of herself (her I) in another. Moreover, in achieving this freedom from particularity, she has opened the way toward more complete, self-determining freedom. In universal self-consciousness, each self-consciousness has proven itself to be free; the proof, the lasting source of the certainty, is its identity with another self-consciousness. Consequently, "Self-consciousness overreaches itself; it contin-ues itself into another self-consciousness; there are not two self-interested [self-consciousnesses] against each other but one self-consciousness; and thereby it is a universal self-consciousness" (*VPGst* 174).[17]

Concretely, we can see ourselves in others only to the extent that we can raise ourselves above the natural and given particularity dealt with in the "Anthropology." Thus, "Human beings must want to rediscover themselves in one another. This cannot happen as long as they are confined to their immedi-acy, their naturalness . . ."(*Enz.* § 431 Z). As long as we see ourselves only in re-lation to particular dimensions of our identity—our cultural background, political and religious commitments, historical situation, etc.—we cannot rec-ognize what we have in common. We identify with others to the extent that our consciousness can transcend the particular circumstances from which we come. A sense of self and identity that rests exclusively in a particular religious identity, for instance, will obscure what one has in common with those from another tradition. While Hegel gives such factors a very important role in our identity, his multilevel anthropology simultaneously holds in focus our ability to abstract from or transcend these.

Universal self-consciousness, then, satisfies the drives left unsatisfied by the I's earlier attempts at self-knowledge: "*Universal self-consciousness* is the affirmative knowing of one's self in the other self. Each self has *absolute independence* as free singularity; but on account of the negation of its immediacy or desire, does not differentiate itself from the other, is universal and objective, and has the real universality as reciprocity—in that it knows itself to be recognized by the free other and knows this insofar as it recognizes the other and knows it to be free" (*Enz.* § 436). Self-consciousness finally knows itself affirmatively, in terms of what it is. The I knows itself to be an I. Because the recognition involved in universal consciousness is reciprocal, the other self-consciousness also identifies me as a self-consciousness, as free. This recognition *by* the other—not just by me *of* the other—provides the enduring proof of what I am, the objectivity to which Hegel refers in the passage above. It is not simply my own intuition or conviction but something that has existence in another's self-consciousness. The knowledge sought first (unsuccessfully) through the consumption or negation of objects is now provided by another self-consciousness.

The centrality of reciprocity, however, also means that my own freedom depends upon others' freedom: "I am free, insofar as others are . . ." (*VPGst* 175). My freedom depends on knowing my independence of particularity, which means knowing what an I is. By having slaves, the ancient Greeks, for instance, demonstrated that they "had not come to think of themselves as human beings, that is, to know freedom as the essence of human beings" (*Rph V*, 150). Fully grasping this pure subjectivity includes grasping it in others. To the extent that my recognition of others' freedom is limited, my own freedom is as well. As long as some are excluded, self-consciousness is not yet fully universal. This is not an all-or-nothing realization; there are degrees of freedom. Accordingly, although Hegel maintains that "modern Western" civil society largely embeds universal recognition within its structures and culture, he acknowledges that those marginalized by this society—specifically the poor—suffer not only because of their material poverty but also due to a lack of recognition (*Rph III*, 195, translated in Tunick 1992, 140).[18]

Hegel's conception of universal self-consciousness is central to his notion of the interconnectedness of individuality and universality. The I is at the core of Hegel's conception of individuality. Through the process of abstraction which constitutes self-consciousness, we overcome or transcend the natural existence we are given. More than simply the ability to subordinate physical needs, this process also entails a transcending of the traditions and mores that provide the content of our habits; it is not simply the overcoming of our own physicality but also the reflection upon all that we have inherited from our cultural setting.

At this level, Hegel does allow for a transcendence of social and historical context that lies precisely in the ability to call any part of this context into question, to realize that what initially appears given or fixed is also subject to transformation. It is a pure subjectivity which, qua I, has achieved an independence of the particularity that determined it from without.

At the same time, this transcendence is made possible by the struggle for recognition or by living in a society in which such recognition is embedded; it involves events out there in the world, not just internal, cognitive processes. Thus, this transcendence requires a cultural context that allows for that context's own overcoming. In contrast to a Kierkegaardian or Heideggerian conception of transcendence in the form of faith or authenticity, it is not a possibility equally open to all people in all cultures. Nonetheless, the underlying potential—not the actual possibility of its realization—is implicit in what it means to be a human being.

Further, it is precisely this same I that, in coming to self-knowledge, comes to know itself as identical with all other I's. In Hegel, the movement toward the extreme individuality of pure subjectivity simultaneously leads to the most extreme communion with others in universal self-consciousness. What distinguishes me from a conglomeration of natural, immediate influences and unconscious habits is my self-consciousness, but the potential for self-consciousness is precisely what I share with every other human being. By overcoming all givenness, all external determination, all that is left is the I relating to itself. The "purity" of this self-relationship is also its universality. It is because of the purity or emptiness of this process of self-relation that such a strong sense of subjectivity can be combined with an emphasis on the social constitution of the self. This inseparability of the moment of most extreme individuality and the most profound bond with others is crucial to Hegel's effort to reconcile the individual and society.

Given the widespread suspicion that Hegel lacks an adequate conception of individuality, the notion of individuality developed here merits careful examination. For Hegel, our individuality is not constituted by a unique set of native endowments, some naturally given qualities or capabilities that only I have. Nor is it any other sort of unique content or eccentricity. Individuality, for Hegel, is not tied to uniqueness, as it often is in modern conceptions.[19] Against those who claim that being an individual means replacing or resisting what we assimilate from the world around us with a unique, "individual" way of behaving, Hegel pushes the question of where the determinants of that action could come from. If the answer is something fixed in my nature—an inborn disposition—then

Hegel, beyond alerting us to the extent to which most efforts at nonconformity are also deeply marked by the context from which they emerge, points out that we are not then acting freely. If what we do is determined by such "given" factors, we are still immersed in the naturalness characterizing the soul's unfreedom. There is no reason to view something forced upon me by nature as any more intimately tied to my identity or subjectivity than something that comes from the society around me: "That's just the way I am" is an appeal to heteronomous determination, not freedom. Thus, a conception of individuality that centers around private destinies would be more a view of animal uniqueness than of a spiritual, free individual.

By contrast, Hegelian individuality is constituted by self-conscious spirit's awareness of itself as more than the given habits and modes of thought that it inherits. By virtue of this capacity to abstract from what we have taken from our culture and made our habits, we can question these things; we can see them as habits acquired from our culture rather than as the only possible way things could be. At the root of this process is our having ourselves as an object. This level of "pure subjectivity," in which the self relates to itself as a self, however, is abstract; the abstractness of the description corresponds to the abstractness of the I itself. The I's freedom from particularity attains expression or actuality not as some absolute transcendence of all determination but in the abstraction from a particular determination. As soon as the I's freedom is given expression or actuality, it inevitably brings in determination, just as it transcends some other particular. Even if the I represents a "pure" subjectivity not impinged upon by particularity—a subjectivity that has overcome particularity—whenever it acts it becomes concrete and thereby inevitably takes on certain particularity. There is no acting, including thinking, as a pure I, without particularity.

The act of calling one of our habits into question, for instance, entails making use of other particular concepts and habits, not questioning from some Archimedean or ahistorical standpoint. Such activity is perhaps most easily illustrated by taking critical thinking as an analogy. We proceed not by negating all of the particular concepts that enable us to think in the first place—such as our conception of causality—but rather by using some of these concepts to question others. We question one belief largely through using others. This freedom from particularity allows us to question—in theory any—inherited belief from the perspective of other beliefs we hold.

Hegel's moment of pure subjectivity, the I, both is free from particularity and takes on particularity whenever it exists as more than a mere abstraction. The ability to utilize some concepts to critique others reflects what it means to be an individual in this Hegelian conception. While it excludes a notion of individuality based on a simply given uniqueness, it does justice to many of our contemporary intuitions regarding a significant space for the individual to think differently from the society, to question conventional wisdom, and thereby to be different. Hegel's conception allows for such individuality without requiring either a universal standpoint or a conception of individuals as determined by some fixed natural instinct or disposition.

### Reason

The third moment of the "Phenomenology" brings together the consciousness that characterizes the first moment and the self-consciousness of the second. In consciousness as such, the subject has grasped that its own determinations constitute the object. In self-consciousness, the I has found itself in another. The concept that determines both is the subject's own concept, the self-moving concept whose development has been traced throughout the system. Insofar as self-consciousness achieves this awareness, it passes out of self-consciousness proper, no longer cleaving to the particular self. In reason, therefore, the subject has itself as an object but with the realization both that this object is itself and that it is the universal (VPGst 175-76). Reason is "the simple *identity* of the *subjectivity* of the concept and of its *objectivity* and universality" (*Enz.* § 438). The subject has itself as an object and recognizes other self-consciousness as such— as it already did in universal self-consciousness. In addition, however, in reason the subject recognizes its own concept as the essence of all objectivity and therefore as universal. Hegel's discussion of this important and difficult point is extremely brief in both the *Encyclopaedia* and the *Vorlesungen über die Philosophie des Geistes*. He can be concise, however, precisely because the crucial claim here is one that should be familiar from the logic: "[I]t is in the determinations of thought and the concept that it [the object] *is* what it *is*" (*WL* 2:560/833). Without this understanding of the logic in the background, it is difficult not to interpret Hegel as making grand metaphysical claims. As I argued in chapter 1, however, such a reading fails to appreciate Kant's influence and saddles Hegel with bold—probably preposterous—claims that he does not make.

Here, self-consciousness, which is now reason, is certain "that its determinations are just as much objective, determinations of the essence of things [*Dinge*], as its own thoughts" (*Enz.* § 439). These self-determinations of the subject constitute the object. Because they constitute both the subject and the object, they are universal. As a result, "The rationality of spirit has this certainty: to find its content in the world, to have before it nothing foreign, nothing impenetrable to it. Spirit says to the world: You are reason of my reason. It knows that it encounters therein nothing other than its reason, its universality, that *its* content is the object" (*VPGst* 177). Reason therefore has its own concept as its object and knows this concept as universal. This, however, is the determination of spirit, so that the transition to the third level of the anthropology has already been made.

# 4 Pursuing Reconciliation
*Theoretical and Practical Spirit*

As the second moment in Hegel's philosophy of subjective spirit, the "Phenomenology of Spirit" presented the moment of division or internal bifurcation, where I distinguish myself from my immediate existence and reflect upon myself. Although its development entailed the implicit overcoming of this division—in the increasing awareness that its object is itself—this reconciliation or overcoming of the internal chasm was not actualized or made real within that sphere. Reason provided only the implicit reconciliation. The next and last stage of subjective spirit, the "Psychology," constitutes the actual overcoming of this division: Hegel's attempt to make the subject whole again. The unity of the first moment, lost in the bifurcation of self-consciousness, is regained. Now, however, it is a mediated unity rather than the immediate unity of the first level. Spirit thus realizes or actualizes its essence and its freedom, providing the basis for the developments of objective spirit.

The reconciliation of this internal division is pursued along two paths. The first is the development of "theoretical spirit" or the intelligence through intuition (*Anschauung*) and representation (*Vorstellung*) to thought (*Denken*). The other is "practical spirit" or the will, which develops from practical feeling through impulses (*Triebe*) and arbitrary will (*Willkür*) to eudaemonia (*Glückseligkeit*). In the 1830 edition of the *Encyclopaedia*, practical spirit ends here and is followed by a third section, "free spirit," in which the will is thinking and rational, constituting a synthesis of theoretical and practical spirit. Although the *Vorlesungen über die Philosophie des Geistes* do not designate a distinct sphere of free spirit, these lectures—as Burkhard Tuschling points out—develop the conception of free spirit decisively beyond the analysis provided in the 1827 edition of the *Encyclopaedia*. Tuschling argues that the *Vorlesungen* are particularly significant as the point at which Hegel develops the conception of free spirit as a stage beyond practical spirit. This conception is incorporated into the structure of the 1830 edition of the *Encyclopaedia*.[1] In both the 1830 *Encyclopaedia* and the *Vorlesungen*, the free, rational will produces the transition to the sphere of objective spirit, in which Hegel provides the concrete content of the spirit's objectification in the world.

While the substantive discussions of the intelligence and the will reveal much about Hegel's anthropology, it is the relationship between these two sides or aspects of the psychology that is most revealing. In this relationship Hegel works out the interconnection of our practical engagement and involvement with the world—through our willing activity—and the cognitive aspects of our development, where belief—including religious belief—finds its place. While Hegel provides important treatments of practical spirit not only in the introduction to the *Philosophy of Right* but also in the corresponding sections of his several series of lectures on the *Rechtsphilosophie*, only the presentations of the philosophy of subjective spirit provide systematic treatments of both theoretical and practical spirit.[2] Consequently, the *Encyclopaedia* and the *Vorlesungen über die Philosophie des Geistes* are the richest sources for examining this complex interrelationship between the theoretical and the practical. Moreover, while all of these presentations define the free will as the will that wills itself, only the anthropology as a whole elucidates this "itself" in all its complexity.

The centrality of practical spirit to the development of free spirit anticipates the centrality of social and political ethics to the development of spirit. It constitutes the foundation for the central role of history in spirit's larger development. Moreover, if practical spirit is as central to Hegel's conception of human beings as I argue, then he is not guilty of abstraction from the concrete materiality of the world, and Marx's attempt to turn Hegel on his head fails to give Hegel credit for how concretely he was concerned with human action. Finally, the understanding of this relationship between the theoretical and the practical will also have profound implications for grasping the impact of theoretical reflection on our activity in the world and vice versa—thus on the relationship between theory and praxis.[3] The question of the relation between theoretical and practical spirit, then, is one of the central questions for the interpretation of Hegel's entire conception of human beings.

## Preliminary Discussion of the Relation between
## Theoretical and Practical Spirit

Significant passages in both the *Encyclopaedia* and the *Vorlesungen* appear to demonstrate an almost exclusive focus on the theoretical, to the neglect of the practical. In the introduction to the "Psychology," for instance, Hegel states that "[t]he knowing reason is spirit" and "reason, which spirit is in and for itself and of which spirit has consciousness that it is, is the concept; and knowledge constitutes the actuality of this reason that exists in and for itself" (*VPGst* 180).[4] Such passages appear to define spirit principally in terms of knowing and suggest that reason is given actuality in knowledge, rather than requiring activity in the world for its actualization. They raise the prospect that spirit can achieve its most important development simply as intelligence, in abstraction from will. Hegel also claims that the most developed will, which wills in accord with reason, has become the thinking will (*Enz.* § 481). Hegel's conception of the will, then, depends upon his conception of thinking and theoretical spirit generally, and spirit's rational self-knowledge is essential to the goal of the teleological development of this sphere. These aspects of Hegel's analysis are central to Edith Düsing's claim that "[t]he systematic connection of all modes of activity of subjective spirit, its innermost center, in which they possess their uniting middle, is for Hegel . . . thought."[5] Emphasizing this side of Hegel, she contrasts the primacy of the will in Fichte with the primacy of the intelligence in Hegel.

Does Hegel's anthropology cheapen human action, viewing it as a dimension of our existence fundamentally subordinate to theoretical reflection? Such an attitude is often attributed to Hegel, but the conclusion should not be drawn so quickly. The passages just cited leave unspecified both the role of practical spirit in the development of this self-knowing and the role of practical spirit in developed spirit. They leave open the will's function as a *means* to the development toward spirit's end and a practical dimension to the *end* of this development. Examining the significance of practical human activity and political activity—including factors such as labor—means investigating precisely this relationship. While certain of Hegel's passages prioritize the theoretical over the practical, the dominant and most convincing account of their relation sees the practical as co-essential with the theoretical, but in a manner that still attributes a specific kind of primacy to cognition.

According to Hegel, the paths represented by the intelligence and the will are inseparable. He describes "intelligence as such" as "one-sided," with the will constituting the complementary side (*VPGst* 239). As Peperzak emphasizes, theoretical and practical spirit each represent complementary modes of spirit's development which are "in their highest completion and deepest origin" the same.[6] Thus, Hegel notes, "The differentiation of *intelligence* from *will* is often misinterpreted, such that each is taken to be a fixed existence, separate from the other, as if volition could be devoid of intelligence or the activity of intelligence could be devoid of will" (*Enz.* § 445 A).[7] Intelligence is also willing, and the will is also intelligent. Practical spirit develops through the will's becoming thinking. Similarly, theoretical spirit develops through coming to know that it manifests its own essence in the world; this only comes about, however, through spirit's transformation of this world through practical activity.

This ultimate inseparability of theoretical and practical spirit entails not only that practical activity has an essential role as a means to the development of knowledge but also that it constitutes a vital element of the end of that development. Early in the "Psychology," Hegel already indicates that an integral aspect of the manifestation of spirit's essence in knowledge is its manifestation in ethical life: "The reality of reason is knowledge. The laws, etc., the ethical in and for itself is reason that realizes itself, is in the citizens" (*VPGst* 180).[8] Hegel's linking of the "reality of reason" with the ethical life manifested in citizens links the fulfillment of knowing to the practical, ethical, political world. The reconciliation of theoretical and practical spirit in free spirit, then, is the stage "in which that doubled one-sidedness is sublated" (*Enz.* § 443). The highest stage in spirit's development is not one that leaves practical activity behind; the knowing that constitutes the end of this teleology is not simply theoretical but also practical: a willing intelligence—as well as an intelligent will. It is not an engagement with the world leading to a departure or withdrawal from it, as in solitary monastic contemplation; nor is it a return simply for the sake of others, as in Plato's *Republic*. Rather, this activity is part of the free spirit in which the development of subjective spirit culminates; the "knowing reason" that constitutes the goal of spirit's development cannot exist in abstraction from willing activity in the world. Edith Düsing's one-sided emphasis on the intelligence over the will, then, fails to do justice to the mutuality of the relation of the two terms in Hegel. Summing up the interrelationship of the theoretical and the practical as both the means of development and its culmination, Fetscher refers to the "the mutually conditioned unity" of theoretical and practical spirit, such that "from the perspective of thought as well, volition cannot be abstracted from, and therein we have before us a reference to the *mutual entwinement of the structure of the theory of human beings*."[9]

## Theoretical Spirit

As the first of the three moments of the "Psychology," theoretical spirit begins with the implicit identity of subject and object attained in reason at the end of the "Phenomenology." While this identity was already implicitly achieved there, it remained an abstract reconciliation, not yet actual in either intelligence or will. Throughout the "Psychology," spirit strives to make this identity actual. Whereas practical spirit will begin with an internal determination that is in tension with the existing world, theoretical spirit begins with something existing, with the intelligence occupied by some object: "The intelligence *finds* itself *determined*" (*Enz.* § 445).[10] Hegel's use in this context of the present participle of "to be" (*ein Seiendes*) emphasizes that the so-called object is not yet construed by the intelligence into an object per se; it is nothing more than a something, which initially appears as an other to the subject. Because this something "fills" the intelligence itself, however, this relationship entails an internal bifurcation, something other within consciousness. Theoretical spirit develops to overthrow this "appearance, from which it [intelligence] in its immediacy proceeds" (*Enz.* § 445). This development is made up of a series of types of mental activity, with each one leading to the next. The advance does not eliminate prior stages but points to the existence of higher forms of cognition. The goal of the development is to overcome the subject-object dichotomy through transforming the being (*das Seiende*) into its own (*das Seinige*), "to posit that which is found as its own" (*Enz.* § 445).[11] In doing so, it makes real and concrete what reason implicitly and merely abstractly knows. Through this process, spirit overcomes the apparent otherness of the object.

Theoretical spirit itself consists of three moments—intuition (*Anschauung*), representation (*Vorstellung*), and thought (*Denken*). Each is a form of cognition (*Erkenntnis*), each aiming and developing toward thought.[12] Although intuition, representation, and thought are the forms of cognition appropriate to art, religion, and philosophy, respectively, these different forms are aimed at the same object or truth: "The moments of its realizing activity are intuition, representation, recollection, etc.; the activities have no other immanent significance; their only purpose is the concept of cognition . . . . It is only when they are isolated that they are presented as being useful for something other than cognition . . ." (*Enz.* § 445 A). They are different (but unequal) forms of striving toward the same truth, which is expressed most adequately in thought and the corresponding realm of philosophy.

Intuition (*Die Anschauung*)

Intuition is a mode of cognition in which the intelligence is immersed in a content that appears to be externally given. It is associated with immediacy, the sensible, and the particular rather than anything abstract or universal. For this reason, Hegel's use of "*Anschauung*" differs from much contemporary English-language usage of "intuition." Hegel's intuition begins as immediately determined by the content of feeling. Through the developments of intuition, the intelligence awakens to its active role in constituting these objects, specifically through the forms of time and space.[13] This awareness directs the intelligence's attention inward, eventually generating the transition to representation.

In the present context, what is most significant is Hegel's extensive discussion of feeling considered as a mode of cognition. As in the soul and in consciousness, "in feeling, as spirit, spirit is likewise immediately determined . . . ." In intuition, however, "it is explicit to it [spirit], that it is only immediate determination and that this is a defect" (*VPGst* 187). Spirit is aware that this is merely an immediate determination and that it is therefore in need of further refinement. This awareness of its own deficiency distinguishes it from the immediacy with which the previous two spheres began, though the contents are the same feelings that made up the lower spheres. It is thus still immersed in particularity.

Though this immersion in feeling represents the most elementary stage of spirit's cognition, Hegel is not as disparaging of it as his emphasis on thought might suggest.[14] Feelings are essential to spirit's development to thought, and are not left behind by the thinking individual. Moreover, Hegel consistently emphasizes the capacity of feelings for development. Although feelings initially appear to us as immediate or given, they transform as a result of reflection and experience: "[W]hat man owes to reflection [*Nachdenken*] and experience, what he has gained from them, enters feeling in an immediate form. . . . There is a rationality in feeling" (*VPGst* 188). Feelings are not simply given but rather cultivated through experience: "*Cultivated*, true sensation is the sensation of a cultured spirit, which has acquired consciousness of specific differences, essential relationships, true determinations, etc. . . ." (*Enz.* § 447 A). Such a developed sensibility responds in accord with thought, even though it may not have achieved the self-clarity of philosophical thought.[15] For those who have achieved this greater clarity and thought—not just intuited this content—the content is still present in feelings as well: "All education, the highest development of spirit through learning, experience, and science, is present in the subject, is also present in feeling" (*VPGst* 188). Feeling is not left behind, even though it is the most basic form of spirit's cognition; Hegel's developed individual is not unfeeling.

Because intuition is one aspect or form of cognition and shares content with the other forms—representation and thought—what is valid in intuition is capable of "translation" into these higher, more universal forms. The process of expressing intuition linguistically, however, does not belong within the sphere of intuition itself; it is precisely such a reflective process that raises a particular content from the sphere of intuition to representation (*Vorstellung*). Language is a more universal mode, which gives objectivity to what is initially only subjective in feeling: "People often speak of the inexpressibility of feeling, i.e., of that which exists only in the subjective manner of feeling. Language has for its content only the universal, true, concrete. What language cannot grasp is the lesser, worse, the merely subjective, the abstract mine. What is true in it is rational, and I can express the rational" (*VPGst* 189). Thus, this denigration of the aspect of feeling that is merely subjective and without universal significance does not entail that feeling as a form is insignificant in the developed individual.

Hegel consistently emphasizes that the most refined state—whether in the realm of ethics or of religion and philosophy—must also be accompanied by corresponding feelings. Further, it is generally through feeling that we have our first, most immediate perception of this content, which is then refined through reflection. In this way as well, intuition plays an essential role in ethical life. Nonetheless, Hegel's emphasis on the rational element in feeling, on the truth of feeling being that which can be expressed in language and thought, seems to deny that feeling or intuition provides any content that thinking reason cannot; there is no ethically relevant insight that can be revealed only through feeling. While Hegel's position contrasts with ethical theories that make emotion central to ethical life, his emphasis on the role of feeling as the basis for the development of universal ethical content as well as the essential accompaniment of proper action by the proper inclination gives a much more important role to feeling in ethics than do many other modern ethical theories.[16]

Hegel's claim that what is ethically valid in feeling can be expressed in thought also entails that feeling cannot be the justification of ethics. Although the question of ethics is not central to Hegel's point here, even in the shorter *Encyclopaedia* version he stresses that "[i]f a person *appeals* to his *feeling* in respect to something, rather than to the nature and concept of the matter, or at least reasons, the general consensus, there is nothing to do but let him alone, since by doing this he opts out of the community of rationality and shuts himself up in his isolated subjectivity, *particularity*" (*Enz.* § 447 A). A reliance on feeling in its particularity rather than as revealing something universal and subject to discussion undermines all possibility of criticism. We can disagree, but if there is no acknowledgment that reflection might be able to express and critique (as well as transform) feelings, there is no justification for ethical claims, there are only opinions. Moreover, such a view does not do justice to the extent to which our feelings themselves are transformed by our reflection on a matter, as Hegel well indicates. It is thus based in an inadequate conception of intuition and its relation to other forms of cognition.

Representation (*Die Vorstellung*)

Throughout the sphere of intuition, the intelligence remains immersed in the particularity of feeling. Through that stage's developments, however, it becomes increasingly aware of its own active role in constituting objects, prompting the inward turn that marks the transition to representation. As the second stage of theoretical spirit, representation or representational thinking is the midpoint between spirit's finding itself determined and the free self-determination of theoretical spirit's final stage, thought. In this middle position, representation contains a content that is still given from without but a form that is entirely its own (*VPGst* 195). Whereas in intuition the intelligence was immersed in its object, in representation this object is "represented" as its own object. While in representation the element of givenness remains, the object belongs to the intelligence because its form is given by the intelligence: "Representation is the general name expressing that the object is mine, in my possession, that I am the subject of it" (*VPGst* 205).

Hegel's analysis of representation, particularly in the *Vorlesungen*, is central to his account of the "expression" or "externalization" that Charles Taylor makes fundamental to Hegel's anthropology. Although some of the most obvious forms of expression or externalization come in practical spirit, the account of language, as the mode of expression appropriate to theoretical spirit, is one of Hegel's clearest discussions of this drive to externalize. For this reason, representation requires a more detailed discussion than that given to intuition.

At the first level of representation, recollection (*Erinnerung*), the intelligence "posits the *content of feeling* within its inwardness . . ." (*Enz.* § 452). The content that it projected outward in time and space in intuition is now taken out of that particular space and time and transformed, for instance, into a mental picture, which can then be preserved in memory. The original particular context of the object is thereby overcome: "[W]hat is properly called recollection is the relation of the image to an intuition, and, what is more, as a *subsumption* of the immediate single intuition under that which has the form of what is universal, under the *representation* which is the same content . . ." (*Enz.* § 454). In representation, the form given to the content by the intelligence is more universal than the original intuition. "The image that is immediate in this manner [of intuition] is bound to a time and place; in contrast, the image belonging to me has preserved the determination of the universal" (*VPGst* 200). While the form is more universal in that it is no longer bound to a particular setting, however, the content is still particular and given by the content of sensation or intuition (*VPGst* 201). Thus, while representation is moving beyond the external determination of intuition, at this first stage it is still largely determined by it.

The next stage of representation constitutes another step toward freedom from external determination. In imagination (*Einbildungskraft*) the intelligence extends its role by creating the links or connections between the particular contents rather than using the connections given by the intuition. Here, "In that the content belongs to the intelligence, this subjectivity of the image is demolished. The connecting point is no longer objective; rather the intelligence is the subject of this content, this content is borne by the subject . . ." (*VPGst* 202). The subject, rather than the object being intuited, is the "connecting point." In the different types of imagination, this takes different forms, ranging from the random association of ideas in stream-of-consciousness thought to the analytic dissection of material under abstract categories. Because the intelligence's productivity here becomes explicit, we begin to see the expressive, self-objectifying activity of intelligence.

The first subsection, reproductive imagination, deals with the intelligence's most basic type of production: its own reproduction of the intuitions it has internalized (*erinnert*). The content here is still that given by intuition, but the connecting point already comes from the intelligence rather than the content of intuition itself (*VPGst* 202). Although the connections are created by the intelligence, however, they are not yet freely determined but rather arbitrarily or accidentally linked (*VPGst* 203).

Hegel's analysis next proceeds through an examination of the nature of the bond or link between the two contents that are connected. The contents here can be any concrete object, a stone or a human being. Essential is only that it is a concrete, unified object (for the subject) with particular characteristics (*VPGst* 202). The intelligence initially associates objects based on one particularity they have in common; in doing so, it abstracts from the objects' other particular characteristics: "This noticing of *one* determination is abstraction or the way of forming universal representations. This universal, which we named associating, appears at first as the linking, the universal, which is common to both" (*VPGst* 204). Through this process of abstraction, we develop the more general concepts that allow us to move away from the particularity of the object and subsume the particular under the general or universal category.[17] For example, "The yellow of the gold is linked with the determinate weight, etc. In that the intelligence removes this yellow, which exists only in relation to other determinations, singles out this determination, it thereby makes it (yellow only as yellow) so that it relates to itself; thereby the determination becomes universal, becomes abstract representation" (*VPGst* 205). The content comes from something given in intuition (the piece of gold), but the concept of yellow is produced by the intelligence's analysis. Because yellow by itself does not exist as yellow, but only as a yellow something, the category yellow sublates the particularity and givenness of the object in the abstract, general category of yellow. We only focus on the color—among the many other characteristics of the object— in light of a category that isolates this particular and thereby subsumes it. Put in terms of the association of two objects, they are only brought together because of some universal already implicitly operating. Although scientific categories are formed through this process of analysis as well, the activity of representation at this point does not presuppose conscious grouping. Rather, the reflective analysis develops out of an unconscious, undirected association of objects or ideas based on commonalities of which we may not initially be conscious.

But in the case of both the relatively unconscious association of ideas and deliberate analysis, the content is still given by the object, even if it is subsumed under the intelligence's abstract category. In the next stage, representation transforms this material through fantasy. Whether symbolic, allegorical, or poetic, fantasy is the "*fundamental* linking" in that it goes beyond the analysis of given objects discussed above. Most importantly, it is the imagination as productive—not simply reproductive or analytic.

In Hegel's treatment of the different modes of fantasy, he describes the subject's efforts to overcome the difference between the given intuition and the representation produced by the intelligence. Simply put, he sees us as driven to make them match up. At this point, "It is the activity of the intelligence to sublate this difference as well, to posit them as identical, to give its abstract, inner, peculiar content externality, representation [*Darstellung*] . . ." (*VPGst* 206). Up to this point, the intelligence has been determining itself internally. Yet it can only show itself that it has grasped what is external by itself constituting the object. In fantasy, this unity is brought about: "Fantasy is the central point in which the universal and being, one's own and what is found, the inner and the outer are completely forged into one" (*Enz.* § 457 A).

The intelligence overcomes this difference by expressing or objectifying itself. After having internalized the content provided by an external object, it now seeks to give objectivity or external existence to its own inwardness (*Innerlichkeit*): "The intelligence has thus come to this inner completion, to recollection [*Erinnerung*], in which it has its own peculiar content and is the impulse to externalize [*äußern*] this content" (*VPGst* 208). Such expression is not simply a process of giving back the objective content that was received. A work of art, for instance, always does more than reproduce something given. The intelligence's own activity has at this point transformed the received content, overcoming the particularity and givenness of the original object. It is precisely the resulting disparity between the inner and outer that is overcome through expression. These two aspects, internalizing (or recollection, both from Hegel's *Erinnerung*) and externalizing, are the twin components of representation: "Just as much as it [representation] is the drive to internalize [*der Trieb der Erinnerung*], it is the drive to externalize [*der Trieb der Entäußerung*], so that the inner is posited as an external . . ." (*VPGst* 208).

This objectification takes many forms. In the first, it is as an object that is "immediately at hand" (*VPGst* 208) in fantasy-constructs (*Phantasiegebilde*). Although they are produced by the intelligence, such constructs are just as immersed in particularity as any other given content. The next stage is the sign, in which the intelligence exercises greater control in its determination of the meaning of the externalized object: "In *signifying*, therefore, the intelligence displays a freer willfulness [*Willkür*] and sovereignty in the use of intuition than it does in symbolizing" (*Enz.* § 458 A). Whereas the symbol's meaning is given by the symbol's objective form—as in a picture of a house—the intelligence gives the sign its meaning, establishing an arbitrary link between the external, objective sign and its meaning, between the signifier and the signified. Because the sign's meaning is determined by the intelligence, the intelligence has overcome the givenness of objective existence, making it its own.

The discussion of the sign culminates in Hegel's treatment of language, in which theoretical spirit gives most adequate expression to its inwardness. In language, the intelligence determines not only the relation between the sign and its referent, but also the form of the language (*VPGst* 210). Language is thus the mode of the intelligence's self-expression and objectification. Moreover, although language finds its systematic place in Hegel's account of representation, it is the most appropriate and adequate expression for theoretical spirit as a whole. As Hegel states in his discussion of thought, "The deed of intelligence is the word" (*VPGst* 226).

In giving objective existence to its own inwardness, intelligence transforms the world around it, creating a new objective existence.[18] Hegel discusses this transformative aspect in terms of "the second existence that immediate things receive by existing in language" (*VPGst* 209). Through naming, the object is given a new existence. The bundle of particular characteristics we call a tree, *become* a "tree," an instance of a general category, through our naming it thus. The thing is no longer just this group of characteristics but a tree: "Through language the content receives a higher existence born from conscious intelligence; the other existence is its not irrational but unspiritual existence" (*VPGst* 209). Language, then, spans the chasm created between the inner and outer, the subjective and objective, as it externalizes its own inwardness by transforming the objective world. This is not to say that language or naming *changes* the characteristics—such as changing the weight of an object by calling it something else—but rather that just as the particular characteristics that together constitute the "object" are brought into a unity only through the mind's forms of time and space, higher order categories also play a role in constituting the object.

The concept of naming, though begun in the analysis of language, creates the transition to memory (*Gedächtnis*). At this point Hegel is struggling to further develop the relation between the sign and its meaning in a manner adequate to spirit. To be adequate to spirit's self-determination, this relationship cannot simply be given by the object, as it is with the symbol. Attempting to overcome this external determination, memory proceeds through overcoming the mediation of the relationship by a sensible image and eventually negates this relationship altogether in the string of "meaningless words" characterizing mechanical memory (*Enz.* § 463).

The first subsection of memory, verbal memory, deals with our internalization of names. Here the meaning of the name—not the name's external characteristics—becomes "what is essential to the word and existence" (*VPGst* 215). What is essential in the sign is what it refers to, not its external form. "Tree" is significant for and identified with what it represents (the concept of a tree), not what is sensible or immediately there, i.e., ink arranged in a particular pattern on a piece of paper.

This identity of the name and its meaning leads into the next stage, reproductive memory. Here the relationship between these two is no longer mediated by sensible material such as an image (*Enz.* § 462). For example, "With the name lion we need neither the intuition of such an animal nor even the image of it, for in that we *understand* it, the name is the imageless and simple representation" (*Enz.* § 462 A). Overcoming this dependence on a picture, "the names are not images, and yet we have the entire content by having the name before us" (*VPGst* 218). Representation as memory "is . . . no longer concerned with the *image*, drawn as this is from intuition, from the immediate unspiritual determinateness of intelligence, but with a determinate existence [*Dasein*] which is the product of intelligence itself . . ." (*Enz.* § 462 A). These representations are— according to Hegel—produced by the intelligence rather than simply taken over or accepted by the intelligence from the external world. Moreover, because they have overcome the particularity and givenness of intuitions, such names are the basis of the most universal activity of theoretical spirit, thought: "We *think* in names" (*Enz.* § 462 A).[19] This overcoming of mediation by sensible material is critical to the development of the intelligence from externally determined to self-determined. While one might object that our understanding of "lion" is never imageless, this objection misconstrues the nature of the development being traced. Hegel's claim is that we have a capacity for cognition that does abstract from all sensible particularity, not that all of our cognition can be purged of sensible content. The concepts "red" and "lion," for instance, may be inconceivable apart from images; Hegel's examples may be poorly chosen.[20] Nonetheless, more abstract concepts—such as "philosophy"—may be conceivable without images. It is the possibility of the latter that reveals, for Hegel, this mode of cognition that is independent of sensible intuition.

While the overcoming of particularity in the second moment of memory can be defended, in the third moment Hegel's attempt to satisfy systematic needs results in a conception of mechanical memory that seems to be more at odds with those requirements than to satisfy them. In memory as such, the intelligence overcomes the remaining difference or distance between the word and its meaning by detaching the latter. The intelligence posits "meaningless words," fixedly ordered (*Enz.* § 463). In this way, the intelligence has given itself an existence as objective being.[21] On the path toward knowledge of its conviction of the identity of the subject and object, the inner and outer, mechanical memory makes the inner completely objective: "Spirit, however, is only *with itself* as the *unity* of *subjectivity* and *objectivity*, and here in memory—after being in intuition initially something external, so that it *finds* determinations and in representation recollecting within itself and making its own *what is found*—it makes itself inwardly into an externality as memory, so that what is its own appears as something *found*" (*Enz.* § 463 A). Making its inwardness something external and objective eliminates a difference between the internal and external. It thereby at least provisionally fulfills "the highest purpose of memory," that "the intelligence be real, that the unity of subjectivity and objectivity come into existence" (*VPGst* 222). The price, however, is high. Mechanical memory seems to bring about this identity only by sacrificing meaningful inwardness. In earlier stages, the name gave external existence to the meaning that existed inwardly. In making the objective just a string of meaningless words, intelligence eliminates the difference between the internal and external by eliminating the internal. While it is apparent why Hegel would seek to overcome this difference, it is more difficult to see how mechanical memory could be an adequate solution to the problem. Even though the "solution" at this point should not be expected to be entirely adequate—since the sphere of thought is still to come—Hegel's culmination of representation in mechanical memory seems to be more of a backsliding than a progression in spirit's development.[22]

The transition from mechanical memory to thought—in Hegel's analysis— is not so much necessitated as bridged by the commonality between mechanical memory and thought: "*Memory* is in this manner the transition to the activity of *thought*, which no longer has a *meaning*, i.e., what is subjective is no longer different from its objectivity, as this inwardness has *being* within itself [*an ihr selbst* seiend *ist*]" (*Enz.* § 464). Thought is precisely the coming to knowledge of the identity of subject and object, inner and outer. To the extent that Hegel does point to an inadequacy in mechanical memory that drives the transition to the next level, it is in terms of memory's being "the exclusively external mode of thought, the one-sided moment of its *existence*..." (*Enz.* § 464 A). Calling the objectivity of mechanical memory a defect hints at the problem of the absence of inwardness identified above. Nonetheless, Hegel seems to view this inadequacy only as what calls for the development to thought, not as a reason to believe mechanical memory could only be a step backwards at this level in spirit's development. At the least, however, it points generally to an inadequacy or one-sidedness that thought must function to overcome.

## Thought (*Das Denken*)

The ultimate sphere of theoretical spirit, thought, constitutes the final step toward the intelligence's self-determination, such that "the content is determined by it" (*Enz.* § 468). At the culmination of this sphere, being and thought are one: "*its* [intelligence's] product, the *thought*, is the matter; simple identity of the subjective and objective. It knows that what is *thought is*, and that what *is* only *is* insofar as it is thought" (*Enz.* § 465).[23] The truth of the object is known as none other than the determinations given by spirit itself.

Proceeding where representation left off, the first stage of thought, formal understanding (*Verstand*), also has a content that originates in the senses. Formal understanding processes "the recollected representations into genera, species, laws, forces, etc., generally into categories . . ." (*Enz.* § 467). Working inductively, the intelligence subsumes particulars under categories, such as in a classification of animals. While this form of thinking is superseded in the further development of thought, Hegel emphasizes that formal understanding retains a vital role for the intelligence.[24] Thus, Hegel's sublation of this form of thought in reason does not seek to displace understanding as essential to our everyday negotiation of the world. Its one-sidedness does not make it dispensable.

In the second, diremptive moment of thought, the intelligence recognizes that the general categories are not simply assigned by the subject but are the truth of the object. Although this was already implicitly (*an sich*) the case in the first moment, it now becomes explicit for the subject (*für sich*). Thus, "We understand under judgment this: that it is not only something subjective but also something objective, that, for example, the tree within itself [*an ihm selbst*] is differentiated in this manner" (*VPGst* 234). This means that "the former opposition between universality and being" is overcome (*Enz.* § 467). The general category is no longer other than or opposed to the particular, the concept "tree" no longer foreign to the particular tree, because the analysis of the tree corresponds to the truth of the tree. The internal relationships that constitute the totality, however, are still understood as determined by the object itself rather than established in freedom by spirit (*Enz.* § 467 Z). Although the object is grasped in relation to universal thought forms, its characteristics are not grasped as determined by spirit.

The final moment of thought overcomes this inadequacy and with it the final dichotomy within theoretical spirit between the subject and object. Intelligence as reason or "syllogizing understanding" is entirely self-determining; it is "self-determining activity" (*VPGst* 232–33). Whereas until now the content was given by the object, "in *syllogism* . . . it [the thinking subject] *determines content* out of itself, in that it sublates this difference of form. In the insight into necessity, the final immediacy, which still clings to formal thought, has disappeared" (*Enz.* § 467). The intelligence knows that it posits its own determinations. The object, which is now thinking itself, is entirely determined by thought and thus self-determining. Insofar as the intelligence has grasped that it, *qua* spirit, determines the content itself rather than being given it by the object, spirit is free.[25] Moreover, in so doing it overcomes the otherness of the object: "The intelligence that has thus come to itself as thought is *free*, with itself [*bei sich*]" (*VPGst* 228). In returning to itself, thought no longer thinks some object that is other than itself but has only itself as an object. This is not to suggest, however, a turning away from the world. Thought thinking itself does not imply not thinking the world, precisely because thinking posits nature and spirit manifests itself throughout the realms examined by the philosophy of spirit.[26] Hegel's "thought" is not a solipsistic contemplation. The *Encyclopaedia* as a whole illustrates this point by its inclusion of politics and history in the articulation of a philosophical system.

In thought, theoretical spirit has reached the culmination of the drive that motivated the entire development through intuition, representation, and the preliminary stages of thought: "The intelligence has reached its concept to the extent that this is its determination; thus, it wants to think. It wants its intuitions and representations to become thoughts" (*VPGst* 226). This drive toward satisfactory knowledge has been the engine of the entire development of theoretical spirit.

### The Transition to Practical Spirit

Hegel's treatment of the transition from theoretical to practical spirit in the *Encyclopaedia* is remarkably brief—part of one short paragraph. Moreover, although Hegel's transitions generally result from an inadequacy experienced at the previous stage, the *Encyclopaedia* provides little indication of the inadequacy of thought that drives the transition to practical spirit.[27] One suspects that Hegel's not identifying this inadequacy relates to his tendency to emphasize the theoretical over the practical.[28] Further, the appearance of free spirit as a distinct, third moment of the "Psychology" first in 1830 suggests that Hegel was still struggling with the internal relations of this sphere. The discussion in the *Vorlesungen* offers only slightly more, yet it deals more directly with the inadequacy of thought. Consequently, we might surmise that Hegel's conception of this inadequacy (even if it was not as explicitly incorporated into the 1830 *Encyclopaedia*) and his partial development in the *Vorlesungen* of the conception of free spirit are related. Because thought is incorporated into free spirit, Hegel can be more explicit about the inadequacy of the thought in which theoretical spirit culminates. This suggests that at least in his treatment of these issues Hegel was not moving further away from the practical during his time in

Berlin. With this in mind, I turn first briefly to the *Encyclopaedia* treatment and then to the *Vorlesungen*.

In § 468 of the *Encyclopaedia*, Hegel summarizes the point reached by thought, where "[t]hought, as the free concept, is now also free in respect to *content*." He concludes the paragraph—and the discussion of theoretical spirit—with the sentence, "The intelligence, knowing itself as the determinant of the content, which is its own no less than determined as being, is *will*." One key to this brief, cryptic expression of the transition lies in the centrality of process to Hegel's thought. Knowing itself as determining, the intelligence does not simply stop determining. Rather, it comes to determine consciously, and in so doing, it wills.

Yet practical spirit is not simply a continuation of theoretical spirit. Hegel's treatment in the *Vorlesungen* indicates that practical spirit makes actual and external that which is only internal in theoretical spirit: "Thought as reason is free, and the will is free; rational thought and will have this in common: freedom. But the will is then further, to realize this freedom, which the intelligence in itself is—to posit this freedom (that the content, the determinations in the intelligence are its own) in the form of the immediate, not its own" (*VPGst* 237). At this point Hegel makes clear that the reconciliation or overcoming of difference effected by thought is one-sided in that it is still internal. On one hand, even coming to this knowledge requires spirit's acting and willing in the world; spirit comes to know its freedom vis-à-vis its objects only through demonstrating it. Willing thus has an instrumental, pedagogical role, which is one reason willing cannot simply follow thought. On the other hand, Hegel here indicates that practical spirit goes beyond theoretical spirit in complementing thought's one-sided inwardness. Practical spirit actualizes the freedom that the intelligence implicitly is. Thought's inadequacy is that it is a purely internal reconciliation—in thought but not at the level of existence. Thought "returning to" or thinking itself is not solipsistic in that the initial opposition of subject and object has been overcome and thus it does not simply think the subject in the narrow sense of introspection. Nonetheless, the activity is still the internal activity of thinking rather than a process of objectification in the world. Although language has in some sense an objective existence, it does not have the same degree of objective existence as the objectifications of practical spirit. (Moreover, language itself would seem to require the will as well as the intelligence.) In contrast, as we will see below, practical spirit gives external existence to the subject's determinations: "Practical spirit signifies that it brings its determinations back into being, that it be an existing world" (*VPGst* 238). Only in so doing can spirit fully realize its freedom in relation to the immediately given particular. As we have already discussed to some extent at the beginning of the chapter, this relationship therefore entails the ultimate inseparability of intelligence and will: "This transition [from intelligence to will] is not of course present for ordinary consciousness; rather, for representation thought and will fall apart. In truth, however, as we have just seen, *thought* is *what determines itself into will* and remains the first, the *substance* of the latter, so that without thought there can be no will; even the least cultivated person is only will insofar as he has thought; the animal, in contrast, because he does not think, is incapable of willing" (*Enz.* § 468 Z).

## Practical Spirit

With the help of the *Vorlesungen über die Philosophie des Geistes*, then, we can see the inadequacy remaining at the end of theoretical spirit that requires the transition to practical spirit: Practical activity has had a pedagogical role, essential to the progression toward thought, which must now be accounted for; and, more importantly, the reconciliation achieved in thought is now revealed as one-sided. The developments of practical spirit are not only necessary means for achieving the reconciliation at the culmination of theoretical spirit. They also reveal an end beyond the end of theoretical spirit. In addition to establishing the necessity of the transition out of theoretical spirit, the latter point also illuminates the systematic significance of practical spirit, its role in the objectification or externalization of the inwardness of theoretical spirit. In the first paragraph of practical spirit, the *Encyclopaedia* expresses the point in the following terms: "The determination of the *implicitly* existing [an sich *seienden*] will is to bring freedom into existence in the formal will and so to fulfill the purpose of the latter, this purpose being to fulfill itself with its concept, that is to make freedom its determinateness, its content and purpose as well as its determinate being" (§ 469).[29] This giving existence to what exists only implicitly (*an sich*) is the process of externalization so central to Charles Taylor's reading of Hegel. The one-sided, exclusively internal development of theoretical spirit must be overcome by the development into external reality (*VPGst* 239). Spirit must come to know itself not only as capable of transforming the world, positing its determinations into existence, but as actually doing so. Freedom cannot be complete (or "real") if it is only internal ("just a thought") and does not actualize itself in relation to objects in the world. Practical spirit has precisely this role: "Practical spirit is this: to make its determinations also explicit as objective, so that its determinations are not only as implicitly objective but are objective as posited by it, through its activity" (*VPGst* 240). At this level, the motive for spirit's actualization is its freedom: Without such actualization, freedom cannot be real freedom. Concretely and concisely expressed, "theory should be realized [*die Theorie soll realisiert werden*]" (*VPGst* 239).

While this discussion frames the systematic role of practical spirit, it does not by itself set up the internal developments of the sphere. To the contrary, much of this development—particularly once the second moment has been attained—is elaborated not as the progression of the objectification of the inwardness of thought (with which theoretical spirit culminated) but primarily as the increasing "rationality" of the will, which means that the internal determinations that are being objectified or externalized increasingly express reason, or the concept at spirit's core.

Beginning as practical feeling and developing through many stages into the rational, universal will, the developments portray the will's overcoming of its initially external determination to become a self-determining will. "Will" has both the general sense of the agent as practical spirit—paralleling the intelligence of theoretical spirit and encompassing the range of the process—and the specific sense of the fully developed, rational, free will that culminates this process of development. While this development proceeds toward an adequate expression of the thought reached at the end of theoretical spirit, it is neither a development from a less adequate to more adequate expression of that particular level of thought (such that practical feeling also attempts to express thought but the developed will simply does so better) nor a development corresponding to the stages of development of theoretical spirit (such that practical feeling objectifies intuition, impulses and willfulness objectify representation, etc.). Rather, the stages of practical spirit follow their own trajectory corresponding to the development of the inwardness that is to be expressed. Although they too begin with immediate determination (in practical feeling) and move toward a rational self-determination, they begin with a different immediate from theoretical spirit: the immediately given (internal) inclination rather than the immediately given object. Because the intelligence is also active, this difference—rather than a contrast between thought and action—differentiates theoretical from practical spirit.[30] Theoretical and practical spirit thus describe two different paths from immediacy to mediated, free self-determination.

The contrast between the systematic role of practical spirit set out in explaining the transition from theoretical to practical spirit and the internal developments of practical spirit provides two different—but complementary—perspectives on practical spirit. From the first perspective, practical spirit is the objectification of inwardness. While this perspective frames the introduction and systematic position of practical spirit and is central to the transition from the first to the second moment of the sphere, the dominant development of the sphere—which is central to the second and third moments as well as the transition between them—points to another perspective on this sphere: the will's own internal development toward being a rational will, i.e., willing in accord with its own essence. This rational will is also the thinking will; the culmination of the will's development is the thinking will. In the first paragraph of the *Encyclopaedia* treatment of practical spirit—immediately following the passage quoted above in which Hegel discusses the will as the objectification of inwardness—Hegel refers to the path of development actually portrayed in the stages of practical spirit: "Essentially, this concept, freedom, exists only as thought; the will makes itself into *objective* spirit by means of raising itself into thinking will . . ." (*Enz.* §469). If the first perspective reveals the systematic role of practical spirit as a whole, the second reveals the most important internal developments of this sphere. It focuses not on the externalization itself but on the development of the internal determination being externalized. Precisely because these are different, practical spirit must be viewed as possessing its own integrity in relation to theoretical spirit; its internal developments are not determined by theoretical spirit, even if its systematic function is inextricably tied to theoretical spirit.

These two perspectives, however, are related. If the systematic role of practical spirit is to provide the objectification of thought, practical spirit must reach a stage in which it is capable of being a thinking will. But the will does not start out at such an advanced stage. When it first reaches the point of objectifying or externalizing internal determinations—at the level of impulse—the internal determinations are not yet rational. Rather, they initially express the practical feelings we simply "find" ourselves possessing. To become an expression of the thinking will, practical spirit must pass through its own internal stages of development. Within the text, this means that after introducing practical spirit in light of its systematic function to objectify theoretical spirit, Hegel must back up to provide the internal developments of practical spirit to reach a stage at which it can play this role, i.e., be free.

Finally, these two different perspectives on practical spirit also suggest two different relationships to theoretical spirit. The first perspective corresponds to a global relationship in which practical spirit gives expression to theoretical spirit. The second corresponds to an internal relationship in which the will develops toward being an expression of thought, toward being a thinking will. Distinguishing these two helps to make clear that the developments of practical spirit are not simply developments in its expression of thought. The central developments of the sphere of practical spirit—which occur in the second and third moments—deal with the externalization of an internal determination, but it is not this *externalizing* that develops but the internal determination itself. The initial internal determinations—those found or given in practical feeling and impulse—have no direct relationship to theoretical spirit in that they are not expressions of theoretical spirit. They are related to theoretical spirit only by virtue of their telos to develop into the thinking will. Although expressing thought can be viewed as the purpose of the entire development of the sphere, an adequate expression of thought is reached only at the end. If, on the contrary, the entire development of the sphere of practical spirit were the development of the expression of thought, practical spirit would become nothing more than the aftereffect of theoretical spirit. In that way, the significance of practical spirit—and with it practical activity—in Hegel's system would be greatly underestimated.

### Practical Feeling (*Das praktische Gefühl*)

Like theoretical spirit, practical spirit begins with feeling, in this case the immediate, nonautonomous determination Hegel labels practical feeling: "Practical spirit has its self-determination within itself initially in a manner that is immediate and therefore *formal*, so that it *finds itself* as *singularity* determined in *its* inner *nature*" (*Enz.* § 471). It is not a feeling of something given outside the subject (the starting point for theoretical spirit) but a feeling of something given in the subject's own inwardness (such as hunger): "These determinations are immediate. . . . [T]hey are felt thus, but also as belonging to the essence of the subject itself, stepping forward out of it—not externally found, but based in the subject's own essence . . ." (*VPGst* 244).

The feeling "found" here is distinctly practical in that it is oriented toward an activity or different state of affairs. The internal content is related to an external as an ought: "Practical feeling contains the *ought*, its self-determination as *implicitly* existing, *related* to an *existing* particular, which has validity only in its conforming to the former" (*Enz.* § 472). This internal feeling is not indifferent to the way things are. This "ought," however, does not imply a sophisticated or necessarily moral claim; it is a specific desire, such as to be warmer or to eat something sweet. At this level "this relating of *need* to determinate being is the entirely subjective and superficial *feeling* of what is *pleasant* or *unpleasant*" (*Enz.* § 472). The given determination is characterized by particularity rather than universality and indicates merely satisfaction or dissatisfaction.

While this content is particular rather than universal and freely posited, Hegel emphasizes that this inadequacy is not inherent to the form of feeling. As in the discussion of intuition, the specific content of feelings can be either good or bad: "Feeling is, however, nothing other than the form of the immediate, peculiar singularity of the subject, in which this content, like every other objective content to which consciousness also ascribes objectivity, may be posited" (*Enz.* § 471 A). Thus, feelings are neither necessarily in conflict with the determinations of right—i.e., the ethical—nor necessarily in harmony with them. Acting out of feeling does not preclude one from doing the right thing, but neither does it justify an action or prove it is the right action. Because of this openness of the form of feeling to proper content, "[f]eelings, when they are of a true kind, are the same as what virtues and duties are," but "whether a content is essential, or right, is not decided in the sphere of feeling" (*VPGst* 246). This judgment comes only at the higher levels of practical spirit. Even though feelings cannot justify ethics, they are not to be overcome for ethics: "Everything that is in the will, everything that is in us in general *must* exist in the manner of feeling, i.e., in my peculiar, immediate subjectivity, must belong to me as this" (*VPGst* 246–47).[31] Through the cultivation of ethical feelings—one aspect of the process portrayed in the development of practical spirit—the givenness of feeling must be overcome but not the form itself.[32]

## Impulse and Arbitrary Will (*Die Triebe und die Willkür*)

The transition to the next stage of practical spirit, impulse and arbitrary will, is driven not by this inadequacy, however, but by the difference between the ought of feeling and the state of the world. It concerns not the development of the nature of the determination itself but the externalization or objectification of the internal determination: "In order that the will, i.e., the *implicitly* existing unity of universality and determinateness, satisfy itself, i.e., be *for itself*, the *correspondence* of its inner determination and of existence *ought* to be posited through it" (*Enz.* § 473). Impulses concern the overcoming of the difference between the preference of practical feeling and the state of things, i.e., the overcoming of displeasure or dissatisfaction. They are the objectification of the preferences that exist implicitly in the form of practical feeling, "the translation out of the subjectivity of the content, which to that extent constitutes purpose, into objectivity . . ." (*Enz.* § 475). Their content is the same as practical feeling: "Inclinations and passions," which are species of impulse, "have as their content the same determinations as practical feeling . . ." (*Enz.* § 474). The distinction between the level of practical feeling and impulses is not in the content of the determinations or in differences in what is wanted or the sources of this content. Both begin with a content simply found by the subject within itself. The difference, then, lies in the externalization of this interior practical feeling: "Impulse is a lack; that which I am missing is not a matter of the content as such, but rather lies much more in my self-determination, and this subjective determination should be objectified" (*VPGst* 252). The transition from the first to the second moment of practical spirit, then, represents perhaps Hegel's most fundamental treatment of the need for objectification or externalization in the context of human beings (i.e., not simply as a logical process).

The need for externalization, however, is not separable from the internal determination itself. Hegel distinguishes the two in his analysis—in the distinction between the first and second moments of practical spirit—but one cannot exist without the other. Practical feeling would not be *practical* feeling without the drive or impulse to externalization. The telos of practical feeling is precisely the overcoming of the difference between its internal determination and the state of things, i.e., the externalization of the internal. The unity—but not identity—of the first and second moments makes up Hegel's concept of action as both purpose and activity: "An act is a purpose of the subject, and also its activity, which carries out this purpose" (*Enz.* § 475 A). Human action can be grasped only in light of both its (inner) purpose and (external) activity.

At the beginning of the treatment of impulse, this internal determination is simply a practical feeling found as given within the subject. But the need for externalization continues as the internal content develops from this most immediate stage to a rational, mediated content. While practical feeling must be cultivated, its need for objectification will remain. The thinking will is the externalization of the inner, where that inner has developed to thought (though feeling is still present as well, but as cultivated, not in its original, immediate state). While—in Hegel's treatment—impulse has emerged through the development of practical feeling toward externalization, the development out of the sphere of impulse toward the sphere of eudaemonia—the internal development most central to Hegel's treatment of the sphere—consists primarily in the transformation of the internal content that is to be externalized.

Initially, particular impulses are associated with particular feelings and appear to each other as only externally related, i.e., having in common only that they belong to the same subject. My wanting to be warmer is unrelated to my finding my chair uncomfortable. Thus, in addition to having the same content as feeling, inclinations and passions "on the other hand . . . are, as belonging to the still subjective and single will, tainted with contingency and appear to the individual as particular and to each other as external and therefore to be related to as unfree necessity" (*Enz.* § 474).[33] As the expression of immediately given practical feelings, impulses are equally bound by particularity, simply there with no internal relation to each other: "Initially impulses are here only a trivial [*nichtiger*], particular content, and it is this which goes after its satisfaction. The impulse as such does not look around itself but goes after its own satisfaction; the impulse is blind . . ." (*VPGst* 255).

This cacophony of drives inevitably generates conflicts. Not all can be satisfied. The path out of the resulting confusion comes from the subject's differentiation from the particular drives. They are its drives, but they are not it: "As thinking and implicitly free, the will distinguishes itself from the *particularity* of impulses and places itself above their multiple content as the simple subjectivity of thought; in doing so, it is the *reflecting* will" (*Enz.* § 476). The subject that possesses these multiple particular desires distinguishes itself from them. Abstracting from them, the reflecting will is thinking in the sense that "it has the form of universality in itself and under this form relates itself to the particular impulses" (*VPGst* 255). Thus, "thinking" in this context signifies a formal universality: not being committed beforehand to any simply given particularity. In light of the limits that will be revealed to this level of reflection, Hegel does not mean the "thought" that completes theoretical spirit. The will reflects upon or considers the existing impulses.

In choosing among various given impulses, the formally universal will adopts some while rejecting others. The will thereby makes an impulse its own and partly overcomes its simply given or immediate character; it is not simply there but rather chosen by the will: "Such a particularity of impulse is in this way no longer immediate but rather first *its own*" (*Enz.* § 477). Choosing, then, means appropriating a particular impulse: "That is choosing: the will is a particular only when it resolves to be such, posits it as its own" (*VPGst* 257). Moreover, in this activity of choice, the subject "first appears as will in general" (*VPGst* 255). This choosing constitutes willing in its most basic form.[34]

In reflecting upon and choosing between these particular impulses, the subject is guided by the general impulse to satisfy itself as a whole: "the general [*allgemeine*] impulse of the individual is to satisfy *itself*, not just to satisfy the impulse but *itself* in the impulse" (*VPGst* 255). The subject seeks not to satisfy its impulses for themselves but to satisfy itself through satisfying (some of) its impulses—which means the impulses are no longer immediate. The difference between these two sorts of satisfaction is "a difference between the satisfaction of itself as this universal and the satisfaction of itself as this particular" (*VPGst* 255). The subject satisfies itself as something formally universal rather than as captive to particularity.

Although Hegel's conception of the subject at this point appears particularly unified and whole—in contrast to many more recent conceptions of subjectivity—the unity necessary here is the unity of self-consciousness at any given moment, in any instant of reflection, rather than a larger claim about the unity of the self over a period of time. He is dealing with the common experience of deciding what to do when we have conflicting inclinations.[35]

At the same time, Hegel is not claiming that we always have such distance from our impulses, that we can always reflect upon them as ours rather than act upon them immediately, without such mediation. Rather, Hegel's account describes the development necessary for freedom from such impulses; although these impulses are internal, when we act upon them immediately, they are not freely chosen and we cannot be said to be acting freely. The ease with which Hegel's analysis seems to move from these impulses to the subject's ability to reflect upon them should not be mistaken for the claim that the process itself occurs automatically or without effort.

Although action at this point requires the appropriation or adoption of an impulse by a choosing subject, the impulse that is appropriated is still in its origin immediate or given. Its content is thus immediately given rather than determined by the subject itself. The will here chooses among various given possibilities, but without determining what those possibilities are in the first place. For this reason, it is not a fully developed or free will, but what Hegel labels arbitrary will (*Willkür*): "Arbitrary will [is] distinguished from the free will in that arbitrary will has to do with a particular content, not an absolute; free will has to do with absolute content.... Arbitrary will has only impulses for its content, so that it can admittedly choose, but insofar as it rejects this impulse, the other content is only another impulse or another way of satisfying an impulse" (*VPGst* 257). Although this subject's activity is here not determined simply by whatever impulses are present at a given instant—they must first be appropriated—the end result is still the choice of one of those particular impulses and is therefore limited by the impulses that happen to exist. The possibilities then are given to the subject, not determined by the subject itself. Consequently, it is not fully free or autonomous.[36]

At a more abstract level, Hegel expresses this as a contradiction between the will's formal universality (which is not in itself determined by anything particular) and its determination by particular content. Concretely, the result is a subject endlessly seeking satisfaction of its drives but without being able to achieve it: "As the *contradiction* of actualizing itself in a particularity which is simultaneously a nothingness for it, and of having in this particularity a satisfaction which it has at the same time emerged from, will is initially the *infinite process* of diversion, of the sublation of one inclination or enjoyment by another, and of satisfaction, which it is not just as much as it is, by another" (*Enz.* § 478). As long as the subject seeks its satisfaction in the particular, it will remain unsatisfied, ceaselessly pursuing peace through one impulse after another.

At the same time, Hegel's discussion of arbitrary will already emphasizes the interrelationship of theoretical and practical spirit. Even though the reflection involved is not the highest level of thought in which theoretical spirit culminates, it still involves theoretical spirit: "Intelligence is thus reflecting will in general, and thus is the will as arbitrary will, as choosing. To portray will and thought as isolated is ignorant. Insofar as the will is will, thinking is therein; even if it is not abstract, pure thought but relates itself to particularity, it is nonetheless *reflecting* will" (*VPGst* 256). These developments of practical spirit can be seen neither as simply the consequences of theoretical spirit—such that they would begin where theoretical spirit ended—nor as entirely separate from theoretical spirit. Whenever the will has emerged from simply following impulses blindly, whenever reflection on these impulses occurs, the subject is also active as theoretical spirit. Insofar as the subject is spirit, it is both willing and thinking.

Eudaemonia (*Die Glückseligkeit*)

The dissatisfaction and contradiction intrinsic to arbitrary will generate in the subject a general idea or image of happiness or eudaemonia (*Glückseligkeit*).[37] In light of this ideal, the particular drives—because they constitute dissatisfaction—are seen as something to be overcome for the sake of contentment: "In this representation—brought forth by reflective thought—of a universal satisfaction, the impulses in accord with their particularity are posited as *negative* and ought to be partially or wholly sacrificed, partly one to another on behalf of this purpose, partly directly to this purpose" (*Enz.* § 479). The vision of eudae-monia is posited as the positive purpose of activity, with the particular impulses seen as other than this larger end.

In the *Vorlesungen*, Hegel explicitly relates his conception of *Glückseligkeit* to ancient conceptions of eudaemonia, as exemplified in Plato and Aristotle, and thus to a conception of ethics that Kant had largely displaced.[38] Its placement as the third and final moment of practical spirit indicates the high esteem in which Hegel holds it, even if it too is ultimately critiqued. Further, its location suggests the extent to which this ethical conception is formative for Hegel's own ethical outlook and central among the ethical perspectives he seeks to bring together in his own system. As discussed in chapter 1, significant elements of Hegel's project—and particularly his ethical thought—can be framed as an attempt to provide a modern reappropriation of Aristotle that does justice to modern insights, particularly as represented by Kant.

Consequently, it is not surprising that the insufficiency Hegel identifies in eudaemonia is closely related to what he takes from Kant's analysis of freedom as autonomy. At the same time, this inadequacy is not radically different from the one that led to the emergence of eudaemonia itself. Eudaemonia constitutes the emergence—out of the subject's pursuit of its general satisfaction—of this satisfaction as an ideal on its own. Although it does represent a stage distinct from arbitrary will, the difference between the stages is relatively small in com-parison to some of Hegel's other transitions. As a result, the inadequacy of this stage is also closely related to that of the previous stage.

Although the subject views its happiness as a positive purpose or good, this purpose is still formally universal. It is an abstract goal of happiness without any affirmative conception of what this is: "In eudaemonia, general satisfaction is the purpose, but this is so far indeterminate, and satisfaction, if it would be actual enjoyment, is dependent on something particular, single, a content" (*VPGst* 260). Although it posits the desires as something negative, as something over against eudaemonia, they still constitute the only source of the positive content of the drive for happiness: "since eudaemonia has *affirmative* content only in the impulses, it is they that arbitrate, and it is subjective feeling and whim that have to decide where happiness is to be posited" (*Enz.* § 479). Though eudaemonia is conceived as a positive conception, as the good, not simply the satisfaction or quiescence of particular desires, the latter constitutes its only content: "Eudaemonia demands the satisfaction of the universal but is simultaneously a universality that is still in the particular, that has no content other than the particular" (*VPGst* 261). The will still does not determine itself in accord with its own concept. The formally universal concept of eudaemonia remains bound to the particular, such that at this level as well, "arbitrary will reigns" (*VPGst* 261).[39] Consequently, this attempt to overcome the inadequacies of the previous sphere is unsuccessful. The search for eudaemonia is plagued by the same "progress into the infinite [*Progreß ins Unendliche*]" that condemned the second moment (*VPGst* 260). The abstract concept of eudaemonia—as long as it is defined only in relation to the particular content of the impulses—cannot overcome this contradiction.[40] What is needed is a content that is not determined or given by the particular. To be a fitting or adequate source of determination for spirit, it must not be given to spirit—even by an impulse within the subject—but rather determined by spirit itself. Any other conception leaves spirit ultimately unfree.

## Free Spirit

This need for self-determination drives the transition to the final moment of the "Psychology" and simultaneously of subjective spirit as a whole, preparing the following transition to the sphere of objective spirit. In both the *Vorlesungen* and the *Encyclopaedia*, the transition to free spirit clearly emerges out of the inadequacies of the abstract vision of eudaemonia. As mentioned previously, in the 1830 edition of the *Encyclopaedia* this development constitutes a transition to a distinct third moment of the "Psychology," distinguished from both theoretical and practical spirit. While the immediate forces driving the transition are the same in the *Vorlesungen* and the *Encyclopaedia*, the introduction in the latter of a distinct moment makes even clearer that the above contradiction can only be resolved through a synthesis of will and intelligence. It is here that the two paths of theoretical and practical spirit converge; although they were never radically separate, now they form a unity.

In accord with the requirements generated by the failure of eudaemonia, free spirit must produce its content both universally and from within itself: "The determinateness, however, that allows determination within itself, that contains and simultaneously is the *universal* determinateness is *freedom* . . ." (*VPGst* 261). Only a universality that determines particular content within itself—not simply a formal universality that takes on particularity from without—can avoid the contradictions of the arbitrary will. The free will is "the self-posited, *immediate singularity*, which is however to the same extent purified into the *universal* determination of freedom itself" (*Enz.* § 481). The free will generates its own specific content which is both universal and concrete. It is not simply an abstract universal (such as a test for consistency) but has overcome the limitation of particularity and rid itself of contingency or arbitrariness. In Hegel's language, it is individual—both universal and particular.

For spirit, this can only mean a determination by its own essence, such that "[s]pirit that knows itself as free and wills itself as its object" is spirit that has "its essence as its determination and purpose . . ." (*Enz.* § 482). Free spirit has its own essence as its content or purpose. This essence, however, is precisely the concept at the heart of Hegel's system. As manifest within the sphere of subjective spirit, it is the *Anlage* we have been analyzing throughout these last three chapters.

Several concepts necessarily converge here for Hegel. Spirit's universality means its independence of particularity, i.e., its freedom from givenness; spirit's universality is its own power of self-creation and freedom. At this point, Hegel describes this freedom as spirit's essence (*VPGst* 262). In relation to the reason that Hegel has indicated as spirit's essence at other points in his analysis, the common point is the overcoming of the division between subject and object or between what is simply given and what is constituted by the subject. Concretely, in acting practically, i.e., to shape the world, to impose our visions upon it, humans overcome the radical divide between the subject and object as well as overcoming givenness more generally. Through cultivating land, healing the sick, creating works of art, developing social institutions, and an infinite number of other activities, human beings transform the given world. While one may question the limits of such transformation, in its basic structure this aspect of Hegel's point relates to virtually every aspect of our day-to-day lives.

Described in terms of the relation between the will and intelligence, free spirit represents their convergence: "The actual free will is the unity of theoretical and practical spirit; *free will*, which is *for itself as free will*, in that the formalism, contingency, and limitedness of the preceding practical content has sublated itself. . . . The will has this *universal* determination as its object and purpose, in that it *thinks* itself, knows this to be its concept, is *will* as free *intelligence*" (*Enz.* § 481). This universal determination comes about only through a subject that wills intelligently. Not simply a pragmatic or instrumental reflective process, this intelligent will not only calculates but also knows itself as free. Spirit can only become fully free by knowing itself as free.

While the convergence with theoretical spirit entails this knowledge of spirit's own freedom, the culmination of the sphere of subjective spirit also contains another side. While spirit's knowledge of its freedom is a *knowledge* of its own concept, the other side of Hegel's analysis here focuses on actuality (*Wirklichkeit*). At the culmination of subjective spirit, spirit's concept and its actuality have been reconciled: "There spirit has arrived at its true Idea, where the concept is identical with its reality and is identical *for it* [spirit]" (*VPGst* 262). This unity between concept and actuality is what Hegel labels "the Idea." In terms of the anthropology, the underlying structure or *Anlage* has been actualized.

### Concluding Reflections on the Relation of Theoretical and Practical Spirit

While Hegel, particularly in passages such as these from the *Vorlesungen*, suggests that this unity is already realized, in discussing this stage in spirit's development as part of the entirety of its development in part three of the *Encyclopaedia*—i.e., in relation to objective and absolute spirit as well—Hegel emphasizes that the reconciliation here portrayed is only an abstract reconciliation, that it needs to be given concreteness or actuality. Spirit is here "the rational will *in general* or *implicitly* the Idea . . ." (*Enz.* § 482). This relates closely to Hegel's repeated references to the role of objective spirit, e.g., duties, in filling out the positive content determined at this level (*VPGst* 257, 263 and *Enz.* § 482 A). Thus, while Hegel seems to say that objective spirit provides the specific account of the content already being discussed here (the content that is concretely universal), at the same time, objective spirit seems to carry out what is implicit here and in this sense to go further than subjective spirit; objective spirit seems both to be presupposed and to be the consequence.

Seeing how both of these perspectives hold for Hegel requires directly addressing the relation between subjective and objective spirit, particularly since this will also shed further light on the relation of theoretical and practical spirit. Objective spirit does not follow subjective spirit in any temporal sense. Although this is not the case for the stages of development within subjective spirit either, we can frequently see the systematic development of subjective spirit approximately displayed in the development of a particular human being from childhood through adulthood. Subjective and objective spirit, however, must be understood as always accompanying each other. The developments of subjective spirit can only take place within the context created by the objectification of spirit in a social world, and it is these objectifications that "objective spirit" analyzes. This necessity derives not simply from the fact that human reproduction requires the presence of other human beings or from the need to work together to provide for basic physical needs. Rather, while including these points as well, Hegel makes the stronger claim that our consciousness of freedom (and, therefore, theoretical spirit) only develops in a context that actualizes this freedom. Knowledge of our freedom, which is essential to being free, does not come about from abstract reflection alone. It requires seeing and participating in this freedom at least partially demonstrated in the world.

At the same time, these "demonstrations," spirit's objectification in the world, can only be fully comprehended when grasped as the unfolding or further development of what spirit implicitly is, i.e., the implicit structure that Hegel sets out in subjective spirit. Because this structure, this *Anlage*, is a manifestation of the concept first examined in the logic, objective spirit can be said to objectify or express both this *Anlage* and the concept from the logic. Yet the structure developed in subjective spirit plays an important mediating role between the logic and objective spirit. Subjective spirit provides the further determination of the logic's concept necessary for the unfolding of objective spirit. Objective spirit necessarily develops from subjective spirit, not directly from the structures of the logic. Consequently, the content of the sphere of objective spirit—the family, civil society, the state, etc.—is determined by the immanent development of the implicit structure examined in the last three chapters. The construction of this external, objective world, however, is for the most part not a conscious process (whether it can become a conscious process is a central question of the next chapter). Rather, Hegel's treatment of objective spirit, in the *Philosophy of Right* and the next section of the *Encyclopaedia*, is his uncovering of this essence already embodied in the objective sphere, especially the modern state.

Thus, if it is initially puzzling why Hegel thinks that the concept of a universal that wills itself, or freedom that has itself as its content, is any more specific or less abstract than the goals of eudaemonia, his response contains two independent aspects: First, it is precisely this specific content that he is preparing to set forth in the following section, objective spirit. Hegel does not intend to provide the content of his ethics within subjective spirit. Rather, the anthropology forms the substructure for the concrete ethical and political vision to be elaborated in the next segment of the philosophy of spirit. In other words, although the anthropology itself constitutes a "fundamental ethics," to borrow Peperzak's phrase once more, Hegel does not build his ethical home upon this foundation until objective spirit. The content of Hegel's ethics is found there, even though it can only be most adequately grasped as a further development of the anthropological structure.

Additionally, Hegel believes that this content is everywhere around us— as long as "we," the readers, are living in the modern European state as he understands it. Together with Hegel's understanding of objective spirit as the externalization of spirit in the world, this means that the content Hegel refers to so abstractly in subjective spirit is the modern state: "In that spirit wills nothing other than to be free and has no purpose other than its freedom, the state is just a mirror of its [spirit's] freedom, in which spirit has its freedom as something actual, as a world in front of it" (*VPGst* 263). The existence with which the concept of freedom is identical is this state. Moreover, although consciousness of this freedom belongs to the sphere of absolute spirit—in religion or philosophy—this freedom has its actuality in the institutions of the world: "If in religion as such the person knows the relationship to absolute spirit as his essence, even as he steps into the sphere of *worldly existence*, he also has the divine spirit present as the substance of the state, the family, etc. These relationships are cultivated by this spirit and constituted in accordance with it, just as through such existence the conviction of the ethical infuses the individual and he is then *actually free* in this sphere of particular existence, of what is currently sensed and willed" (*Enz.* § 482 A). While this point raises significant questions regarding Hegel's understanding of his own social and historical context as the culmination of spirit's development—questions to be addressed in chapters 5 and 6—what is particularly important here is the vital role of this objectification, *both as a means to theoretical spirit's development and as a constitutive aspect of the end of spirit's development.*

The necessity of this particular social context for spirit's theoretical development points again to the importance to theoretical spirit of spirit's practical activity. Consciousness of freedom does not come about through abstract reflection alone. Although this consciousness of freedom is essential to freedom as well—people are not fully free if they do not know they are free—freedom must also be manifest in the world. To claim that theoretical spirit only fully grasps its own freedom as a result of taking part in spirit's practical freedom, however, is not to say that theoretical spirit does not also influence the development of practical spirit. While the discussion of the reflection involved in choosing among competing impulses indicates one aspect of this influence, Hegel indicates another in the discussion of freedom in *Enz.* § 482 A. There, he contends that freedom is one of the most misunderstood of concepts and that many epochs had no consciousness of the concept. While some parts of the world—according to Hegel—still have no understanding of it, the idea of freedom was introduced in the West by Christianity. Its existence at the representational level in Christianity, however, did not immediately correspond to or translate into the worldly existence of this freedom. To the contrary, it required the entirety of European development from the emergence of Christianity until the emergence of the modern state, following Napoleon's defeat, for this concept to achieve adequate—or at least almost adequate—expression in the world. Only as a result of this external existence of freedom could the representations of Christianity be raised into the concepts of Hegelian philosophy.

This account suggests one of the dominant models for understanding a certain priority of theoretical over practical spirit in Hegel's system. Practical human action—insofar as it is a distinctly human act and not simply a response to stimuli—actualizes what we might call a pre-understanding, to employ a term from hermeneutics. Depending upon the reflection that precedes the action, this pre-understanding may be more or less conscious or articulable. It may, for instance, be a vision of freedom that can be represented in symbols but not yet expressed in discursive and systematic language; it may be something like a hunch. As we act on this pre-understanding, embodying it or giving it an existence in the world, we are then able to reflect more cogently upon it, to better articulate the understanding that motivated—and was thus expressed in—that action. Again, depending upon a variety of factors, the post-activity understanding may be more or less articulate; the road to self-knowledge may be a long one with many intermediate steps. Hegel's point, however, is that it is precisely through such actualization of a pre-understanding that we come to a greater understanding. In the process, the starting point is transformed as well. The pre-understanding is no longer what it was. This indicates something about both how we understand our practical activity and how we understand the advancement of our knowledge—since each post-understanding also contributes to a pre-understanding for a new action. Thus, while it is fair to say that theoretical and practical spirit inform each other, in a dialectical fashion, the dominant model in this context is one of pre-understanding, actualization, and comprehension. At the same time, since spirit is an ongoing process, this comprehension is not an end or conclusion but itself eventuates further practical activity.

This, in turn, helps us to see more clearly another perspective on the complex relation between theoretical and practical spirit. Although practical spirit does not follow theoretical spirit in the sense of coming after the end of theoretical spirit, as long as we are talking about distinctly human willing—not simply the blind following of impulses—practical spirit actualizes an inward, "theoretical" pre-understanding. This pre-understanding is theoretical in the sense that it deals with cognition broadly speaking, including at the most basic level a very rough intuition. As Hegel points out in his discussion of the role of reflection in eudaemonia, for instance, even the calculations involved in trying to quell desires require intelligence. Moreover, particularly by the stage of eudaemonia, there is clearly a concept—which we might call a pre-concept—of the good operating, which the subject seeks to actualize through its activity. It is these efforts, and their failure, that bring about the transition to free spirit. Thus, it is the objectification, even when unsuccessful, that brings about the knowledge integral to free spirit. Correspondingly, the *Vorlesungen über die Philosophie des Geistes* ends: "What is most important is that spirit know itself; γνῶθι σεαυτόν was the call that went out to the Greeks. Spirit is only to know what it is. To contribute to this knowledge has been the goal of these lectures" (*VPGst* 263–64). This final cognition, however, cannot be taken as separable from the practical. Here then, we see a certain priority to the theoretical combined with a co-essentiality of the theoretical and practical.

To conclude this chapter, let us sum up the relations that have been revealed between theoretical and practical spirit. Hegel is explicit that will and intelligence are inseparable. They represent two different paths of development which—without directly corresponding to each other—interpenetrate. The intelligence develops only by virtue of practical activity, and the will develops only by virtue of theoretical activity. Theoretical spirit comes to more adequate self-knowledge as a result of practical activity. Practical spirit comes to be more developed and free will by reflecting upon its impulses and purifying them into rational form. Each is instrumental to the development of the other. This mutual interdependence expresses the role of each, viewed from the perspective of the other.

From the perspective of free spirit, however, we see that their developments must converge, that a genuinely free spirit must be both thinking and willing. Here, both constitute essential aspects or dimensions of the end of spirit's development. Practical spirit, willing—not just the thinking intelligence—is integral to the purpose or end of spirit's development.

Viewed from the perspective of our experience of the world, the relation of the theoretical and practical can be expressed in terms of a constantly recurring sequence of pre-understanding, actualization, and comprehension. This model seems to reflect Hegel's broadest understanding of the relation of thought and action, providing one of the most illuminating perspectives on the movement of the "Psychology" as a whole. It gives a certain priority to the theoretical, both as the pre-understanding and the self-knowledge that culminates the process, while still doing justice to the role of practical activity in forming the theoretical understanding. In so doing, this conception gives practice an integral role in the purpose of the entire process as well.

Finally, this account also illuminates the relationship between Hegel's account of the individual subject's will and intelligence and the larger schematic of spiritual development. Pre-understanding/action/comprehension is the expression at an individual level of the developmental dynamic of spirit as a whole, characterized at the most comprehensive level as abstract/manifest/comprehended.

# 5 From Anthropology to Ethics (1)
*Theory and Practice*

What is rational is actual;
and what is actual is rational.

The treatise, therefore, in so far as it deals with political science, shall be nothing other than an attempt *to comprehend and portray the state as an inherently rational entity*. As a philosophical composition, it must distance itself as far as possible from the obligation to construct a *state as it ought to be*; such instruction as it may contain cannot be aimed at instructing the state on how it ought to be, but rather at showing how the state, as the ethical universe, should be recognized.

A further word on the subject of *issuing instructions* on how the world ought to be: philosophy, at any rate, always comes too late to perform this function. As the *thought* of the world, it appears only at a time when actuality has gone through its formative process and attained its completed state. . . . When philosophy paints its grey in grey, a shape of life has grown old, and it cannot be rejuvenated, but only recognized, by the grey in grey of philosophy; the owl of Minerva begins its flight only with the onset of dusk. (*PR* 24/20, 26/21, 27–28/23)

These three passages from the preface to Hegel's *Philosophy of Right* are frequently taken to entail that philosophy has no role to play in informing practice, especially political practice. They have contributed greatly to Hegel's reputation as a conservative apologist for the Prussian state, urging quiescence and declawing philosophy of its critical capacities. To the extent that they suggest no critical role for theory, they threaten to undermine the entire ethical and political significance of Hegel's thought, at least for anything other than a conservative political agenda. More fundamentally, they appear to challenge the very idea that a philosophical anthropology could have constructive ethical implications. Consequently, the attempt to move from the anthropology set out in subjective spirit to the ethical and political implications developed in objective spirit must begin by confronting these passages.

These passages are among the most discussed of any in Hegel's corpus. Despite frequent conservative explications of these texts, a significant number of interpreters have emphatically rejected any such reading.[1] Considerations important to this challenge include the immediate political context of the writing of the preface (soon after the Carlsbad Decrees), the significant contrast between the state portrayed in the *Philosophy of Right* and any state existing at that time, and Hegel's own attempt in § 6 A of the *Encyclopaedia* to clarify his claim regarding the actual and the rational. Some have stressed the critical dimension of Hegel's linking of reason and actuality, insofar as this relationship entails that the world becomes more rational and free.[2] This scholarship has made invaluable contributions to the interpretation of Hegel's preface and should undermine any simplistic conservative reading; but central questions about the relationship between theory and practice in Hegel's thought remain unanswered.

Regarding the political context, for instance, Allen Wood emphasizes that Hegel rewrote the preface to avoid censorship. The recent Carlsbad Decrees of 1819 were central to a reactionary shift in the Prussian government at the time, and Hegel was concerned that the *Philosophy of Right* would be censored. This concern arguably motivated the quiescent tone of the preface. Thus, according to Wood, "the Preface in particular is designed to quiet any possible suspicions the censors might have concerning Hegel's political opinions."[3] While the political context is of course significant, however, it cannot on its own explain the apparently reactionary claims in the preface, precisely because these claims—particularly those regarding the actual and the rational—draw heavily on broader themes in Hegel's thought, such as his account of reason in history.[4] Similarly, to make the point that Hegel's account of the state in the *Philosophy of Right* differs from the existing Prussian state may rule out his having been an apologist for Prussian reactionaries, but it does not address whether fundamental elements of his thought are in tension with any notion of theory as critical. Because these passages from the preface relate to basic movements in his thought, any adequate grappling with them must consider this possibility.

Much of the recent literature on the preface seeks to do just this by stressing the distinction between actuality (*Wirklichkeit*) and reality (*Realität*) or "mere existence" (*bloßes Dasein*). This distinction is crucial to understanding Hegel's claim that "What is rational is actual; and what is actual is rational," which Hardimon, following Henrich, refers to as the *Doppelsatz*.[5] While the actual consists of that which manifests spirit in the world, "mere existence" refers to that which is only accidental or contingent. Explaining the comment about reason and actuality in the preface to the *Philosophy of Right*, Hegel states in the *Encyclopaedia*, "what is there is partly *appearance* and only partly actuality [*daß überhaupt das Dasein zum Teil* Erscheinung *und nur zum Teil Wirklichkeit ist*]. In common life people may happen to call every brain wave, error, evil, and suchlike '*actual*,' as well as every existence however wilted and transient it may be" (*Enz.* § 6 A). Hegel makes the same distinction at several points throughout his work—in the *Philosophy of Right*, the philosophy of history, and the logic—making it impossible to read his comment on the rationality of the actual as an endorsement of everything—including all suffering and injustice—in the world.[6]

As important as this distinction between actuality and mere existence is, however, it does not on its own provide the key to the relationship between theory and practice. If one sees too little relation between actuality and what happens to exist, then the actuality of the rational is reduced to a tautology, as Hardimon notes.[7] That is, if the actual is defined as what manifests reason, then the claim that the actual is rational is emptied of all meaning. Moreover, a central thrust of the *Lectures on the Philosophy of History* is the manifestation of reason in history. Actuality is not to be understood so abstractly as to be removed from lived experience. Although often translated as "actuality," *Wirklichkeit* is the everyday German term for reality. Given Hegel's conception of spirit's manifestation in the world, actuality cannot be some artificial philosophical conception radically different from the world we encounter; we cannot interpret it so abstractly that the intimate relationship between actuality and what we generally think of as reality or existence is lost. This much follows from both the discussion of the actualization of reason in history in the philosophy of history and the systematic role of objective spirit.[8] Finally, if actuality and reality have nothing to do with each other, the critical moment of Hegel's thought is also lost. Philosophy will be unable to guide us in our interactions in the world and will remain an exercise in otherworldly contemplation. While such an understanding might disable conservative implications of Hegel's thought, they would simultaneously disable any relevance of his thought for social or political critique.

One initially tempting but ultimately inadequate possibility would be to understand the actual as a sort of outline form underneath the details of concrete, particular existence. Then a society would be a manifestation of reason when the basic structures and guiding principles were in accord with reason, though the particular details would be left to the level of mere existence and contingency. Actuality would be the branches of a tree, which are "filled out" or covered by the leaves; although the structure is given by the branches, the final, external form is composed of the leaves. At one point in particular Hegel suggests this interpretation himself: "For since the rational, which is synonymous with the Idea, becomes actual by entering into external existence [*Existenz*], it emerges in an infinite wealth of forms, appearances, and shapes and surrounds its core [*Kern*] with a brightly colored covering [*Rinde*] in which consciousness at first resides, but which only the concept can penetrate in order to find the inner pulse, and detect its continued beat even in the external shapes" (*PR* 25/20–21). As a result, philosophy should not concern itself with details such as whether passports should contain a painting of the individual, as Fichte had recommended (*PR* 25/21). However, the last element of the quotation—regarding the "continued beat" of reason even within the "external shapes" of existence—makes Hegel's meaning here indeterminate. While the point that reason and therefore philosophy cannot determine all the details of how to run a state (which means that some aspects of existence will always be contingent rather than rational, i.e., actual) is evident, the last element of the passage raises once again the question of the relation of the actual and merely existing. Are these "external shapes" in the end actual or merely contingent existence? The first part of the passage suggests the latter, while the idea that the pulse of reason beats in them suggests the former. Moreover, this passage must also be read in conjunction with the centrality of reason in history, where Hegel claims that "the sole aim of philosophical inquiry is *to eliminate the contingent*" (*VG* 29/28). Although some details may be left at the level of contingency, the development of freedom requires that freedom not be dependent upon or subject to contingency. Where "freedom" depends upon accidents of birth for instance, no one is genuinely free (cf. Hardimon 1994, 118). Although some details of government regulation, for instance, may not affect freedom, many of the "details" do. Actuality must concern itself with such details for precisely this reason. An interest in an adequate manifestation of freedom must include concern with details that can determine our freedom on a daily basis. Consequently, an understanding of actuality as concerning only the underlying structure cannot do justice to the manifestation of reason and development of freedom in history.

An adequate understanding of the relationship of actuality and mere existence must focus on the centrality of process or movement. An understanding of the relation between these two terms as static or fixed will inevitably fall to one or the other of the extremes: actuality and reality will either be completely separated, so as to disable the critical leverage of theory, or they will be simply identified, so that Hegel appears as an apologist for all suffering and injustice in the world. Conceiving of this relationship in dynamic and developmental terms accords both with fundamental elements of Hegel's conception of history and with the formulation of the *Doppelsatz* found in the 1819/20 lectures on the *Rechtsphilosophie:* "What is rational becomes actual, and the actual becomes rational" (*Rph III*, 51).[9] This formulation entails that the relation between actuality and mere existence is itself transformed through history, which represents not only the manifestation of spirit in the world but also the overcoming of the accidental by the necessary, the rational. Consequently, when understood in terms of a process of becoming, the rationality of the actual does not preclude a practical, critical theory. Nor does it limit the "practice" recommended by theory to quiet reconciliation to an existing order. Moreover, the telos of the actualization of the basic anthropological structure, the increasing rationality of the world, itself implies a need for change. It generates a critical perspective within Hegel's thought. The need—articulated in practical spirit—for reason to become actual entails the need for freedom to be manifested in the social and political world. It indicates that freedom is something to be achieved in the world, and that this concerns the concrete aspects of politics and society, not simply an inner freedom.

In itself this doctrine of the rationality of the actual does not indicate how this greater rationalization is to be brought about. It suggests the need for change but not the role of humans in this process, i.e., the extent to which human beings can or cannot be conscious agents of freedom's realization. Thus, it brings us precisely to the question of what role reflection has in bringing about a rational and free world—in Hegel's terms, in providing an adequate manifestation of spirit in the objective sphere. In what sense can or should theory be practical?

Locating an answer to this question in Hegel's thought is not easy. His most explicit pronouncements on theory and practice are the three we have cited from the preface to the *Philosophy of Right*. I have already argued that the *Doppelsatz* does not provide the material necessary to answer the question. Moreover, none of the passages comes from a systematic presentation of his thought; rather, they are attached prior to the beginning of the systematic treatment.[10] More importantly, even though they draw on central motifs in Hegel's thought, they are not necessarily the most adequate account of the implications of the rest of the system for the relation of theory and practice. A more adequate response to this question must base itself more deeply in Hegel's system. Other interpreters have sought this in their appeals to Hegel's treatment of actuality in the logic. To complement that appeal and address the relation between theory and practice in a way the logic cannot, however, one must turn to another aspect of Hegel's system, the "Psychology" discussed in the previous chapter. Here, Hegel's complex account of theoretical and practical spirit— particularly as elaborated in the *Vorlesungen über die Philosophie des Geistes*— promises to provide a more comprehensive account of the relation between theory and practice. The extended treatment in the *Vorlesungen*, which yields greater insight into the transition between theoretical and practical spirit, con- tains the most adequate account of the dialectical relation between the theo- retical and the practical. It is here that we find a Hegelian basis for a view of theory and practice as informing, shaping, and inducing each other, a view that undermines arguments against the very possibility of "Hegelian critique."

In appealing to Hegel's "Psychology" to address this issue, I seek to shift the accustomed approach to the discussion of theory and practice in Hegel. I acknowledge the inadequacy of the preface to the *Philosophy of Right* for deter- mining the implications of Hegel's thought for the relation between theory and practice; other interpreters have made powerful cases that the preface to the *Philosophy of Right* need not be understood as precluding critical theory. On the other hand, it is difficult not to read the final of the three passages as denying that philosophy should "*issu[e] instructions* on how the world ought to be." Acknowledging the complexity of this situation, I agree with Sean Sayers in rejecting the "tendency . . . to greet Hegel's doctrine either with uncomprehending outrage or with uncritical sympathy."[11] Thus, rather than claiming that the preface unqualifiedly supports my own view, my interpreta- tion reads Hegel's "Psychology" against some of the claims in the preface. In doing so, however, I am seeking the position on this issue most adequate to his thought as a whole.

I begin by discussing what is meant by the terms "theory" and "practice," both more broadly in the Western tradition and specifically in the present treat- ment of Hegel. Next, I examine how a focus on the relation between theory and practice that stresses the centrality of process or development casts the consid- eration of issues from the preface in a different light. Having established this context, I argue that Hegel's "Psychology"—specifically as elaborated in the

*Vorlesungen über die Philosophie des Geistes*—provides the basis for an appropriately dialectical understanding of the relationship between these two terms.

## Defining Theory and Practice

The question of the relation of theory and practice includes not only theory's role in informing practice but also practice's role in informing theory. Most generally expressed, the question concerns both how our practical activity affects what we think and how what we think affects our practical activity—in Hegel's language, how the will and the intelligence interrelate. Within the Western tradition, the discussion of theory and practice is generally traced to Aristotle.[12] Consequently, despite their differences, elucidating Aristotle's use of the terms provides useful tools for the discussion of Hegel.[13]

Aristotle distinguishes not only theory and praxis but also praxis and poiesis. Praxis has been the principal term of contrast with theory in Aristotle's thought, as well as in much of the Western tradition. For Aristotle, praxis does not designate just any activity in the world but rather specifically ethico-political action. It is contrasted with poiesis, which concerns production or making, such as building (*NE* 1140a). These two types of activity are distinguished by their ends: "For production [poiesis] has its end beyond it; but action [praxis] does not, since its end is doing well itself" (*NE* 1140b). Whereas poiesis concerns productive activity, such as the work of an artisan, praxis concerns living well, the good life, which includes the citizen's active participation in the polis, not just an ethics for the individual. Poiesis transforms the world outside the subject, whereas praxis first and foremost transforms the subject, though it may also—as in political activity—change the world. In English, the two terms correspond roughly to "making" and "doing," respectively. Compared to the life of theory, only the life of praxis is a possible rival, though praxis is a much narrower conception than the idea of "practical" as it is often understood today: in dealing specifically with politics and ethics, it excludes business and other activities aimed primarily at the satisfaction of physical needs. Both the life of theory and the life of praxis presuppose the satisfaction of basic physical necessities.[14]

In contrast to a life dedicated to praxis, Aristotle's life of theoria concerns itself with what is eternal and unchanging. Theoria does not simply involve abstract ideas that can then be applied; nor does it relate to the sphere of practical human activity. As Nicholas Lobkowicz observes, "[O]ne philosophizes in order to escape from ignorance, not because one expects some use from philosophy."[15]

Because Hegel's analysis of these dimensions of human existence transforms the Aristotelian categories, I use "praxis" to designate distinctly ethico-political action and use "practice" as a broader term encompassing praxis, poiesis, and the satisfaction of basic needs, just as practical spirit for Hegel includes the most basic desires as well as the highly developed will.[16] Much of the scholarship on theory and practice in Hegel has focused on practice as ethico-political practice, for the justifiable reason that these discussions have been concerned primarily with the political implications of Hegel's thought. It is important to emphasize, however, that Hegel's conception of practice is broader than an Aristotelian conception of praxis and encompasses making and doing—both internal and external ends—as well as more specifically economic activity.

Hegel's conception of theory is likewise related to but more inclusive than Aristotle's. On one hand, Hegel emphasizes that the "thought" (*Denken*) characteristic of philosophy as a science (*Wissenschaft*) is quite distinct from everyday thinking: "[S]ince philosophy is a peculiar [*eigentümliche*] mode of thinking—a mode by which thinking becomes cognition, and conceptually comprehensive cognition at that—philosophical thinking will also be *differentiated* [*eine* Verschiedenheit *haben*] from the thinking that is active in everything human and brings about the very humanity of what is human . . ." (*Enz.* § 2).[17] At the same time, however, this is a distinction within a larger unity. Thus, Hegel continues this same sentence: ". . . even though it is also identical with this thinking, and *in itself* there is only *One* thinking. This distinction is connected with the fact that the human content of consciousness, which is based on thinking, does not *appear in the form of thought* straightaway, but as feeling, intuition, representation—which are *forms* that have to be distinguished from thinking *itself as form*" (*Enz.* § 2).[18] The relationship between philosophy and everyday perceptions is thus one of differentiated unity. As we also saw in the account of theoretical spirit in chapter 4, the insights of philosophy exist first in the forms of intuition and representation. In philosophy, these insights are purified of the particularity and partialness characterizing them at lower levels. This thinking then permeates our intuitions and representations.

Even more significantly, unlike Aristotle's conception of theory, Hegel's philosophy includes within its object spheres of practical concern: "It is equally important, on the other hand, that philosophy should be quite clear about the fact that its content is nothing other than the basic content that is originally produced and produces itself in the domain of the living spirit, the content that is made into the *world*, the outer and inner world of consciousness; in other words, the content of philosophy is *actuality*. The first consciousness of this content is called *experience*" (*Enz.* § 6). As we see in objective spirit in particular, the objects of philosophy include spheres of human activity and will. Joachim Ritter makes this point in the following terms: "*Hegel equates traditional metaphysical theory directly as such with knowledge of the age and the present.* Philosophy *as* knowledge of being is *at the same time* 'its own time apprehended in thoughts.'"[19] Not only is the political realm an object of philosophy; the comprehension of this realm is intrinsically interrelated with and inseparable from comprehension of the essence of human beings, of spirit. Though we need to draw distinctions between the two realms, our understanding of them is profoundly interconnected, such that no line can be drawn to separate two types of theory here. Given Hegel's conception of practical as well as objective spirit, such a conception is unavoidable.[20] Moreover, these insights achieved in the form of thought in philosophy are developed on the basis of their prior existence in the less developed forms characteristic of everyday consciousness.

In its concern with much that Aristotle saw as practical, the dimension of Hegel's theory with which I am here concerned encompasses Aristotle's phronesis as well as theoria and fits into what Jeffrey Stout has identified as "a modern effort to break down classical distinctions between theoretical and practical reason . . . ."[21] Certain aspects of Hegel's thought would resist this move, and fully defending this point would require further discussion. Nonetheless, we can confidently claim that particularly in those aspects of Hegel's thought relevant to the connection between his anthropology and his ethics, "theory" includes views of the absolute, spirit, as well as the practical, worldly matters that are central to objective spirit. (Consequently, one cannot resolve the issues raised by the preface simply by claiming it is not the task of philosophy to criticize, though it may be the task of other, non-philosophical theory. Insofar as the criticisms draw upon philosophical considerations—as Hegel's own writings on contemporary political affairs do, for instance—they involve philosophy at least indirectly "issuing instructions."[22])

### Locating the Question of Theory and Practice in Hegel

Hegel's account of the relationship between theory and practice is deeply permeated by the central role of development in his thought. Because human consciousness is central to what develops through history, Hegel does not generate a single conception of the relation of theory and practice that is valid for all time. Spirit's self-consciousness, knowing that its essence is spirit and therefore free, should have a tremendous impact on the practical effect of theorizing. Although in the past people may have lacked the self-consciousness necessary to determine deliberately the course of spirit's development, this does not preclude this possibility for spirits with the self-consciousness Hegel claims for himself and others of his context. In Hegel's terms, how could one who has achieved the "absolute knowledge" with which the *Phenomenology of Spirit* culminates be completely deceived by the "cunning of reason" which is given such an important role in the philosophy of history? Admittedly, in the past reason has made its progress and manifested itself in the world without being the conscious intention of the human actors who have brought about these changes. At times, world-historical individuals have a vague conception—at times not even this—of the new shape of spirit they are working to bring about, but most who have participated in bringing about a new level of spirit's development have done so without any idea of what they are doing (*VG* 97–97/83–84). Whether we are talking only about those directing the action or a broader spectrum of the population, we must ask, must it always be so? This question is essential for a grasp of the relation of theory and practice that does justice to the central role of historical development in Hegel's thought.[23]

Framing the question in these terms recommends a different set of secondary literature than that usually brought to bear on the preface to the *Philosophy of Right*. Two interpreters whose work encompasses much of the debate and serves to introduce its fundamental themes are Jürgen Habermas and Michael Theunissen. Habermas's interpretation of a purportedly anti-practical older Hegel is grounded in passages from Hegel's philosophy of history, specifically in the discussion of the role of war in bringing about higher manifestations of spirit: "[C]oncrete right appears to be actualized only historically in the struggle between powers, above all in war between states. As a universal which is mediated into the particular, without violating its particularity, the concrete right comes into being behind the backs of living individuals, as a result of the struggle of interests between powers whose uppermost principle is the unwritten law of concrete self-assertion."[24] Though human actions, such as war, bring about spirit's advancement, the progress happens without humans' consciousness, as an unintended consequence of the pursuit of self-interest. This is the "cunning of reason," which here looks much like Adam Smith's invisible hand projected onto the whole of world history.[25] While this is an important aspect of Hegel's philosophy of history, Habermas extrapolates from this point a more universal claim regarding the role of theory: "With this conception, the claim by revolutionary consciousness of directly realizing the universalities, reasonably formulated in the Natural-Law theories, is rejected conclusively. On the other hand, the possibility that theory may become dialectically practical, which Hegel once had considered, is also rejected."[26] According to Habermas's reading of Hegel, the disjunction between human intentions and spirit's development is not to be overcome; reason will always remain cunning and work "behind the backs of living individuals." Theory can never become practical with a critical intent.[27]

Whereas Habermas looks back at history, Michael Theunissen's claim for the unity of theory and practice is based in an analysis of the culmination of historical development in the final stage of the consummate religion, the cultus, as well as in the drive toward a more adequate actualization of reason in the future. These correspond to the two major senses of the unity of theory and practice that Theunissen discusses.[28] The first focuses on the conception of the cultus as involving both self-consciousness and practical activity: human activity "develops in the Christian cultus into the free act of spiritual self-consciousness.[29] At this historical juncture, spirit no longer functions behind the backs or beyond the consciousness of human subjects. Rather, humans act in full self-consciousness. Moreover, the activity here discussed is not simply that of religious ritual or devotion; nor is it directed away from this world toward some divine other: "[I]n Hegel's genuinely New Testament view, love of God implies love of fellow human beings. Therefore the practical activity of the cultus must without exception take place in the medium of human intersubjectivity as well. . . . To be precise, the intersubjectivity inseparably bound to these activities is in essence not that of a private community in flight from the world but a public intersubjectivity of a society that is in principle worldwide . . . ."[30] The most adequate cultus is not an exclusive group of religious devotees but the ethical life of an entire society.[31] Spirit's development through history produces a society that acts in accord with its self-consciousness; reason is now transparent, no longer cunning.

Similarly, the second sense of the unity of theory and practice Theunissen discusses involves the realization or actualization of the reconciliation accomplished at the level of thought in Hegel's philosophy itself. In Theunissen's interpretation, Hegel's system brings to the level of thought the absolute reconciliation brought about by the Christ event. In line with the centrality of actualization for Hegel, this reconciliation in thought must be given actuality.[32] The end of the *Lectures on the Philosophy of Religion* "sets out the equality, proclaimed by Christianity, of all human beings, nearly radically socialistically, as the real freedom of each individual, as it likewise can only be realized in a future social order." [33] The reconciliation announced by Christianity cannot be brought about through religion, however. It is in philosophy that the unity with practice is achieved.[34] Though Theunissen may not distinguish precisely between theory calling for or guiding practice and a complete unity of theory and practice, his point is that at this historical juncture theory can direct practice.

While Theunissen's account says something about the endpoint of the development and Habermas's account something about an earlier stage of this relationship, both are freeze-frame images of the relationship at a particular point in time. Neither provides a broader, systematic perspective for viewing the relationship as a whole—i.e., its development—within which the two particular emphases can be located; as a result, neither seems to account for the other's interpretation. By focusing on the (systematic) drive toward actualization, Theunissen effectively indicates much about what would be necessary for a satisfactory culmination of the development—that it cannot be merely at the level of theory. Nevertheless, his reference to this general principle does not reveal the particular basis within human subjects on which this actualization depends. It thus does not set out the substructure that allows this development to take place. Although Habermas's attention to the question of the revolutionary consciousness raises the question of the role of the individual,[35] his analysis does not draw on or contribute to an understanding of Hegel's anthropology.

By contrast, exploring the relation between theory and practice through an examination of the implications of the anthropology—particularly the "Psychology"—produces the account most adequate to Hegel's systematic conception of the spheres of spirit. It uses the intrinsic structure of human beings elaborated in the philosophy of subjective spirit to comprehend the developments in the higher spheres. By grasping spirit's developments in objective and absolute spirit in the context of the more basic elements of spirit elaborated in subjective spirit, this approach grounds the interpretation more deeply in Hegel's thought than a static image from a particular point in the systematic development. In particular, it provides a more reliable account of the implications of Hegel's thought for the relation of theory and practice than the pronouncements found in the preface to the *Philosophy of Right*. Further, this analysis focuses directly on the significance of the relationship for the individual, revealing more regarding what this means for the particular human actor and therefore having a more practical and concrete significance.

## Implications of Hegel's Anthropology for Theory and Practice

Within the anthropology, it is the relation between theoretical and practical spirit as developed in the *Vorlesungen über die Philosophie des Geistes* that bears most directly on the present concerns. Drawing on the discussion in chapter 4, the present section seeks to make explicit the implications of that analysis for the relation between theory and practice. To examine this relationship, I focus on two pairs of questions:

(A1)   Is theory sufficient or adequate on its own or does it generate practice?
(A2)   Does practice depend upon prior theory?
(B1)   Is practice sufficient or adequate on its own or does it generate theory?
(B2)   Does theory depend upon prior practice?

(A) focuses on the movement from theory to practice, viewed first from the perspective of theory and then from that of practice. (B) focuses on the movement from practice to theory, viewed first from the perspective of practice and then from that of theory. Examining Hegel's response to each of these questions generates a comprehensive account of his conception of the interrelation of theory and practice, insofar as we are dealing with the type of theory that concerns not only absolute spirit but also ethical and political matters, as outlined in the first section of the chapter.

(A1)   Is theory sufficient or adequate on its own or does it generate practice?

The systematic place and function of practical spirit—discussed in the opening of the treatment of practical spirit—reveals its function as the objectification or externalization of the inwardness of theoretical spirit. The one-sidedness of theoretical spirit drives the transition to practical spirit and must be overcome by external realization, i.e., practical activity (*VPGst* 239). Practical activity in the world represents the effort to give reality or actual existence to the determinations of theoretical spirit, to demonstrate its freedom. Theory's actualization in practice is not some optional, possible application of the theory; it is intrinsic to spirit. To sever theory from practice in this direction would be to terminate a process that is not complete. As Hegel states, "theory should be realized [*die Theorie soll realisiert werden*]" (*VPGst* 239). From the individual's perspective, this means that in my activity in the world I will act upon my understanding of what I am, seeking to realize my essence.

The point also follows from Hegel's conception of spirit. Because spirit as a whole is self-manifesting in the world, contemplation of spirit is not of something eternal, unchangeable, and separate from this world. To the contrary, to grasp spirit includes grasping its manifestation in subjective and objective as well as absolute spirit. A claim that theory does not inform practice presupposes an object of theory that has nothing to do with human activity in the world, nothing to do with politics or ethics. The entire conception of subjective spirit belies such a vision.

Although the point seems clear in light of the discussion in chapter 4, Hegel's utterances regarding the impotence of theory in the preface to the *Philosophy of Right* require that it be adequately emphasized. Moreover, precisely because this comes relatively early in the elaboration of the conception of spirit—i.e., in subjective, rather than objective or absolute spirit—its centrality to Hegel's thought must not be underestimated. And because it intimately coheres with the larger conception of spirit, this claim cannot be said to be peripheral. Although Hegel sometimes expresses himself in such terms, one cannot understand his thought as implying a passive acceptance of every status quo or as requiring that spirit always develop "behind our backs" without doing substantial violence to central threads of his thought.

At the same time, precisely the conception of the pursuit of adequate expression suggests that—until the endpoint of the development is reached—the expression will be fraught with inadequacy. Theoretical spirit does not first begin to externalize itself when it has reached the self-clarity of pure thought. Even in early stages of its development, the intelligence cannot be separated from the will. Consequently, to say that theory must inform practice is not to say that practice will always be the product of the thought with which theoretical spirit culminates. Because this theory is still developing, not perfect or absolute, theorizing will not necessarily produce the intended consequences. The adequate actualization of theoretical spirit—i.e., of theory—is a goal, not a presupposition of the actualization. Thus, Habermas's position has a basis as long as one is dealing with spirit in its earlier stages of development.

The progressive but always partial overcoming of this inadequacy corresponds to the pre-understanding/action/comprehension model discussed at the conclusion of the last chapter. This model—understood as ongoing, such that the comprehension resulting from one action becomes the pre-understanding for another—points to the need for revision in this process. Hegel's conception of the actualization of theoretical spirit in the practical does not entail a claim to produce the perfect state out of abstract reflection alone. It is not simply the actualization of an abstraction, as Hegel understood the French Revolution to have been.

More concretely, this means that Hegel's analysis of objective spirit does not function merely to reveal the rationality of existing institutions. Within the *Philosophy of Right*, much of Hegel's analysis, particularly of various forms of differentiation, functions in this manner; and an important aspect of political analysis should continue to be the examination of the insights motivating and embodied in particular institutions. Nonetheless, the role of practical spirit in manifesting theoretical spirit indicates that this should not be the only function of ethico-political theory. It should also function to critique existing institutions where they fall short of the demands of spirit's essence, reason, and spur action such that this essence is more adequately realized.

Hegel himself provides an example of this type of critique in "On the English Reform Bill," his last published writing other than revised editions of previously published works. Because the work draws upon his philosophy, it illustrates that the condemnation of practical engagement on the basis of philosophy in the *Philosophy of Right* was not his only position on the topic. Central to Hegel's analysis is the question whether existing (and therefore positive) laws are also justified by reason: "But at no time more than the present has the general intelligence been led to distinguish between whether rights are only positive in their *material content* or whether they are also inherently [*an und für sich*] right and rational" ("ERB" 88/299). The demands of spirit's contemporary development are that rule be rational, not justified by power alone. The connection to Hegel's present underscores the interconnection of the development of self-consciousness—which Hegel connects with the modern world—and the demands for rational government, not simply the continuation of tradition. Moreover, merely by juxtaposing the self-interests of the classes in power and the demands of reason, Hegel rejects the idea that spirit must always advance behind our backs in the company of the victor. The piece as a whole is an argument for acting politically in accord with the demands of theory. In itself, it is an effort to influence practice with theory and to consciously determine the course of political events. While Hegel seeks to avoid revolution, he is quite clear that England is in need of change and that this change should be as rational, deliberate, and self-conscious as possible.[36] This is precisely the role for theory that the anthropology indicates it should have.

(A2)  Does practice depend upon prior theory?

The first question, A1, deals with the issues that have been central to most discussions of theory and practice in Hegel. Less frequently asked but also important to understanding the relation of theory and practice is whether one can
properly speak of practice that is not informed by theory. As discussed in the
last chapter, the account of practical spirit can be seen from two perspectives:
the externalization of the interior determination and the development of this
internal determination. Throughout its development, practical spirit entails
the actualization of some internal determination. This begins as practical feeling, a desire for some change in the external world, and ultimately develops
into the rational will. At various levels, this internal determination can be seen
as a more or less developed form of pre-understanding. Nonetheless, in its
early stages, this determination cannot be said to be theoretical in the sense of
determined by theoretical spirit. A feeling of comfort or discomfort, for
instance, is not necessarily determined by the intelligence, even if it can be formulated into a pre-understanding in the broadest sense. The telos of its development, however, transforms this internal determination such that it becomes
more and more an expression of intelligence or theoretical spirit. Thus, while
the most basic stages of practical spirit involve activity that actualizes given
rather than theoretical determinations, practical spirit itself develops such
that it can become the expression of theoretical spirit. Practical activity is not
always the actualization of theory, but the most developed practical activity—
the will proper—is.

   The different levels of the internal determination that is actualized, however,
reveal the contrast between Hegel's broader conception of practical activity and
the Aristotelian notion of praxis. Although Hegel's practical spirit culminates
in the rational, self-conscious will that forms the basis for the political aspect of
objective spirit, it involves much more than this ethico-political praxis. Also
essential to practical spirit is the transformation of the world, not simply the
subject itself (see *Enz.* § 470). Practical spirit thus includes poiesis: It is concerned with producing as well as doing. The shift from Aristotle here is twofold:
First, practical spirit encompasses making things of the sort that Aristotle
would have understood as the result of poiesis—transforming the world
through fashioning a tool or a house, for instance. Second, ethico-political
activity is taken to include making, i.e., transforming of the world, as an integral element, not simply as secondary to the subject's transformation. The end
of such ethico-political activity is thus both internal (in the transformation of

the subject) and external (in the transformation of the world, creating the institutions of the sphere of objective spirit).

At the same time, productive work that is not distinctly political also transforms the subject, not simply the external world. As Guy Planty-Bonjour argues, "Hegel found out that making is that kind of activity by which an agent by producing something produces himself."[37] Like political activity, productive activity—work—has an end both within and beyond the agent. Planty-Bonjour traces this aspect of Hegel's thought to the influence of Adam Smith, who "demonstrated the importance of the activity of production in the life of modern societies," such that "Hegel found in *The Wealth of Nations* the deeper meaning of work for industrial society. . . . Smith helped Hegel to perceive that work (Aristotle's *poiesis*) is not simply an activity whose sole effect is to change the external world. Work is first and foremost an economic activity: both transformation of a thing and intersubjective action."[38] The result is that activity directed toward making also transforms the agent, just as activity directed toward doing also transforms the world.[39] With regard to question A2, this means that while not all practical activity actualizes theory, both explicitly ethico-political and intentionally economic activity actualize some theoretical understanding of the world and other human beings.

For Theunissen, Habermas, and Fulda as well as the broader debates over the significance of the preface to the *Philosophy of Right*, the central question has been whether theory informs practice, generally with the presupposition that if Hegel answers no to this question, he advocates only a conservative acceptance of the ruling powers. A complementary concern, however, is that Hegel's apparent emphasis on the priority of theory gives practice no role in informing theory, with the possible consequence that an abstract, utopian conception justifies the perpetration of any terror in the world in order to realize the vision—that the world must be forced into the categories of the logic regardless of the practical, human consequences. Questions B1 and B2 both address this issue; B1 looks at the movement from practice to theory from the perspective of practice, while B2 looks at this same movement from the perspective of theory.

In this context, the emphasis in the last chapter on the mutual influence of theoretical and practical spirit gains its full significance. Just as practical spirit expresses the theoretical, practical spirit only comes to be what it is through its reconciliation with theoretical spirit. While the movement from pre-understanding to activity corresponds to the first aspect, the movement from activity to comprehension corresponds to the second. Attending to this aspect of the theory-practice relation is vital if we hope to comprehend not just the posited end of this development—such as described in the account of the Christian cultus—but also the path toward this end. That is, while Theunissen's and Fulda's examinations of the culmination of this relationship is helpful, they are less informative when trying to grasp this relationship in a socio-political context that falls short of an adequate manifestation of reason, e. g., in situations of injustice. Focusing on this side of the relationship also provides a better understanding of the kind of comprehension that follows practice, the type of relationship dominant when spirit develops through the "cunning of reason" rather than the conscious designs of human beings. It thus provides a perspective within which we can include Habermas's account of the relation of theory and practice in Hegel without seeing this as the entirety of the relationship or as precluding theory's informing of practice as well.

(B1)  Is practice sufficient or adequate on its own or does it generate theory?

Examining whether practice is sufficient on its own or necessarily leads to the production of theory requires looking at the developments at the end of the "Psychology," where subjective spirit's development ends not within practical spirit proper, but in the unity of theoretical and practical spirit in free spirit. Throughout the sphere of practical spirit, the subject seeks its satisfaction, only to be constantly thwarted and left unsatisfied. In the transition from eudaemonia to free spirit, spirit becomes conscious that it can achieve satisfaction only insofar as it wills in accord with its own essence—which requires reflection on this essence, i.e., anthropology. The developmental character of Hegel's account means not only that we will not be satisfied without this manner of theorizing but also that the impulses driving practical activity lead us to this theorizing for the sake of their own satisfaction. Practice cannot be satisfied without inducing theoretical reflection. This entails that the highest development of the will is not simply practical activity but self-conscious, rational practical activity that is equally theoretical spirit. Not satisfied by activity alone, spirit drives to comprehend its action.

Concretely, we can perhaps best envision this development in relation to social movements such as the civil rights movement. Many of the people involved in such movements are initially driven by visions that may be vague and less than fully theorized. Active engagement leads to reflection, i.e., an attempt to articulate precisely the underlying claims as well as to better define the goals of the movement. Though for some this reflection will not be what Hegel would characterize as philosophy, for others it will inevitably involve serious philosophical engagement with underlying claims regarding what it means to be a human being. Thus, this theorizing process moves beyond the more intuitive sense of injustice that often sparks such movements; and as we saw above, it will also motivate and inform future action. In this sense, practice is not sufficient unto itself but necessitates theory. Theory, philosophy, or comprehension stands after as well as before practice.

(B2)  Does theory depend upon prior practice?

This claim that the highest level of spirit's development, free spirit, comes about only as a synthesis of theoretical and practical spirit entails that practical activity must play an essential role in theory's development. The previous chapter examined at length the role of the will in the development of intelligence. At a more abstract level, this claim is already implicit in the "Concept of Spirit" discussed in chapter 1. Here, spirit is fundamentally self-manifesting. Because spirit reveals itself through its objectification in the world, one does not comprehend it through abstract thought or contemplation alone. This point is most apparent in relation to social and political issues, yet Hegel's own view on the issue goes further. He argues in the preface to the *Science of Logic* that even the study of logic should be infused by "the higher standpoint reached by spirit in its self-consciousness" over the last twenty-five years (*WL* 1:13/25; see also *WL* 1:15/26). This self-consciousness of spirit, actual in human beings, could not have arisen without world-historical changes, i.e., practical activity. Theorizing cannot ignore actual events in the world. Spirit can only be grasped (which means that we can only understand ourselves) through comprehending actual events in the world through which spirit manifests itself.[40] To know itself, spirit must know itself in its manifestations. This is the compelling and powerful aspect of Hegel's claim that "philosophy, too, is *its own time comprehended in thoughts*" (*PR* 26/21), though this need not imply a passive, all-accepting expression of its time.

Both of those discussions remain quite abstract, however; and the second applies just as much to other people's practice as to one's own. The issue can be made more concrete by asking whether there is a necessary connection between the practice of a particular individual and that individual's theorizing. Because the unity of theoretical and practical brought about in free spirit is something to be realized in individual human beings, it concerns the practical activity of the individual. As we saw in chapter 4, it is the subject's own active pursuit of satisfaction that drives the transition to free spirit. The culmination of the anthropology thus consists of the unity of intelligence and will—not simply intelligence about the will of others. We will grasp freedom more adequately if we have tried to actualize it in the world. As Hardimon notes with respect to civil society, for instance, "Hegel also holds that these self-understandings are *engendered* by the practices of civil society. It is precisely as a result of participating in civil society that modern people come to think of themselves as selves and as bearers of separate and particular interests."[41] The point is not simply a rule of thumb or unique to civil society; it is a basic principle of the development of spirit's self-knowledge.

At the same time, it is essential to emphasize that Hegel's position does not imply that political practice automatically or mechanically results in or justifies knowledge. Practical activity does not do away with the need for philosophical reflection. Rather, it informs and shapes this reflection, sometimes consciously, sometimes unconsciously. This point indicates the continuing relevance of Hegel's discussion of empirical science in the philosophy of nature. As discussed in chapter 1, he there maintains that "the *origin* and *cultivation* of philosophical science have empirical physics as a presupposition and condition," yet experience cannot constitute its foundation, which must be constituted by the concept (*Enz.* § 246 A). Much the same relationship applies to this aspect of the relation between practice and theory: The larger systematic structure entails that practice is a presupposition and condition of theory, but practice does not thereby replace or constitute an argument on its own. To conceive of practice in that manner would be to invoke an appeal to immediate experience whose possibility Hegel has already undermined. Practice thus plays an essential role in informing theorizing, but it cannot in and of itself constitute a reason. The latter is the work of theory itself. This account of the role of practice in informing theory is undeniably abstract, in some sense vague. While it might be viewed as a weakness of Hegel's "Psychology" that it does not produce a more detailed account of this relationship, the generality is more likely due to the topic itself, such that we should bear in mind Aristotle's injunction: "Our discussion will be adequate if its degree of clarity fits the subject-matter . . . ."[42]

Examining these relationships between theory and practice has established the first step in moving from Hegel's anthropology to his ethical and political thought. The entire project depends upon theory generating normative claims on practice—specifically, anthropological theory generating normative claims on ethico-political practice. Without two crucial connections—between anthropological and ethico-political theory and between theory and practice—the very project of developing an ethical theory on the basis of the anthropology would be undermined. Hegel's anthropology supports both.

# 6 From Anthropology to Ethics (2)
## Tradition, Criticism, and Freedom

In tracing the stages of Hegel's anthropology within the sphere of subjective spirit, we have anticipated important elements of his ethics. As we turn now to objective spirit, we will grasp the comprehensive role of his anthropology in his ethical and political thought. In the sphere of objective spirit, habit reappears as a prereflective ethical life, in which we completely identify with the inherited norms and conventions of the religious and cultural world we inhabit. Self-consciousness undergirds morality, where we reflect explicitly on the norms of our behavior, distinguishing ourselves from them and pursuing the (abstract) good for its own sake. Free spirit develops into a self-conscious, reflective ethical life, in which we recognize the existing norms of the world or tradition around us as just and consciously will them—not simply because they exist, but because they are manifestations of our own essence and the substance of freedom.

The anthropological foundations of Hegel's ethics provide the most encompassing perspective for examining whether his ethics entails that after reflection upon the customs of our own society and the religious views that support them, we will necessarily find these just. A number of interpreters have stressed that Hegel's conception of freedom includes not only adhering to just norms but also consciously endorsing them. Mark Tunick expresses the point precisely: "Hegel claims that human beings are born into a community in which they live unreflectively. This community shapes who they are; it is their substance. But they are truly free only by fulfilling the demands of this community when they choose their commitment to it upon reflection and with an insight into the rationality of the demands this commitment entails."[1] Interpretations such as this one highlight the point that subjective agreement with norms is essential to Hegelian freedom, but they have hardly examined the anthropological basis of Hegel's position. They thereby exclude an essential element of Hegel's justification and systematic grounding of this conception, which almost invariably leaves his more robust claims appearing indefensible. Specifically, without drawing upon the anthropology, one cannot adequately account for Hegel's claim that this reflective acceptance of norms as rational—when it occurs—is based in the realization that these norms and the associated institutions are themselves manifestations of my own essence.[2] Put more simply, an account of freedom in which *self*-determination is central cannot dispense with a more extensive account of the "self" than most readers of the *Philosophy of Right* provide.[3] Examining how the distinct elements of Hegel's anthropology are manifest in the sphere of objective spirit enables us to present and justify the latter in terms of Hegel's more basic systematic claims.[4]

Moreover, in elaborating the respective roles of tradition and criticism in Hegel's thought, analyzing objective spirit in terms of these three levels also provides a more concrete elaboration of the anthropology itself. The larger significance of the elements of subjective spirit, such as habit and self-consciousness, can only be grasped in light of their role in the higher spheres of spirit. Because these later manifestations of basic elements also incorporate other, later elements of subjective spirit (higher-order habits require language, for example), we cannot see their role in objective spirit before Hegel has presented the remaining stages of subjective spirit. As a result, Hegel cannot discuss the full significance of these elements when they are first introduced in subjective spirit, and the connection between the concepts introduced there and their consequent manifestations is often lost.[5]

What is needed, then, is an examination of Hegel's total picture of human beings and his ethics that relates these two levels of analysis. Only by doing so can we adequately interpret Hegel's anthropological observations at other points in his system, such as his claim that "[e]ach individual, at any given moment, finds himself committed to some essential interest of this kind; he finds himself in a particular country with a particular religion, and in a particular constellation of knowledge and attitudes concerning what is right and ethical" (VG 52-53/46). Reading such comments in conjunction with the philosphy of subjective spirit is critical to understanding both the justification behind them and the sense in which the givenness of a way of life is overcome. Each of these dimensions is crucial to Hegel's ethical and political thought. By seeing the religious and ethical customs which we initially "find" as constituting us at the level of habit, we are able to investigate the impact of consciousness and of becoming free spirit upon our relationship to these customs we inherit. It thereby allows us to separate the question of whether or in what way we can be critical of these customs from the account of their role in constituting us.

Hegel structures his accounts of objective spirit in terms of the actualization of the free will, the concept of which is set out in practical spirit and recapitulated in the introduction to the *Philosophy of Right*.[6] The will unfolds in three sections: abstract right, the most immediate shape of right, in which property, contracts, and wrong are dealt with; morality, in which the self-conscious I relates itself to the good; and ethical life, in which the previous spheres are sublated and freedom obtains actuality. Though the *Philosophy of Right* is structured by the actualization of the will, our treatment of the "Psychology" in chapter 4 revealed that the will is inseparable from the intelligence and only develops on the basis of other elements of the anthropology. Hegel's claim that "[i]t is only as *thinking* intelligence that the will is truly itself and free" entails that in the achievement of freedom, nothing incorporated into the culmination of the anthropology is left behind (*PR* § 21 A). The foundation of the *Philosophy of Right* that Hegel discusses in terms of the will cannot be viewed as excluding other elements of subjective spirit. The account of the will is embedded within the larger anthropology, which therefore provides a comprehensive perspective from which to interpret what is actualized in freedom. The anthropology therefore justifies an analysis of objective spirit structured by the moments of subjective spirit. Unlike Hegel's structure, this one roughly tracks the developments as they occur in the lives of individuals.[7] We therefore return to the fundamental moments of the anthropology set out in chapters 2 through 4, beginning with habit, moving through self-consciousness, and concluding with free spirit, as each of these is manifested in the sphere of objective spirit.

### Habit as Prereflective Ethical Life (*Sittlichkeit*)

The first level of the anthropology, habit, finds its principal expression in objective spirit at the beginning of the third major section of the *Philosophy of Right*, ethical life (*Sittlichkeit*): "Ethical life is the *Idea of freedom* . . . . [It] is accordingly the *concept of freedom which has become* [1] *the existing world and* [2] *the nature of self-consciousness*" (*PR* § 142). Being the "Idea" of freedom means being both its concept and its actual existence. It is not a mere possibility but actuality. This concept of ethical life consists of two aspects: It is both an "objective" existence in the world [1] and the accompanying consciousness [2].[8] These constitute the objective and subjective dimensions of freedom. A highly developed ethical life includes not only the existence of these relations in the world but also the consciousness of their being the actualization of freedom. The element of consciousness is central to the sphere of morality, the second part of the philosophy of objective spirit; consequently, ethical life must incorporate consciousness.[9]

Although consciousness constitutes one side of Hegel's concept of ethical life, it must be developed; it does not begin in its advanced form. That is, while consciousness has a role in Hegel's discussion of ethical life from the very first, ethical life should not be conceived as beginning only when this fully developed consciousness emerges. To the contrary, the individual's initial relationship to the "existing" aspect of ethical life—the ensemble of norms, values, and institutions which make up the substantial content of the society in which we live—is far from the self-conscious, reflective relationship required in the highest freedom. The individual begins, not with this consciousness, but in immediate identification with ethical life as an existing system of customs and values. At this level, "what we are dealing with is the initial [mode of] ethical life so to speak, ethical life in its immediacy" (VPR 2:535).[10]

Hegel expresses this development very concisely in a handwritten note to PR § 146: "Subject αα) is ethical [sittlich]—is in unity—is in accordance—ββ consciousness of α) relationship to duties, they are, fixed—γγ) gives testimony—has itself therein—will—spirit..." (PR § 146 N).[11] Hegel seems to be indicating the various levels of the subject's relation to the norms that constitute the ethical world. At the first level, the subject is in complete unity with these customs; it cannot properly be said even to have a relation to them, insofar as "relation" implies a distinction (see PR § 147 A). Here, I act in a certain way without any consciousness of the norms that guide my actions. At the second level, consciousness, the subject relates to them as an object. There are many levels of this consciousness and the level of questioning reflection illustrated in morality is one of the higher ones. For example, I can ask myself what I should do and articulate relevant norms without necessarily reflecting critically on the justification of my action; the early forms of consciousness do not entail such profound questioning. Finally, at the third level, the subject consciously identifies itself in these customs and norms.[12]

By attending to these different stages of the relationship, we see that, although Hegel's discussion of ethical life has a central role for the consciousness developed in the second section of the philosophy of subjective spirit, it also contains a great deal that corresponds to the prereflective level of habit. More precisely, because ethical life is based in the customs (*Sitten*)[13] of a particular community, it is based upon the norms, traditions, and ways of life that we first acquire unconsciously, in the form of habit.[14] Even though fully developed ethical life incorporates self-consciousness, it can only develop on the basis of customs that have already become second nature. (As we have seen, the education (*Bildung*) of children consists largely in this shaping by societal norms.[15]) Thus, while the discussion of ethical life points us beyond the level of spirit's development discussed in Hegel's "Anthropology" (to the second and third moments), it also points us back to the level of habit.

In *PR* § 151, Hegel explicitly connects the subject's initial relationship to the ethical world with the first level of the anthropology: "[I]n simple *identity* with the actuality of individuals, the ethical [*das Sittliche*] appears as their general mode of behavior, as *custom* [*Sitte*]—the *habit* of the ethical as a *second nature* which takes the place of the original and merely natural will and is the all-pervading soul, significance, and actuality of individuals' existence . . . ." The subject's identification with the actuality constituted by the customs is not initially mediated by consciousness; in its simplest form, it is an immediate identity with these norms. Before we have a consciousness of these norms, we *are* them. Although it is important to emphasize that the moments of spirit's development do not constitute a strict temporal succession in an individual's life, different moments have more or less dominance in an individual's life at a given point in time, and there are often rough correspondences between the development traced here and the developments experienced by individual human beings as we go through life. Hegel's discussion of the changes that accompany age explores these correspondences (*Enz.* § 396). Thus, while it is not the case that we first live entirely out of habit, then develop consciousness, consciousness about our customs does tend to develop after we have already largely appropriated the customs of our society. Consequently, we can justifiably speak of our first relationship to these customs being largely one of habit, upon which we can then reflect. At this level, they constitute our "second nature," because they have become our habits. And they are distinctly spirit because they involve an overcoming of natural drives—just as Hegel has set out in the discussion of habit in the philosophy of subjective spirit.[16]

At the same time, though Hegel uses the term "habit" (*Gewohnheit*) in both subjective and objective spirit, the habits in each case tend to be of different orders. The treatment of habit in subjective spirit focuses primarily on the subject's overcoming of particular sensations. Elementary examples include the ability to remain sitting upright without focusing on the physical sensations involved or walking without concentrating. Although these habits involve the overcoming of natural determinations, they do not necessarily replace these with culturally transmitted norms that we would describe as customs or values. These first-order habits, the most basic form of overcoming natural determination, however, can also be overcome through higher-order habits that are culturally transmitted, such as sitting up straight or walking in a particular manner. Higher-order habits are more properly customs and in some cases ethical norms, such as not stealing. Habits, then, can replace not just natural determinations but also other habits. Because these higher-order habits frequently make use of language, which comes only later in subjective spirit, Hegel cannot deal with them substantially within the "Anthropology," though he refers briefly there to the "religious [and] moral" content of habits (*Enz.* § 410 A). Since these higher-order habits overcome both natural determinations and other habits, they differ somewhat from first-order habits. They are more distinctly spiritual and involve a greater degree of remove from natural drives; they also require some degree of consciousness to learn, though not the self-consciousness that entails critical reflection. Nonetheless, their developmental structure is the same as that of first-order habits. Hegel's use of the term "habit" to describe the various orders of habit indicates this, as do the commonalities in his discussions of habit in subjective and objective—as well as absolute—spirit.[17] Common to all levels is the absence of a reflective consciousness.

Customs and behavioral norms—which in the *Philosophy of Right* provide the basis for ethical life—constitute the particular habits that fill out the content of the individual. This account is still abstract because the particular norms that might be constitutive for any given individual have not been filled in. These norms could not be part of any *general* anthropology or theory of human beings precisely because they vary from one culture or tradition to another.[18] Socially accepted norms for relations between the sexes, inheritance patterns, attitudes toward work, and religious rituals are all examples. Nonetheless, by including those customs that make up the ethical world among the habits under discussion, the account is now more concrete than it was or could be in the philosophy of subjective spirit.

In the philosophy of subjective spirit, Hegel talks about habits constituting who we are; in the *Philosophy of Right*, he discusses ethical norms in similar terms: "[T]he determinations of ethics . . . are the substantiality or universal essence of individuals . . ." (*PR* § 145 Z).[19] Hegel's accompanying point, that individuals relate to the ethical substance "as its accidents" (*PR* § 145), has often provoked criticism for subordinating the individual to the collective, but reading this passage in conjunction with the conception of habit shows that this is not the case. We are our habits, and these habits are preconscious appropriations of ethical norms and customs; thus, this ethical substance constitutes our essence, and we are the accidents in which it achieves reality (*PR* § 145). This in no way precludes, however, our moving beyond our first, immediate identification to a position of reflective, critical consciousness.

Hegel goes on to describe the relationship between the individual and constitutive customs as even closer, more identical than faith and trust: "Faith and trust arise with the emergence of reflection, and they presuppose representation and distinction [*Vorstellung und Unterschied*]. For example, to believe in pagan religion and to be a pagan are two different things. That relationship—or rather, that relationless identity—in which the ethical is the actual living principle [*Lebendigkeit*] of self-consciousness, may indeed turn into a relationship of faith and conviction and into a relationship mediated by *further reflection*, into insight grounded on reasons . . ." (*PR* § 147 A). In the subject's most immediate identity with these norms, they constitute what the individual *is*. We do not simply *believe* in a particular set of values; we are these values and commitments. They constitute who we are.[20] Through mediation, i.e., consciousness, this immediate identity can be transformed into a relationship; and when the individual self-consciously finds herself in and identifies with this ethical world, a more developed ethical life has been attained. The "content" of the self, which initially exists in the form of habit, then, is retained in spirit's more developed stages.[21]

Although the particular ethical worlds into which different people are born vary immensely, we are always born into—and, more importantly, socialized and educated within—an already existing ethical life. Through the process of habituation, this world's customs come to constitute who we are long before we are conscious of the process. The implications for Hegel's conception of human beings is that we appropriate as our own identity the traditions of the society in which we are raised. If and when we achieve consciousness of this situation, we find ourselves already constituted by the way of life of a particular ethical world.

One might take exception to the universality of this portrayal by imagining a child raised entirely separate from society. In relation to this possibility, Hegel suggests that the attempt to remove a child from the world by raising her in the country—as in Rousseau's *Emile*—would not be enough to keep out the spirit of the age: "Even if young people have to be educated in solitude, no one should imagine that the breath of the spiritual world will not eventually find its way into this solitude and that the power of the world spirit is too weak for it to gain control of such remote regions" (*PR* § 153 Z). One might go further, however, and imagine the child brought up among wolves, with no human contact whatsoever. In this case, the individual would remain largely at the level of natural determination. Consequently, although the person might be implicitly spirit, her existence would be entirely natural—as contrasted with spiritual—such that Hegel might qualify the sense in which we would call this individual human.

Both with regard to spirit and in general, Hegel stresses development. A Hegelian anthropology has a large teleological component. It does not seek simply to describe a set of properties that all human beings share, but rather focuses on the development of a potential inherent within us all.[22] That some individuals develop very little is not in itself a challenge to Hegel's conception of human beings. To the contrary, it is precisely this possibility of limited development that provides the ethical leverage in Hegel's anthropology: "The human being is what he should be only through education [*Bildung*], through discipline; what he is immediately is only the possibility of being that (that is, rational), of being free—only the determination, the ought" (*VG* 58/50). If an anthropology simply describes how we all are, it will likely have little to say about ethics or will have difficulty grounding the normativity of such claims. In contrast, if an anthropology, like Hegel's, describes what (or how) we could and should become, it already generates ethical norms.

The ethical world or substance discussed in the *Philosophy of Right* has a central role in the philosophy of history. Within Hegel's system, world history—the subject of the philosophy of history—constitutes the final section of the sphere of objective spirit, though Hegel also treated it separately in his *Lectures on the Philosophy of History*. The philosophy of history merits special discussion in order to demonstrate how Hegel's conception of habit challenges an interpretation of certain controversial passages as radically subordinating the individual to society. Much of the introductory discussion of ethical life in the *Philosophy of Right* emphasizes the developed consciousness involved in an advanced ethical life that subsumes morality and characterizes modernity. In contrast—because, according to Hegel, levels of reflection were severely limited for most of human history—the philosophy of history most often treats these norms as not yet mediated by consciousness. This distinction between the modern and the premodern precisely reflects the world-historical import Hegel attributes to a modern Western emphasis on self-consciousness. Further, from the broad perspective of history, naïve and self-conscious identifications with one's society may not look very different. For both of these reasons, much more of the discussion of ethical norms in the philosophy of history corresponds to the prereflective level of habit than does that in the *Philosophy of Right.*

In tracing spirit's development in history, Hegel is concerned with the consciousness of spirit attained by particular "national spirits" (*Volksgeister*). "Consciousness" in this context, however, does not necessarily entail the degree of mediation that is achieved in the "Phenomenology of Spirit" within the sphere of subjective spirit or through morality in objective spirit. Lutheranism, for example, constitutes an understanding of spirit, and in this sense a "consciousness" of spirit; yet not all Lutherans reflect self-consciously upon the beliefs and practices they have inherited. People can be Lutherans largely out of habit, i.e., prereflectively. There is a consciousness here, in that these customs together make up an ethical life that both implicitly (in these norms and institutions) and explicitly (in art, religion, and philosophy) expresses a particular understanding of spirit, but the single individual who follows these norms and participates in these institutions merely out of habit has not achieved the more specific "consciousness" developed in the second section of subjective spirit.

Like the *Philosophy of Right*, the *Lectures on the Philosophy of History* have a different goal than the present exploration of Hegel's anthropology, which means that we must uncover the relevant observations, realizing that these are not always the focal issues in Hegel's analysis. Hegel's philosophy of history examines the actualization of reason, as spirit, in history.[23] Although spirit has no actual existence other than in particular individuals, from the broader perspective of history, spirit is manifested in national spirits: "Spirit is essentially individual, but in the field of world history, we are not concerned with particulars and need not confine ourselves to individual instances or attempt to trace everything back to them. Spirit in history is an individual which is both universal in nature and at the same time determinate: in short, it is the nation in general, and the spirit we are concerned with is the *spirit of the nation* [*Volksgeist*]" (*VG* 59/51; see also 52/45). The philosophy of history also looks at particular individuals—world-historical individuals—who bring about the next stage of spirit's manifestation, but it is not centrally concerned with developing a theory of human beings.

At the same time, because it is concerned with the functioning of national spirits and these nations or peoples are made up of particular individuals, the philosophy of history reveals a good deal regarding the relationship of particular individuals to the ethical life of the nation in which they are educated to overcome their natural determinacy and become spirit. The spirit of a nation represents the way of life to which the individual habituates herself. The "nation" or "people" [*Volk*], shaped by a common worldview and way of life, constitutes the broader context or world that the individual, largely preconsciously, appropriates. The activity of the spirit of a nation

> consists in making itself into an existing [*vorhandenen*] world which also has an existence in space. Its religion, ritual, ethics, customs, art, constitution, and political laws—indeed the whole range of its institutions, events, and deeds—all this is its own creation, and it is this which makes the nation what it is. . . . And then the individual finds his nation already in being, as a complete and firmly established world into which he must become assimilated. He must take over its substantial being as his own, so that his outlook and abilities are in accord with it, in order that he may himself become something in turn. (*VG* 67/58)

Interpreted in light of Hegel's conception of habit, such passages do not have the authoritarian implications some critics would see in them. Further, the preceding passage makes explicit that the existing or available [*vorhandene*] world, the one in which we find ourselves, includes religious as well as more narrowly ethical and political dimensions of existence, thus elucidating the broad range of factors to which we initially relate in the form of habit.[24] Together, all of these factors make up the way of life and the "consciousness" of a particular community or people.

The individual's appropriation of this way of life is not a matter of taking on something foreign. Rather, this consciousness "is the substance that underlies the spirit of a nation, even if individual human beings are unaware of it and simply take its existence for granted. It is like a necessity, for the individual is brought up within its atmosphere and does not know anything else. But it is not merely education [*Erziehung*] or the result of education; for this consciousness is developed out of the individual himself and is not instilled in him by others: the individual *is* in this substance" (*VG* 59-60/52). These mores and habits are not something external to the individual, something *other* than the individual's true essence or nature, but rather make up the individual's substance. The entire heritage of a people, its history, deeds, and traditions, "constitute their [individuals'] substance, their being" (*VG* 122/103). It makes us who we are; it defines the individual, just as it defines the nation. At the same time, as the multiple levels of Hegel's anthropology reveal, it does not exhaustively define us. There is more to us than this first level of the anthropology.

One concern with Hegel's analysis here is that it seems to assume a homogeneous and static social context quite unlike most parts of the world today. We might consequently understand a rejection of certain of society's norms as an endorsement of other trends within that same society—perhaps as in a conflict between a deep commitment to human rights and a cultural identification with a group violating them. While this point constitutes a reasonable counter to Hegel's assumptions regarding the simplicity of identifying the norms of one's society, it can be accommodated within the framework of his anthropology, even while suggesting that some of our habits may conflict rather than fit smoothly together. Moreover, an anthropology such as Hegel's may prove particularly useful in understanding such conflicts, especially the internal conflict that is part of them.

While we can never be fully free when acting merely out of habit or custom, our constitution by customs or ways of life plays an essential role in Hegel's conception of freedom. Because these norms have a role in constituting us, Hegel believes that acting in complete freedom must involve acting in accord with them. Even if we have reflected upon and become conscious of these norms as the particular traditions of a given society, they still make up much of who we are. To act against them would be to act at least in part against ourselves and thus not entirely freely. Hegel consequently sees following the conventions of one's land not simply as conformism but as "being true to oneself"; for Hegel, the two coincide.[25] By living according to these norms, we are living in accord with our own values and goals. In those cases where the individual rejects significant elements of her society's norms, Hegel's analysis suggests that she is not only violating the standards that constitute the substance of the society, but also acting against a part of herself, alienated from some aspect of her own essence.[26] Although the highest freedom requires being able to recognize these norms as a rational manifestation of spirit (and thus living in a society where it is possible to do so in good conscience), this does not mean that freedom will entail acting other than in accord with these norms.

Hegel's claim is not that following society's norms automatically makes us free; most, perhaps all, societies are far too unjust or undeveloped for that to be possible. Consequently, the conservative conclusion that one must simply endorse the prevailing norms regardless of what they are is not at all justified by Hegel's claim. Rather, Hegel's point is that we will be able to attain the highest degrees of freedom only in a society where we can in good conscience follow the society's norms; otherwise we will be acting at least partly against ourselves. Being able to act in accord with society's norms is thus a necessary but far from sufficient requirement for complete freedom.

It is essential to distinguish Hegel's claim about the rationality of the ways of life of particular nations—a claim we might reject—from his analysis of individuals' relations to these ways of life. In order to do that, we must differentiate between the prereflective identification with this way of life and the possibilities for reflecting upon and reflectively identifying with this way of life that emerge as the next stages in Hegel's anthropology. While on one hand these mores constitute us, on the other hand this initial, immediate identification with them is only the lowest, simplest level of our relation to them. Without these distinctions, made clearly in the *Vorlesungen über die Philosophie des Geistes*, certain passages from the *Philosophy of History* will appear to call for individuals to conform uncritically to their society, no matter how irrational and unjust it may be. Reading these passages in conjunction with the discussion of habit in the philosophy of subjective spirit illuminates this distinction as well as provides the meaning of the claim that these mores constitute our substance; it clarifies both what Hegel is claiming here and what he is not. Given the concerns of the philosophy of history, particularly its interest in nations or peoples rather than individuals, it is no surprise that he does not make explicit this distinction between prereflective and critical social conformity. From the perspective of history as Hegel conceives of it, it makes little difference whether individuals performed deeds reflectively or unreflectively, whether they lived in immediate or mediated identification with their society. From an individual's perspective, however, the difference can be decisive.

### Self-Consciousness as Morality

As prereflective ethical life is the level of ethics corresponding to habit—the first moment of subjective spirit—so morality is the principal level corresponding to human beings as consciousness, as I's—the second moment of subjective spirit. Just as the I constitutes one dimension of what we are, so morality constitutes one dimension of human ethics; it is the level of ethics that has the self-conscious I for a subject. While abstract right also has the I, abstracted from particularity, as its subject, abstract right lacks the self-consciousness that is central to morality.[27] Introducing critical reflection, morality moves beyond the stage of habit; but just as the I proves itself not to be the final dimension of the human subject and is sublated by spirit, so morality shows itself to be inadequate on its own and is sublated by a reflective ethical life. Corresponding to the subject as abstract and free from particularity, morality consists largely of

Hegel's appropriation of Kant's ethics, while his account of its inadequacy is largely his critique of Kant's ethics.

A central issue in Hegel's treatment of morality is the extent to which he both accords morality—or the moral point of view—a role and overcomes it. If "sublation" includes both retaining and negating, precisely what does this mean for our understanding of Hegel's account of morality? What of morality is lost in its sublation and what is incorporated into the higher level of ethics? In order to see that the immediate identification with society's norms represented in habit is not Hegel's last word on ethics, we must respond adequately to these questions.

By focusing on the anthropological basis of Hegel's treatment of morality, we can see both how Hegel's "morality" reveals the ethical consequences of this aspect of his anthropology and how the underlying anthropology illuminates the conception of morality. Examining the relationship between self-consciousness in the sphere of subjective spirit and morality in the sphere of objective spirit is essential to identifying which aspects of morality are preserved in developed ethical life and which are left behind. It thus avoids an interpretation of morality exclusively in the form where it is totalized and taken to be all of ethics, instead revealing morality as one dimension of Hegel's complex ethics—corresponding to self-consciousness as one dimension of his complex conception of human beings.[28] In both cases, this is the dimension in which subjective freedom and the individual come to the fore. And in both, this individuality will reveal itself to be formal and lacking in content.

Hegel's frequent references to the moral "point of view" emphasize that the concept of morality refers not to a particular set of moral norms or rules but rather to the subject's relation to these norms, whatever particular norms they may be. Morality deals centrally not with precepts, such as not lying, but with intention, conscience, and an abstract conception of the good. This exclusive focus on the relation rather than content is ultimately responsible for the lack of content which necessitates the transition to the next sphere.

Already in the transition from abstract right to morality, Hegel expresses the central principle: "[T]he infinite subjectivity of freedom, which now has being *for itself*, constitutes the principle of the *moral point of view*" (*PR* § 104). The subject which is a subject "for itself"—i.e., is conscious of itself as a subject—constitutes the perspective that is morality. This perspective or standpoint is the subject "viewing" its own action, having its action as an object of reflection.

Through this perspective, the subject overcomes the immediate, given character of its action—it is no longer determined simply by habit—and therefore achieves a degree of freedom from this particularity. Because the moral standpoint constitutes freedom from prereflective, habitual mores, "[a] higher *ground* has thereby been determined for freedom" (*PR* § 106). Morality is the dimension of ethics that allows human beings to overcome the particular norms of the society in which they are born and thus achieve a higher level of freedom. It is the basis for the overcoming of givenness, the transition to a genuinely free, self-determining agent (see *PR* § 107).

Whereas subjective spirit dealt with the I as a dimension of human existence, in morality objective spirit deals with the subject's attempts to express or actualize this dimension. No longer acting simply out of habit, the subject seeks to realize its purposes. This extension beyond subjectivity to existence in the world locates morality within the sphere of objective spirit and constitutes one of its essential aspects. Throughout the sphere of morality, the I attempts to act (*handeln*) in accord with its own purpose and intention rather than simply to do (*tun*) out of habit; the I wills, rather than unconsciously "going through the motions." That is, in morality the subject attempts to demonstrate in the world that it possesses self-consciousness, that it is a subject and not simply an object. Although the I was already the acting subject in abstract right, in morality it acts to express its consciousness of itself as an I. Thus, though the entire *Philosophy of Right* deals with the actualization of the will, it is in morality that we first see the self-conscious will coming forward, trying to determine what should happen: "[T]he Idea's aspect of *existence* [*Existenz*], its real moment, is now the *subjectivity* of the will. Only in the will as subjective will can freedom, or the will which has being *in itself*, be actual" (*PR* § 106). The will as subjective, as the conscious will of a subject or an I, becomes actual in the sphere of morality. Seeing the I as the most abstract form of this freedom illuminates why Hegel describes morality as its actual side.[29] Hegel is not simply forcing his analysis of right into a logical scheme with actualization as the second element; rather, in morality, the subject first acts as a subject, i.e., as self-conscious and willing, and attempts to express this subjectivity in an external sphere.

The first subsection of morality, "Purpose and Responsibility," deals with the I's attempt to express itself in relation to a given, external object. The act changes this external object and has responsibility for it "insofar as the abstract predicate '*mine*' attaches to the existence so altered" (*PR* § 115). The I is here concerned with the individual aspects of a larger set of circumstances: "Every individual moment which is shown to have been a *condition, ground,* or *cause* of some such circumstance and has thereby contributed *its share* to it may be regarded as being *wholly,* or at least *partly, responsible* for·it" (*PR* § 115 A).

The objectives of a subject's action, however, are not limited to particular objects. "Intention and Welfare," the second subsection of morality, takes up the point that the subject's concern with particular objects or events has its full meaning only in light of larger intentions: "The external existence [*Dasein*] of an action is a manifold connection which may be regarded as infinitely divided into *individual units* [*Einzelheiten*], and the action itself can be thought of as having *touched* only *one of these units in the first instance*. But the truth of the *individual* [*des Einzelnen*] is the *universal*, and the determinate character of the action for itself is not an isolated content confined to one external unit, but a *universal* content containing within itself all its manifold connections" (*PR* § 119). Actions can be described in terms of individual aspects or components, such as the movement of my finger as I type, but they can only be fully understood in light of their contribution to a larger intention, such as my intention to type a certain word. But "intention" does not stop there. I type a word in order to express a certain thought, in order to make an argument, which in turn plays a role in a larger vision of my life. The same cannot be said when I act strictly out of habit unless I have deliberately, consciously acquired the habit. When consciousness is involved, the action is determined by this larger goal: "[T]he subject, as reflected into itself and hence as a *particular* entity in relation to the particularity of the objective realm, has its own particular content in its end, and this is the soul and determinant of the action" (*PR* § 121). The character of the action is determined by the larger intention.

I have an interest in the action because of its role in my larger purposes. At this level, however, ends are given or found rather than generated by the I itself (*PR* § 123). Hegel calls the satisfaction of the needs, inclinations, and passions with which we find ourselves "*welfare* or *eudaemonia* [*das Wohl oder die Glückseligkeit*]" (*PR* § 123). They are not part of the individual's freedom; they are based in our boundedness to material givens: "Insofar as the determinations of eudaemonia are present and given [*vorgefunden*], they are not true determinations of freedom . . ." (*PR* § 123 Z). Nonetheless, their satisfaction is essential to the I's satisfaction. Hegel seems to include here basic physical needs such as food and shelter. Even though these are immediate and not determined by the I, Hegel views their satisfaction as essential and justified because human beings exist only in physical form; there is no "higher" possibility (*PR* § 123 Z). Hegel here ties the satisfaction of material needs to more distinctly spiritual possibilities. Although their satisfaction is not constitutive of freedom, it is an essential prerequisite.

In this second section, one sees Hegel working to develop a complex, multi-layered ethic that integrates a wide range of intuitions regarding what a conception of freedom must include. Beyond emphasizing the importance of fulfilling basic needs, he is strongly committed to the individual's right to fulfill individual, subjective desires. Just as the analysis of the I pointed to Hegel's treatment of individuality, the corresponding section of objective spirit elaborates the aspect of his ethics—subjective, individual freedom—that is most often closely associated with individuality. In both cases, he sees a close link to the modern world: "The right of the subject's *particularity* to find satisfaction, or—to put it differently—the right of *subjective freedom*, is the pivotal and focal point in the difference between *antiquity* and the *modern age*" (*PR* § 124 A). Although this personal, subjective satisfaction does not constitute the highest end of ethics for Hegel, it is an essential moment or aspect of the highest form of ethical life: "The essence of the modern state is that the universal should be linked with the complete freedom of particularity and the well-being of individuals . . . ; but the universality of the end cannot make further progress without the personal knowledge and volition of the particular individuals [*der Besonderheit*], who must retain their rights" (*PR* § 260 Z).[30] Subjective desire does not in itself justify, but it must accompany, the attainment of the highest ethical goal in order for them to constitute this highest ethical life. Though it is still better to remain unsatisfied than take advantage of the innocent person who happens to be sitting next to you on the bus, when the only reason you are not doing so is obedience to a moral norm, you are far from a fully ethical life. The analysis of morality functions largely to develop this subjective side of freedom, the side dealing with the subject's attitude toward objective, existing mores (*Sitten*).

Nonetheless, this right to subjective satisfaction is trumped by the requirements of freedom: "My particularity, however, like that of others, is only a right at all insofar as I am *free*. It cannot therefore assert itself in contradiction to this substantial basis on which it rests; and an intention to promote my welfare and that of others—and in the latter case in particular it is called a *moral intention*—cannot justify an *action which is wrong*" (*PR* § 126). The limitation of subjective satisfaction in light of higher demands of freedom, however, is not unique to Hegel and is certainly not what distinguishes him from liberals.

Whereas welfare is determined in light of a totality of given or immediate ends, in the third level of morality, "The Good and the Conscience," the good is defined in terms of a universal determined not by particulars but by abstraction from particularity: "Within this idea, welfare has no validity for itself as the existence [*Dasein*] of the individual and particular will, but only as *universal* welfare and essentially as *universal in itself,* i.e. in accordance with freedom . . ." (*PR* § 130). Correspondingly, "True conscience is the disposition to will what is good *in and for itself;* it therefore has fixed principles, and these have for it the character of determinacy and duties which are objective for themselves. In contrast to its content—i.e. truth—conscience is merely the *formal aspect* of the activity of the will, which, as *this* will, has no distinctive content of its own" (*PR* § 137). The conscience wills the good, but the conscience is incapable of determining the content of the good on its own.

The account of the good and the conscience, then, adds a further dimension to the requirement for subjective agreement. The I seeks to will in accord with its own essence, its freedom from particularity; it seeks to will the good itself, not just welfare. This requirement, however, concerns the form of the willing (the need for universality) without being able to determine the content. This is the level of morality developed in Kant's practical philosophy:

> Hence all that is left for duty itself, insofar as it is the essential or universal element in the moral self-consciousness as it is related within itself to itself alone, is abstract universality, whose determination is *identity without content* or the abstractly *positive,* i.e. the indeterminate.
>
> However essential it may be to emphasize the pure and unconditional self-determination of the will as the root of duty—for knowledge [*Erkenntnis*] of the will first gained a firm foundation and point of departure in the philosophy of *Kant,* through the thought of its infinite autonomy (see § 133)—to cling on to a merely moral point of view that does not make the transition to the concept of ethical life reduces this gain to an *empty formalism,* and moral science to an empty rhetoric of *duty for duty's sake.* . . . One may indeed bring in material *from outside* and thereby arrive at *particular* duties, but it is impossible to make the transition to the determination of particular duties from the above determination of duty as *absence of contradiction,* as *formal correspondence with itself,* which is no different from the specification of *abstract indeterminacy* . . . . (*PR* §§ 135, 135 A)

The self-conscious subject can will something universally, but it cannot determine what should be willed universally. The subjective aspect of ethics, then, is also a formal one.

In examining this formal requirement at the highest level of morality, how-ever, Hegel addresses the possibility of justified disagreement with the reigning ethos. The claim that subjective will must accompany the highest ethical life does not presuppose that moral agreement is always possible or justifiable, that it is called for in all cases, or that assenting to (or willing) a set of norms will make them more ethical. Hegel is not calling for people to be seduced by what-ever society they live in or saying that people can be ethical simply by willing the norms around them. To the contrary, he provides the example of Socrates as someone who was forced to turn away from society because its customs were in greater conflict with the demands of freedom than were his own reflections: "In the shapes which it more commonly assumes in history (as in the case of Socrates, the Stoics, etc.), the tendency to look *inwards* into the self and to know and determine from within the self what is right and good appears in epochs when what is recognized as right and good in actuality and custom [*Sitte*] is unable to satisfy the better will" (*PR* § 138 A). Hegel is not claiming that every-one everywhere should conform to the world around them. Although he thinks that the reigning ethical norms are the highest possibilities available to most individuals, he sees an essential role for individual questioning and reflection, and believes that such independent thinking can at times produce something higher than the common customs. It is precisely here, in the sphere of morality, that we find the basis for individuals' at least partial transcendence of the norms they inherit through habituation.

At the level of politics, the theory of morality produces a requirement of subjective, conscious agreement in the most ethical society. This entails both the freedom to make individual choices that do not bear on the ethical good of the society—choices about flavors of ice cream, for instance—and the need for agreement with a society's norms.[31] "Need" in this context signifies that such agreement is necessary for a life that develops the spiritual potential intrinsic to human beings, but it does not in itself say anything about valid and invalid ways of trying to bring about this agreement or when it would be justified. The point is simply that if we view a society's norms—both those expressed in laws and those expressed otherwise—as nothing more than external regulations imposed on us against our will, we will not be fully free. We will be alienated from the society in which we live and most likely be internally divided or alienated from ourselves. But none of this is to deny that in certain societies we would be made even less free by conforming. Hegel's treatment of Socrates illustrates that the individual can at times achieve something higher by disagreeing with society's norms than by agreeing with them. At the same time, Socrates' fate shows that following one's beliefs alone is not all that is required for a flourishing life, even if it may create the highest instance available in certain circumstances.

Thus, while morality may say a great deal about what must be included in ethical life, it also leaves a great deal still unspecified. It does not in itself indicate when the "right to choose" is trumped by higher ethical demands. Without denying the differences between Hegel's ethics and a conventional liberalism, it is important to keep in mind that both place limits on personal choice; the distinction between the two has to be located more precisely, in the specific justification of such abrogation of choice. For Hegel, this limitation depends largely upon the higher ethical goods that are explicated in the theory of ethical life, the final section of the *Philosophy of Right*.[32]

The limitations or inadequacies that drive the development of morality to a higher level are located in morality's inability to generate norms out of itself. The self-consciousness seeks to will freely; this entails transcending the norms and customs that it has merely appropriated through habit rather than identified as rational. The early section of morality involved content or goals that came from outside of self-consciousness and appeared as givens, whether they concern the desire for food or the desire to follow social and ethical conventions. At that level, the self-consciousness determined the form of willing but not its content. Seeing the contradiction between its attempt to will freely and its taking its content as something external and immediately determined, the subject seeks to produce the content of its will from itself:

> This subjectivity, as abstract self-determination and pure certainty of itself alone, *evaporates* into itself all *determinate* aspects of right, duty, and existence [*Dasein*], inasmuch as it is the power of *judgment* that determines solely from within itself what is good in relation to a given content, and at the same time the power to which the good, which is at first only an imagined [*vorgestellte*] good and *obligation*, owes its *actuality*.
>
> The self-consciousness that has managed to attain this absolute reflection into itself knows itself in this reflection as a consciousness that cannot and should not be compromised by any present and given determination. (*PR* §§ 138, 138 A)

This self-conscious subject knows that the givenness of society's customs does not justify her allegiance to them; as a result, she seeks to generate norms from within herself, to become entirely self-determining.

The pure formality of self-consciousness, its abstraction from all particularity, however, renders it incapable of providing this content on its own: "In its vanity toward otherwise valid determinations and with the will in a state of pure inwardness, the self-consciousness is capable of making into its principle either *the universal in and for itself,* or the *arbitrariness* [*Willkür*] of its *own particularity,* giving the latter precedence over the universal and realizing it through its actions—i.e. it is capable of being *evil*" (*PR* § 139). The I abstracting from particularity leaves behind the content necessary to determine what is good. In claiming the right of our own subjectivity to determine the good, we create the possibility of evil just as much as the possibility of a more universal good, because the I can just as easily and self-consistently act out of arbitrary will as in accord with a higher good.

Absolutizing the I, as if it were the only dimension of the self, can produce several possible distortions of the will, each of which can be understood as the totalizing of one element of the anthropology. This "*subjectivity* [that] *declares itself absolute*" falls into hypocrisy, probabilism, an exclusive focus on personal conviction, and—lastly—irony. The last represents the peak of subjectivity, in which the subjectivity "*knows* itself as that power of resolution and decision on [matters of] truth, right, and duty . . . . Thus, it [this subjectivity] does indeed consist in knowledge of the objective side of ethics, but without that self-forgetfulness and renunciation which seriously immerses itself in this objectivity and makes it the basis of its action" (*PR* § 140 A). The I knows the objective good but holds itself apart from this and thereby absolutizes one dimension of itself while losing sight of other dimensions. This places the individual subject above customs, norms, and laws: "It is not the thing [*Sache*] which is excellent, it is I who am excellent and master of both law and thing; I *merely play* with them as with my own caprice, and in this ironic consciousness in which I let the highest of things perish, I *merely enjoy myself*" (*PR* § 140 A). Hegel here critiques that extreme subjectivity which knows the ethical content but still sees this content as something other and lower than itself. Though the subject knows the objective side of ethics, he has not grasped the role of this ethics in constituting the world that makes him who and what he is, nor been able to view it as a manifestation of his own essence.

In this final stage, the duality created in the self by self-consciousness has been totalized. The moral point of view, the aspect of ethics corresponding to the I, has been taken to be everything rather than as one dimension of a more complex concept. Reading morality in relation to the anthropology illuminates that, for Hegel, just as the conception of the I must be incorporated into a more complex theory of the human subject, so morality must be incorporated into a more complex ethical conception, not made to stand on its own.

While Hegel's critique at this stage is not of the emptiness of an ethics reduced to morality, that is, Kantian morality, the underlying inadequacy remains: Morality constitutes only the formal, the subjective, not the objective side of the ethical whole. This inadequacy drives the transition from morality to ethical life: "For the *good* as the substantial universal of freedom, but still as something *abstract*, determinations of some kind are therefore *required*, as is a determining principle (although this principle is *identical* with the good itself). For the *conscience* likewise, as the purely abstract principle of determination, it is required that its determinations should be universal and objective. Both of them [i.e. the good and the conscience], if raised in this way to independent totalities [*für sich zur Totalität*], become the indeterminate which *ought* to be determined" (*PR* § 141). Self-consciousness alone, when absolutized into the most extreme subjectivity, still does not produce the necessary objective side of ethics that can be given actuality in the ethical life of a society. For this, we must turn to the developed conception of ethical life, which is the aspect of objective spirit corresponding to the third part of subjective spirit, the "Psychology."

### Free Spirit as Self-Conscious, Reflective Ethical Life

A reflective ethical life brings together the identification with customs represented in the earlier discussion of ethical life and the reflective self-consciousness of morality. It signifies a self-conscious, mediated identification with these ethical customs as manifestations of one's own essence. As in the third moment of subjective spirit, the subject is distinctly spirit, both subject and object, knowing and acting. Overcoming the bifurcation within the self represented in self-consciousness and in morality, developed ethical life recuperates the content of habit yet preserves the consciousness of morality. It recognizes this content, these norms and duties, as rational and as the substance of freedom.

Hegel's discussion of ethical life consists largely of his filling out of this content, explicating the customs and ethics that manifest freedom in the modern (Western) world as he sees it. Chapter 7 will examine several themes central to this content. The present section focuses, as did the discussion of habitual, pre-reflective ethical life, on the *concept* of ethical life, but dealing now with the conception of a developed, self-conscious ethical life: Because my terminology might suggest that these are two different forms of ethical life, it is important to emphasize that the later form is not some other version but the developed form of the earlier, the form toward which ethical life as a whole moves.

Ethical life provides the content that was found lacking in morality. To return to the passage with which we opened the discussion of "Habit as Prereflective Ethical Life": "Ethical life is the *Idea of freedom* .... [It] is accordingly the *concept of freedom which has become* [1] *the existing world and* [2] *the nature of self-consciousness*" (*PR* § 142). In light of the discussion of morality, we can now grasp the first element, which also made up the content of habit, as the content missing from morality. This constitutes the objective side of ethical life: "The objective sphere of ethics, which takes the place of the abstract good, is substance made *concrete* by subjectivity *as infinite form*. It therefore posits *distinctions* within itself which are thus determined by the concept. These distinctions give the ethical a fixed *content* which is necessary for itself, and whose existence [*Bestehen*] is exalted above subjective opinions and preferences ..." (*PR* § 144). These are the norms and customs that tell us what to do and how to behave. They are determined by and thus manifestations of the concept. Because of the anthropology's mediating position between the abstract concept of the logic and the sphere of objective spirit, they are also—and more directly—manifestations of the elements of Hegel's anthropology. Together, they constitute a system of ethical life (*PR* § 145). According to Hegel, they tell us concretely what good is, replacing the merely abstract concept that morality produced.

While this concrete content was present in habitual ethical life as well, it was not recognized there for what it is. Thus, the second constitutive aspect of ethical life, consciousness, newly emerges in reflective ethical life and distinguishes it from merely habitual ethical life. We still do what we did purely out of habit, but we now do it out of the conviction that it is right. As Mark Tunick writes, "When the citizen returns from his withdrawal [the moment of division or alienation], he has knowledge of why he should obey the laws; he obeys the laws, as he always had done, but for completely different reasons. The laws are justified to him, and he is genuinely free by obeying them, for he understands them to be his own, the product of his own will."[33] We self-consciously, freely will, because of its rationality, that which is simultaneously asked by society's norms. Attending to the anthropology reveals that without the integration of self-consciousness into ethical life, genuine freedom is not possible.[34] Without this integration, free spirit as developed in subjective spirit could find no adequate expression in objective spirit. The fundamental movement of Hegel's own position would thereby be undermined.[35]

This self-conscious ethical life entails a reflective recognition that the customs and ethics of the "existing world" are right, just, and rational. We are able to recognize these demands as rational because these norms are—for Hegel—rational manifestations of spirit in the objective realm. They express my own essence:

> In this way, *ethical substantiality* has attained its *right*, and the latter has attained *validity*. That is, the self-will of the individual [*des Einzelnen*], and his own conscience in its attempt to exist for itself and in opposition to the ethical substantiality, have disappeared; for the ethical character knows that the end which moves it is the universal which, though itself unmoved, has developed through its determinations into actual rationality, and it recognizes that its own dignity and the whole continued existence [*Bestehen*] of its particular ends are based upon and actualized within this universal. Subjectivity is itself the absolute form and existent actuality of substance, and the difference between the subject on the one hand and substance as its object, end, and power on the other is the same as their difference in form, both of which differences have disappeared with equal immediacy. (*PR* § 152)[36]

The stage in which conscience and self-will pit the subject against the demands of the existing world has been overcome through the individual's recognition that these demands are manifestations of our own essence. The thinking will grasps that in willing in accord with these norms it is willing its own essence, which is precisely what it means to be willing itself, self-determining, and thus free. These demands, which at the level of morality appeared external and simply given, are not arbitrarily imposed, irrational customs.[37] The distance between the subject and these objectively existing norms that is initially created by conscious reflection is overcome, and a mediated identity achieved. Thus, by highlighting the anthropological structure manifest in objective spirit, we can fully grasp the meaning and justification of another of Hegel's formulations of ethical life: "The abstract concept of ethical life is the unity of subjective and objective will, the universality of the will as identical with the subjectivity of the will" (*Rph VI*, 395).[38] The will's universality and subjectivity can be identical only because both are manifestations of the same *Anlage*.

As a result, the concrete determinations of ethical life—insofar as it is a developed ethical life—also fulfill the demands set forth by morality. Kant is right to demand universalizability; the point is not that this requirement is not valid but that it alone cannot provide the concrete content.[39] The replacement of the abstract good, the culmination of morality, with society's accepted mores is a matter of going beyond rather than back upon the requirements of morality.

Because for Hegel these existing norms manifest my own essence, living according to them is living in freedom—living in accord with myself, not being subject to some external control or command. I find my "*right . . . to subjective determination*" fulfilled in them (*PR* § 153). Any other source of determination— such as a random impulse or arbitrary desire—would be an external, heteronomous source, but these norms are themselves manifestations of what I am. Thus, "In duty, the individual liberates himself so as to attain substantial freedom" (*PR* § 149). Only by fulfilling these duties am I living freely, with my action determined by my own essence. It is only in this light that Hegel's conception of freedom through obeying social norms can be understood.

Hegel's vision of developed ethical life thus weaves together the various components of freedom that he has been elaborating to produce a remarkable coincidence of desire, society's expectations, and right. Perfect freedom, for Hegel, entails all three. Only such a convergence can constitute the self-determination in which spirit finds itself genuinely "at home."

Hegel certainly does not think that all three coincide anywhere and everywhere. This developed ethical life is not present in all societies. At the very least, however, he thinks that post-Napoleonic Germanic states, specifically Prussia after the Restoration, have come very close (the significant contrasts between the Prussian state and the state portrayed in the *Philosophy of Right* notwithstanding). In the last paragraph of the *Philosophy of Right*, he declares, "the present has cast off its barbarism and unjust [*unrechtliche*] arbitrariness, and truth has cast off its otherworldliness and contingent force, so that the true reconciliation, which reveals the *state* as the image and actuality of reason, has become objective" (*PR* § 360).[40] While this highest level of reconciliation requires the knowledge acquired only through absolute spirit—which means that it cannot be achieved at the level of objective spirit alone—it entails a recognition of the existing world as a manifestation of freedom. Only in his own time and place, Hegel thinks, has a society been achieved that possesses the ethical relations, customs, and consciousness necessary for the requirements of freedom to come together. Only there can individuals reflectively recognize the mores and ethics of the society and religious tradition as manifestations of reason, thereby accepting them freely and finding their freedom in accepting them.

As Peperzak argues, the transition from objective to absolute spirit in the *Encyclopaedia* makes clear that "the nation state cannot be an adequate form of spirit," i.e., that a perfect reconciliation cannot be achieved in this finite world.[41] But Hegel does seem to claim that the manifestation of freedom achieved by the modern Germanic state, though perhaps not perfect, is verging on the highest that can be attained in the objective sphere itself. It is not a fully adequate manifestation, but it is an adequate objective manifestation. There seems to be, according to Hegel, no further tension between the actual manifestation and the highest possible objective manifestation.[42]

For the interpretation of Hegel's ethics and politics, however, the crucial point is that Hegel thinks this highest stage of ethical life is possible because, as a result of the historical development of spirit, the modern Germanic state is at least a roughly adequate objective manifestation of our essence. If members of that society reflect on the conventions around them, they will ultimately not find them oppressive or objectionable. This world can be reflectively appropriated in this manner not simply because it exists, but because it manifests freedom. Its capacity to produce, support, and maintain free individuals—not its mere being there or even its being part of one's habits—makes it right and compatible with the highest possibilities of ethical life. Consequently, the content, as compared to the fundamental concept, of the section on ethical life consists of Hegel's demonstration of the rationality of the existing Germanic world. Even if we do not find that Hegel has succeeded in this task—and find profoundly alarming any claim to have achieved a society that adequately manifests the essence of humanity—it is essential to be clear about the nature of Hegel's project: to demonstrate, not to presuppose, that the existing world is a rational manifestation of freedom.

The result is that it is possible to separate any claim that Hegel's society, or the modern West in general, is a satisfactory manifestation of freedom from the notion of reflective consideration and judgment of a society's norms regarding the extent to which they manifest freedom. It is precisely the focus on Hegel's anthropology that allows us to pry apart the conception of ethical life, revealing both a habitual and a conscious, reflective side. The process of moving between the two reveals an opening out of which we can draw Hegel's conception of human beings and the implications for ethics without being committed to the confidence Hegel often—though not always—expresses in the rationality of the status quo.[43]

Distinguishing these levels of the anthropology and analyzing their relevance to higher levels of spirit acknowledges the role of ethical and religious traditions in constituting us, even as it submits them to critical inquiry. Like other inherited norms, the mores and customs that embody these traditions can be critically examined for their potential to actualize our essence and thereby make us free. To the extent that they do have this potential and are therefore rational (in the sense the term has been used here), they can be justified and consciously appropriated on this basis rather than simply because we happen to have inherited them—i.e., simply because they make up our tradition. In integrating this reflective, critical moment within the basic structure of his anthropology, Hegel does not provide a guarantee that any particular traditions will be found rational, but he does produce an account of what it would mean to find them rational, justifiable, and worth defending in a critically self-conscious culture.[44]

To find one's tradition and society deficient with regard to freedom does not invalidate the conception of freedom as the coincidence of desire, society's expectations, and right; but it means that this ideal will not be completely attainable in these circumstances. Although we can transform ourselves somewhat, deliberately acquiring new habits, we are often unable to depart completely from even those customs we find unjust; they frequently continue to make up part of who we are. Even as we reflect, we do not leave behind habit altogether. Our thinking and feeling will be largely affected by the social world in which we live. A variety of views regarding the self-clarity possible for human beings could be fit into this Hegelian framework as different judgments of how much of our lives we can move beyond the level of habit and bring to self-consciousness. The framework itself does not presuppose that habit as a whole can be left behind. This enduring role for habit means that in an unfree society we will almost inevitably be divided against ourselves to greater or lesser degrees. In Socrates' situation, for instance, true freedom was unattainable. The same point regarding an internal conflict can be made with regard to existence in any society—and this may be virtually every society today—where the social and ethical conventions do not form a coherent system, where members inherit multiple traditions with conflicting expectations.

This point raises larger questions regarding the idea of a fragmented self, which has played a significant role in many contemporary discussions of what it means to be a human being. Hegel's anthropology does not deny the possibility of such fragmentation but rather explains why, for instance, growing up in two different societies can produce something like a dual identity. The anthropology points to the internal conflict that a dual identity can generate, particularly when the two sides remain disjunctive rather than being forged into a single, new identity. The pervasiveness of habit, moreover, suggests how difficult—and most likely always only partially completed—such a task of fusion will be.

The difficulty of attaining this freedom, however, does not render it irrelevant. These requirements are best understood as a definition of complete freedom. Even if we do not think this freedom will ever be perfectly attained, we may find it a compelling account of the freedom toward which we should strive. Moreover, having this as our conception of perfect freedom does not prevent us from distinguishing forms and degrees of unfreedom; it does not make all incomplete manifestations of freedom equal. It allows us to critique some social arrangements as less free than others without deifying any one of them, thereby avoiding the idolization of any existing state.

# 7 Equality, Differentiation, and the Universal Estate

In examining the role of habit, self-consciousness, and free spirit in the sphere of objective spirit, the previous chapter considered a crucial dimension of the relation between subjective and objective spirit. Attending to the anthropological basis of Hegel's ethical thought revealed that ethical life encompasses two distinct relationships possible between the individual subject and the existing ethical order: one prereflective and habitual, the other self-conscious and deliberate. The present chapter considers another aspect of the import of Hegel's anthropology for objective spirit. It focuses on whether Hegel's account of objective spirit is adequate to the *Anlage* or potential that subjective spirit articulates as intrinsic to being human. Whereas the previous chapter drew on the anthropology to identify essential but often overlooked distinctions within objective spirit, the present one argues that significant elements of Hegel's account of this sphere are in fundamental tension with the egalitarianism inherent in an anthropology defined by universal human potential.[1] For this reason, it develops an immanent, "Hegelian" critique of Hegel's claims regarding social differentiation.

Objective spirit constitutes the further development of the system from the point at which it arrives at the conclusion of subjective spirit—free spirit. Insofar as Hegel conceives of the system as developing immanently, objective spirit is not a simple repetition of subjective spirit considered in a different light or context. Insofar as it is a development of spirit "in the form of *reality*," however, it is a development and manifestation of spirit (*Enz.* § 385). Consequently, it must be expressive of and adequate to what spirit has already revealed about itself in subjective spirit. In this sense, subjective spirit generates requirements for what could constitute a satisfactory objectification of spirit "in the form of *reality.*" In accord with the drive to realize its potential, when such satisfaction is not attained, spirit—i.e., human beings—will continue, consciously or unconsciously, to transform the objective sphere to produce a more satisfactory expression of our essence. Precisely because subjective spirit elaborates a telos of development based in a universal human potential, it must be realized in all human beings, not just a particular subset of the population. A political vision that necessarily excludes some members of society from the highest level of freedom ultimately fails to satisfy the demands set forth by Hegel's anthropology.[2] Moreover, given the role of universal recognition in spirit's path to self-knowledge, a system that precludes self-realization for part of the population does so, at least to some degree, even for the most privileged members of society.

Much of Hegel's account of the content of ethical life is inadequate to his anthropology in this regard. He introduces various types of hierarchical differentiation or stratification that structurally condemn significant segments of society to incomplete self-realization and therefore to unfreedom. In his treatment of gender, estates, and the difference between civil society and the state, he assigns groups to live the majority of their lives in modes of existence that fall short of free spirit. The lives of these groups are dominated by habit (in the case of women and the agricultural estate) or the internal division expressive of self-consciousness that has not been sublated in free spirit (in the case of the estate of trade and industry and civil society). Examining these aspects of objective spirit in relation to the anthropology therefore produces an immanent critique of several of Hegel's most problematic political claims. Despite these inadequacies in Hegel's treatment, his conception of the state and the universal estate that identifies its interests with the state provides a model of the relation to the state that would constitute a freedom adequate to this anthropology.

Exploring both the inadequacies of Hegel's account and the egalitarian elements implicit in his treatment of the state requires particular attention to the objective side of ethical life. The previous chapter focused on the subject's relation to the existing life, i.e., the subjective element. In discussing the family, civil society, and the state, the present chapter considers this existing side per se—the specific customs, norms, and institutions that Hegel sees defining the modern, free state and making freedom actual.[3] I do not, however, follow Hegel's systematic unfolding of this material.[4] In examining these issues, this chapter elaborates an immanent critique, based on his anthropology, of Hegel's account of objective spirit. In concluding, I will suggest a strategy for framing the ethical contributions of Hegel's anthropology—in light of these criticisms—that does not require a complete rewriting or reelaboration of the sphere of objective spirit.

## Ethics as Social and Political

As even the introduction to the structure of ethical life indicates, Hegel's ethics concentrates on the social, political, and economic institutions necessary for the development of individual human beings into the free spirit discussed at the end of subjective spirit. This focus, however, does not entail the subordination of the individual to the community or state.[5] A good society is good not simply in itself but because it produces and sustains individuals who realize the potentials set forth in the philosophy of subjective spirit; they realize, both practically and theoretically, their spiritual essence. To provide such possibilities is what it means for a society to be free and to manifest the essence of spirit. The "knowing thyself" with which the development culminates is something done always by individual—but never isolated—human beings. The endpoint is a freedom that only attains concrete existence in human beings, regardless of how essential particular societies are for these developments.

This self-actualization, however, can take place only in certain kinds of societies, which makes the concern with this kind of society central to ethics. The culmination of the development in free spirit is in spirit's knowledge of itself as free, but this knowledge comes about only through the demonstration of this freedom in the world. This demonstration is the existence of a free society in which human beings actively and self-consciously participate. Thus, just as the free spirit at the culmination of the anthropology brings together theoretical and practical spirit, this free society must include both an adequate consciousness of what we as human beings are (the self-understanding dealt with specifically in absolute spirit) and institutions that provide for this flourishing.

In relation to other ethical theories, this means that Hegel's most concrete discussions of ethics focus on what can be called social ethics: The principal, though by no means exclusive, concern is with social, economic, and political structures and institutions. As Ritter states, "Hegel thereby, however, brings ethics at the same time back into the context of 'politics.'"[6] Ethics and politics are here inseparable, so that one can refer to his "ethico-political" thought. Hegel concentrates on these factors not as ends in themselves, but precisely because of their essential role in undermining or fostering—as well as providing a space for—human freedom. Although this social ethics is based in an anthropology, it is not based simply in the extension of personal ethics or their application to the social sphere. An emphasis on personal virtues, Hegel contends, arises precisely where the ethical relations and customs of a society are inadequately developed: "Within a given ethical order whose relations are fully developed and actualized, *virtue in the proper sense* has its place and actuality only in extraordinary circumstances, or where the above relations come into collision. . . . This is why the form of virtue as such appears more frequently in uncivilized societies and communities, for in such cases, the ethical and its actualization depend more on individual discretion and on the distinctive natural genius of individuals" (*PR* § 150 A). Virtue is not thereby made insignificant (and we may believe that "collisions" occur more frequently than Hegel suggests), but the concern with an ethical social order functions at a more fundamental level than the concern with individuals' virtues. Though the two concerns are related, they are not identical. The former is based in the concept of a society that can produce free individuals—where free is understood in the encompassing sense of Hegel's conception of free spirit as the culmination of human self-actualization. This concern of ethics with creating a society that produces "developed," free individuals highlights that the sphere of objective spirit does not follow the sphere of subjective spirit in any temporal sense. The developments of the individual traced in chapters 2 through 4 do not precede in time the developments of objective spirit. To the contrary, they are made possible and sustained only by certain types of societies, and the sphere of objective spirit functions to analyze social structures. Precisely because of this interrelationship of social and individual concerns, however, the characterization of Hegel's ethics as social ethics should not imply that it is radically different from a more personal ethics. It represents an alternative center of attention, on socioeconomic, cultural, and political issues.

## Three Forms of Differentiation

Charles Taylor views Hegel's greatest contribution as closely tied to his conception of differentiation. This contribution lies in Hegel's identification and analysis of the central problem of modern Western society: homogenization.[7] With the breakdown of traditional social orders, the looming concern is that people will no longer identify with the larger order of which they are a part. Without institutions that mediate between the individual and the state as a whole, society becomes an undifferentiated, homogenous mass, incapable of providing identity for its members. The result is alienation, "when the goals, norms or ends which define the common practices or institutions begin to seem irrelevant or even monstrous, or when the norms are redefined so that the practices appear a travesty of them."[8] Individuals will have no means to realize that the community constitutes them rather than simply stands over against them. The response is either a vicious attack on all differentiation—as in the Terror of the French Revolution—or an attempt to produce such identity through nationalism—as in Nazi Germany.

In Taylor's reading, Hegel responds to this challenge primarily through his conception of society as articulated into three estates (*Stände*), corresponding to each of the basic moments in his thought: the substantial estate, comprised of those tied to agriculture; the estate of trade and industry; and the universal estate, comprised primarily of civil servants. The estates provide the differentiated units through which individuals can identify with a body larger than themselves. By mediating between the individual and the entirety of the state, they provide a workable basis for identity. According to Taylor, Hegel thought only the estates could "provide what modern society needs . . . . And this is a ground for differentiation, meaningful to the people concerned, but which at the same time does not set the partial communities against each other, but rather knits them together in a larger whole."[9] The estates do not oppose each other but together make up an organic whole. Only they enable individuals to identify with something larger than themselves without dividing the larger society or state against itself.

Taylor thinks that the actual homogenization achieved by modern Western societies proves Hegel wrong regarding the role the estates could play in preventing such a development.[10] Additionally, Taylor seems to find such a hierarchical vision to be in too strong a tension with the emphasis on freedom that characterizes the modern West. But if Taylor rejects Hegel's solution as irrelevant, he nonetheless thinks Hegel got the problem facing modern democracy right: alienation produced by homogenization.

While Taylor's reading focuses on Hegel's attempt to provide differentiation within society through the estates, Shlomo Avineri emphasizes the mediation provided by the three spheres of ethical life, especially the autonomy enjoyed by civil society in relation to the state. Hegel's treatment of ethical life divides into three moments: the family, characterized by particular altruism (one acts for the good of another, but only the good of a particular, closely related other); civil society, characterized by universal egoism (each member acts according to self-interest); and the state, characterized by universal altruism ("a mode of relating to a universe of human beings not out of self-interest but out of solidarity, out of the will to live with other human beings in a community").[11] Most (male) members of society participate at least to some degree in each of these spheres, but different groups dominate within as well as have their consciousness characterized by each of the spheres. The substantial or agricultural estate corresponds to the family, the estate of trade and industry to civil society, and the universal estate to the state. Nonetheless, the spheres of ethical life should not be identified with the estates that dominate them; the difference between them corresponds to the different focal points of Avineri's and Taylor's analyses. Avineri focuses on the autonomy of civil society in relation to the state, Taylor on the difference between the people dominating the two spheres.

Civil society, the sphere of universal egoism, finds "[i]ts most acute and typical expression [in] economic life, where I sell and buy not in order to satisfy the needs of the other, his hunger or his need for shelter, but where I use the felt need of the other as a means to satisfy my own ends."[12] As in classical economists' models of the free market, society is treated as a mere instrument for the satisfaction of one's needs and desires. These needs, however, are not fixed or given. They continue to multiply, with the satisfaction of one need followed by the creation of another. This freedom from natural determination "drives human society to the endless pursuit of commodities," creating "the inner restlessness of civil society . . . ."[13]

This unending pursuit of ever greater accumulation produces not only wealth but also its opposite: poverty. Poverty is not due to inefficiency or an inability to create enough goods; it is intrinsic to the system itself. Society's inability to solve the problem of poverty becomes particularly significant because it is more than material deprivation of part of the population. Its greatest import in Hegel's view lies in its propensity to create a "rabble" (*Pöbel*), "a heap of human beings utterly atomized and alienated from society, feeling no allegiance to it and no longer even wishing to be integrated into it."[14] If their numbers are large enough, they pose a serious threat to the society as a whole.

Despite the inevitability and significance of poverty, Hegel does not call for a state-led transformation of the sphere of civil society. He preserves the latter's autonomy in relation to the former. And precisely here, one sees—in Avineri's reading—that Hegel's commitment to the autonomy of civil society is so great that he resists a state-based solution to the most significant social problem for which he does not have an answer: "Hegel's dilemma is acute: if he leaves the state out of economic activity, an entire group of civil society members is going to be left outside it; but if he brings in the state in a way that would solve the problem, his distinction between civil society and the state would disappear, and the whole system of mediation and dialectical progress towards integration through differentiation would collapse."[15] The state intervenes in small ways, but it does not fundamentally alter the civil society described in free-market economic theories, because the differentiation this sphere represents is essential, despite the irresolvable problem it creates.

Allen Wood focuses on the need for differentiation to provide expression to two basic principles—the substantive and the reflective—which Hegel sees as manifest principally in women and men, respectively.[16] The substantial principle "shows itself in the human character dominated by habit and feeling, and in social institutions emphasizing trust and tradition or concrete relationships between individuals."[17] It represents an immediate, unreflective identification with the world and institutions directly around one. "On the other side is the modern *reflective* principle, which favors personal insight and reason, in the guise both of self-interested calculation and of impartial, impersonal moral thinking. Reflection also predominates in the specifically modern social institutions, civil society, and the modern political state . . . ."[18]

While the reflective moment is specifically related to the modern world, both principles must be manifest and reconciled in modern society, and it is here that Wood focuses the need for social differentiation: "Hegel's theory of this reconciliation is founded on his idea that a developed ethical order must be 'articulated' (*gegliedert*)—an organism composed of differentiated social institutions with complementary functions. (Generally speaking, the substantial principle has its place in private family life, whereas the reflective principle predominates in the public domains of civil society and the political state.) Next, Hegel holds that differentiated institutions require a social differentiation among individuals. Each principle must have its proper representatives and guardians."[19] Modern society must incorporate both principles and does so by having different members of the society represent each of the two principles. They are reconciled within society but not within individuals. In the estates, the agricultural estate embodies the substantial principle, while the other two estates embody the principle of reflection. Freedom finds its most adequate realization, then, only in the latter two estates. For Wood, however, the most important division appears to be that between men and women, the substantial principle being associated with women and the reflective principle with men.

Wood sees this assignment of the lower principle to one gender and the higher principle to another as in fundamental tension with Hegel's commitment to the idea "that all individuals are equally persons and subjects."[20] As a result, Wood suggests that

> One attractive way out of Hegel's problem might be to reject his idea that the substantive and reflective principles should be assigned each to one gender. Instead, it might be proposed that we integrate both principles within each human personality. On this view, every human being should be a whole . . . .
> Hegel never considers this option.[21]

According to this option, differentiation would be located within each individual—perhaps in our different activities and relationships—rather than distributed among different members, genders, or classes of society. Wood suggests this possibility as an alternative to what many of us today find objectionable in Hegel's attempt to provide a hierarchical or vertical form of differentiation.

## Family

With these three models of differentiation and the concerns they raise framing the analysis, I turn now to a more detailed consideration of the significance of the anthropology for the content of ethical life. While the sphere of ethical life as a whole can be characterized by either immediacy or self-consciousness, in the family immediacy predominates. As Wood emphasizes, the family represents "the *immediate substantiality* of spirit" (*PR* § 158), which has love at its foundation.[22] Being prereflective, it is characterized by the unity of feeling, trust, and faith rather than the dichotomy of consciousness. It is the setting in which individuals express and satisfy their emotional needs.[23] Natural love, however, is characterized as much by accident and contingency as by reason or our essence. To overcome this contingency at least partially, love must be given an external, ethical significance recognized by others through marriage: "Marriage is still only the immediate ethical Idea and thus has its objective actuality in the inwardness of subjective disposition and feeling. This accounts for the basic contingency of its existence" (*PR* § 176). Because its origin is something contingent, the family is always only an immediate rather than a spiritually developed unity. Like the initial conception of habit in the "Anthropology," the family raises natural determinations to a more spiritual level, yet it lacks the internal differentiation that is dominant in civil society and that is incorporated into a mediated unity in the state. Consequently, "It lies in the nature of marriage itself, as immediate ethical life, that it is a mixture of substantial relationship, natural contingency, and inner arbitrariness" (*PR* § 180 A). Although the family belongs to ethical life, every family is still largely shaped by accident rather than determined by our essence.

The family culminates in and is ultimately overcome by the production of a child. The child produced by the parents symbolizes the unity of the family (*PR* § 173), and a central task of the family is the raising of children. Not surprisingly, Hegel emphasizes that this task is largely a matter of instilling proper habits to overcome the immediacy of nature:

> As far as their relationship with the family is concerned, their *upbringing* [*Erziehung*] has the *positive* determination that, in them [children], the ethical is given the form of immediate *feeling* which is still without opposition, so that the heart therein, as the *basis* of ethical life, lives its first life in love, trust, and obedience. But in the same connection, their upbringing also has the *negative* determination of raising the children out of the natural immediacy in which they originally exist to self-sufficiency and freedom of personality, thereby enabling them to leave the natural unity of the family. (*PR* § 175)

Hegel's description accords precisely with the earlier treatment of habit; the analysis here is the more concrete account of the principal context in which individuals acquire the habits discussed at an abstract level in the "Anthropology." In raising the child, the parents must overcome the child's initial, natural determination by supplanting it with ethical habits. These too will be only partially free; they are a second nature, still in the form of feeling and unmediated by reflection. Nonetheless, this is the first appropriation of a society's norms and values, which make it possible for the individual to participate in that society; they are the foundation for ethical life.[24] Moreover, they enable the child to leave the family and participate in society as an independent person; they thus provide the transition to the next level, civil society.

Although the family is only the most immediate moment of ethical life, Hegel contends that it must be preserved in a rational society. It is one of the essential forms in which immediacy is given objective existence and is a key to Hegel's conception of a differentiated society. For many men, however, the family constitutes only a part of their lives. One aspect of their lives is in this immediate form, but they also participate in civil society and/or the state and achieve greater degrees of freedom there.

For women, according to Hegel, the situation is different. Hegel thinks the center of women's existence should be in the family. They should play virtually no role in civil society or the state and therefore have their lives dominated by family life. Whereas "[m]an . . . has his actual substantial life in the state, in science, and so forth," in the family woman has "her substantial determination and in this *piety* her ethical convictions" (*PR* § 166). Women are inherently characterized by feeling and intuition, and in the family "[t]he *natural* determinacy of the two sexes is given *intellectual* and ethical significance by virtue of its rationality" (*PR* § 165). What Hegel sees as natural differences between men and women correspond to different moments within the concept—or levels of the anthropology. As a result, he claims they can be given an ethical significance without being significantly transformed.

As we saw, Wood argues that this claim conflicts with Hegel's belief "that all individuals are equally persons and subjects."[25] The analysis of the anthropology, however, allows us to express the problem more precisely. Insofar as this anthropology applies to both men and women, people whose lives are dominated by participation in the family as Hegel conceives it live primarily at the level of habit, the lowest distinctly human potential. Consequently, they have not come close to fulfilling the potential that, according to the anthropology, is inherent in them. A social or political system that endorses this is inadequate to Hegel's anthropology. For this reason, it will be destabilized by spirit's intrinsic drive to self-realization and freedom.

Although Hegel does not discuss them under the family, there is another group in Hegel's state that is also characterized by this state of mind. The life and activity of the agricultural estate is largely determined by nature—its rhythms and progress. This estate's activity, "because of the conditions to which it is subject, . . . retains the character of a [mode of] subsistence in which reflection and the will of the individual play a lesser role, and thus its substantial disposition in general is that of an immediate ethical life based on the family relationship and on trust" (*PR* § 203). Like the family, this estate retains a large element of natural determination and lacks the reflection and self-consciousness characterizing higher spheres: "The human being reacts here with immediate feeling as he accepts what he receives; he thanks God for it and lives in faith and confidence that this goodness will continue" (*PR* § 203 Z). The estate's daily activity—work in agriculture—is conducive to a particular ethical and religious attitude.

As in the discussion of the other estates, Hegel demonstrates here the profound consequences of the relation between practical and theoretical spirit. Different types of activity foster or inform different forms of self-consciousness. An individual whose principal activities consist of practices that express only a one-sided, partial account of what we are will generally be unable to come to a comprehensive consciousness of herself. Rather, she will usually develop a correspondingly limited self-understanding. She will not be able to view herself as what she essentially is—free—or to understand what it would mean for the state to manifest freedom. The anthropology, then, and not objective spirit itself, explains why Hegel views each estate as characterized by particular ethical attitudes.[26]

While Hegel agrees that existence in the agricultural estate is not fully free, he sees such an estate as, like the family, essential to providing for differentiation within society by giving external reality to the first moment—whether of the concept or the anthropology. As was the case for women confined to the family, men who belong to this estate and therefore have their activity and convictions dominated by this first moment have not realized the potential inherent within them; they have not become fully what they are and have not fulfilled the most fundamental ethical demands of the anthropology.

### Civil Society

The next sphere of ethical life, civil society, is defined by the element of difference lacking in the first moment. Whereas the family dealt with a small group of people in immediate identity with each other, civil society concerns many individuals who define themselves primarily in contrast to other members of society, corresponding to the self-differentiating, individualistic aspect of self-consciousness in the "Phenomenology." This self-understanding, as a particular end whose own satisfaction is not intrinsically related to that of others, is the most explicit and conscious principle of civil society—and is the dominant one in Avineri's treatment. Nonetheless, there is another equally important yet largely hidden principle of civil society, one of relationship and mutual dependency. As in the "Phenomenology," extreme individualism conceals a universalism within itself. In the first paragraph of the section on civil society, Hegel defines the concept of civil society in terms of these twin principles of particularity and universality: "The concrete person who, as a *particular* person, as a totality of needs and a mixture of natural necessity and arbitrariness, is his own end, is *one principle* of civil society. But this particular person stands essentially in *relation [Beziehung]* to other similar particulars, and their relation is such that each asserts itself and gains satisfaction through the others, and thus at the same time through the exclusive *mediation* of the form of *universality*, which is *the second principle*" (*PR* § 182). With regard to this first principle, "[i]n civil society, each individual is his own end, and all else means nothing to him" (*PR* § 182 Z). Here, the conception of the free market developed by British political economists is central (*PR* § 189 A). As Avineri rightly emphasizes, the market dominates civil society as Hegel conceives of it. Civil society's other principle, universality, necessarily remains concealed or misunderstood as long as we remain within this sphere. Civil society is defined by the apparent separation of the two principles, in spite of their intrinsic unity (*PR* § 184; *Rph III*, 201–2).

To complement Avineri's treatment of the first side of civil society, its other principle—universality—must be stressed. Viewing themselves as the only important ends, individuals in civil society initially acknowledge the importance of others merely as means (*PR* §§ 182 Z, 187). They can achieve their own goals most effectively by working together with others, as in the division of labor to increase production. The individual's satisfaction is thus mediated by others (*PR* § 192). The ethical and universal significance of such collaboration is initially lost on the individuals; yet without being fully conscious of it, "[i]n furthering my end, I further the universal, and this in turn furthers my end" (*PR* § 184 Z).

Concretely, this produces not only the division of labor but also a schooling of desire such that my pursuit of my own welfare is coordinated with others' welfare. By working to earn money and then using this money to purchase goods I desire, I support an economy that allows others to do the same. Hegel also thinks that we will be led to desire largely what others desire. Conformity requires less effort and is therefore more satisfying: "To this extent, everything particular takes on a social character; in the manner of dress and times of meals, there are certain conventions which one must accept, for in such matters, it is not worth the trouble to seek to display one's own insight, and it is wisest to act as others do" (*PR* § 192 Z). Thus Hegel explains why a society that self-consciously emphasizes individual satisfaction can lead to such high degrees of conformism. This largely unconscious process, however, develops the universal dimension of civil society; it gradually exposes, though only partially, what we share, the extent to which we do not simply stand opposed to one another.[27]

Initially, to the extent that individuals are conscious of this relationship to others, they see it as a limitation; collaboration is a necessary means, not an end in itself: "This unity [of particularity and universality] is not that of ethical identity, because at this level of division . . . , the two principles are self-sufficient; and for the same reason, it is present not as *freedom*, but as the *necessity* whereby the *particular* must rise to the *form of universality* and seek to find its subsistence in this form" (*PR* § 186). Because of this apparent antagonism between particularity and universality, civil society is inadequate as an ethical ideal: "Ethical life is here lost in its extremes" (*PR* § 184 Z). Individuals whose consciousness is dominated by this sphere remain profoundly unaware of their own essence.

This estrangement of particularity and universality is partially overcome within civil society itself, and civil society as a whole can be seen as the process of overcoming this internal division. Yet this overcoming is the development within the sphere whose culmination marks the transition to the next sphere, the state. Accordingly, the institutions that make up civil society are not only businesses. As a middle level between the family and the state, civil society includes other forms of organization that mediate between these two. Common interests lead members of the same profession to band together into what Hegel calls corporations, which are trade associations closer in resemblance to guilds than to what we call corporations today (*PR* § 251).[28] Such groups form a kind of second family, which Hegel identifies, following the family, as the "second . . . *ethical* root of the state" (*PR* § 255). Corporations are groupings larger than the family that define their own interests commonly in relation to other members yet over against the interests of nonmembers. Like a union or industry coalition, they are thus more universal than the lone economic actor yet still particular and exclusive in relation to those outside the group. For this reason, they form an important step toward the sphere of the state and come at the end of the discussion of civil society.[29]

Such steps toward overcoming egoism as the only explicit and conscious principle of civil society are, however, always only partial insofar as we remain within civil society. Correspondingly, the estate whose life is centered in this sphere has its consciousness dominated by an attitude of antagonism toward others. This is the estate of trade and industry, which "relies for its livelihood on its *work*, on *reflection* and the understanding, as well as essentially on the mediation of the needs and work of others" (*PR* § 204). Because members of this estate seem to provide for themselves, their mutual dependency is concealed and they think of themselves as independent (*PR* § 204 Z). Their daily activity to provide for themselves and pursue their own self-interest shapes a consciousness that prioritizes independence and freedom from external restraint.[30] Even their corporations are established to promote a collective but still limited self-interest.[31] Freedom is thus a central value to this group, but it is understood—or rather, misunderstood—principally as negative freedom. Moreover, this estate's ethical views are dominated by the moral standpoint (*PR* § 207), failing to achieve the reflective ethical life essential to the full realization of freedom. By failing to grasp the fundamental connection between genuine self-interest and the common good, this estate remains divided against itself, unable to realize its true essence and thus—as Avineri fails to recognize— profoundly unfree. It is consumed by the pursuit of material well-being, with little appreciation of higher goods.[32] In calling for a civil society so conceived, Hegel calls for a large segment of society to fail to fulfill the demands of his own anthropology.

In addition to revealing why individuals who "thrive" in civil society are less than fully free, Hegel's anthropology yields further insight into his account of the "rabble." The unending attempt to satisfy ever-increasing desires leads to extremes of both wealth and poverty:

> On the one hand, as the connection of human beings through their needs is *universalized*, and with it the ways in which means of satisfying these needs are devised and made available, the *accumulation of wealth* increases; for the greatest profit is derived from this twofold universality. But on the other hand, the *specialization* and *limitation* of particular work also increase, as do likewise the *dependence* and *want* of the class which is tied to such work; this in turn is tied to an inability to feel and enjoy the wider freedoms, and particularly the spiritual advantages, of civil society. (*PR* § 243)

This result is intrinsic to the dissociation of self-interest and the common good that defines civil society.[33]

In the first place, the poor are "more or less deprived of all the advantages of society, such as the ability to acquire skills and education in general, as well as of the administration of justice, health care, and often even the consolation of religion" (*PR* § 241). Hegel is remarkably sensitive to the concrete difficulties faced by the poor. They remain unconsoled by religion in part because the poor man "cannot go to church in rags," and ministers often prefer to go to "the houses of the rich than the shacks of the poor" (*Rph VI*, 606; see also *Rph III*, 194). At an even deeper level, the inability to provide for oneself and enjoy the benefits of the society contributes to alienation from this society and its values, "to the loss of that feeling of right, integrity, and honor of supporting oneself by one's own activity and work" (*PR* § 244). Hegel's account of the rabble is one of his most concrete discussions of the connection between practical activity and consciousness. Being able to provide for oneself through one's own practical activity contributes to a conviction of independence; doing so through participation in a society's institutions contributes to a belief in the overall justness of those structures. When this is not possible, people tend to lose confidence in and become alienated from these institutions. Hegel emphasizes that this is not a mechanical relationship: "Poverty in itself does not reduce people to a rabble" (*Rph VI*, 609). Yet this practical (rather than theoretical) condition is connected to the rabble *mentality*, which is "the disposition [*Gesinnung*] . . . naturally associated with poverty: inward rebellion against the rich, against society, the government, etc." (*Rph VI*, 609). This is a prime example of the mutual imbrication of theoretical and practical spirit discussed at a more abstract level in subjective spirit.

To limit the impact of misfortune—at both an individual and societal level—Hegel emphasizes the state's right to regulate markets (*PR* § 236) as well as the need to provide structural help rather than just alms for the poor (*PR* §§ 242, 242 A). Inherent in the demand for freedom is the requirement that it not be subject to luck. Concretely, this means that within a society, the individual has the right to demand a subsistence: "No one can assert a right (in the true sense) against nature, but within the condition of society . . . hardship at once assumes the form of a wrong inflicted on this or that class" (*Rph VI*, 609; see also *PR* §§ 230, 240 Z; *Rph III*, 195).[34]

Poverty is an injustice, but Hegel sees no way of solving it and identifies it as one of the most vexing problems of modern society (*PR* § 244 Z). He also sees that further industrialization will only increase the problem (*Rph VI*, 612). The creation of poverty is so intrinsic to civil society as Hegel conceives it that there is no way to eliminate the former without eliminating the latter.[35] Since Hegel sees civil society as essential to society's differentiation, he is unwilling to suggest this step. Perhaps more importantly, the problem is not simply a lack of material goods but the absence of an opportunity to provide for oneself and thereby achieve "the feeling of self-sufficiency and honor" (*PR* § 245).[36] Consequently, even were it possible to provide for the material needs of all members of society through a welfare program, for instance, this dimension of the problem would remain unaddressed. Despite both the numerous mechanisms

Hegel recommends to combat poverty and his unambiguous claim that the poor have a right to subsistence, he never offers a solution that he thinks will succeed: Poverty "will always exist in society, and the greater the wealth, the greater it will be" (*Rph V*, 702; see also *Rph VI*, 612).[37]

This unfreedom of civil society—for those on top as well as those on the bottom of the economic ladder—renders it inadequate to the conception of free spirit. Here again, Hegel incorporates a significant group of unfree individuals into his political vision, such that his concrete political views render unattainable the end of self-realization central to his anthropology.

## The State

The inadequacies of the two previous spheres reveal themselves most fully when contrasted with Hegel's conception of the state. The developed state represents the culmination of the development of modern political society. According to Hegel, it provides the objective realization of spirit's freedom and therefore can satisfy the multiple requirements of Hegelian freedom. As a result, although much of Hegel's treatment considers the institutional structures of the free state—the monarchy, houses of government, civil servants, etc.—he emphasizes that the state is not simply these institutions themselves but just as much the consciousness of members of the state. Because this consciousness reveals the ethical significance of the anthropology more than the institutional arrangements do, my discussion focuses here.

As Hegel describes in the opening paragraph of the section on the state, "The state is the actuality of the ethical Idea—the ethical spirit as substantial will, *revealed* and clear to itself, which thinks and knows itself and implements what it knows insofar as it knows it. It has [1] its immediate existence in *custom* [*Sitte*] and [2] its mediated existence in the *self-consciousness* of the individual, in the individual's knowledge and activity, just as self-consciousness, by virtue of its disposition [*Gesinnung*], has its *substantial freedom* in the state as its essence, its end, and the product of its activity" (*PR* § 257). As the ethical *Idea*, the state includes both the existing practices and institutions—the objective, external side—and the consciousness of these institutions for what they are, the actualization of human freedom. Moreover, this is the consciousness of individual human beings in the state, not some supraindividual entity. Hegel's state, then, does not exist simply over and above individuals but in them. Individuals must be able to see the state as the realization of their own essence and as providing, through their own activity, the actualization of the potential implicit in them. Concretely, it is only because of the kind of society provided and maintained by the institutions of the state that individuals can successfully pursue their own most fundamental interests and self-realization. For this reason and this reason alone, the state is their end. As Allen Wood argues, "it is a serious distortion of Hegel's view to say that he regards true freedom as the freedom of a collective rather than the freedom of individuals. The state is an objective and collective end, but the freedom it actualizes is the freedom of the individuals who are active in its behalf."[38] When Hegel writes of the "*highest duty*" of individuals as being membership in the state, this is because it is only here that individuals can fully realize themselves; it is thus simultaneously a duty to realize oneself (*PR* § 258). Only in this light can we adequately grasp Hegel's emphasis on the state as the proper end of human existence and his claim that spirit realizes itself in states. Without this perspective, Hegel's state can appear to be the totalitarian danger that it is sometimes accused of being.[39]

Entailed in this consciousness, however, is that the individual's subjective desires and inclinations have been raised to the universal. Whereas in civil society individual interest is conceived as over against a common or universal interest, in the state these are united such that both can be fulfilled: "Considered in the abstract, the rationality [of the state] consists in general in the mutually interpenetrating unity of universality and individuality [*Einzelheit*]. Here, in a concrete sense and in terms of its content, it consists in the unity of objective freedom (i.e., of the universal substantial will) and subjective freedom (as the freedom of individual knowledge and of the will in its pursuit of particular ends)" (*PR* § 258 A). This unity is achieved not by sacrificing individual interests but by comprehending where the individual's true interests lie, through the awareness that individuals can only realize themselves by self-conscious participation in and identification with such a state:

> The state is the actuality of concrete freedom. But *concrete freedom* requires that the personal individuality and its particular interests have their full *development* and *recognition of their right* for itself (within the system of the family and of civil society), and also that they should, on the one hand, *pass over* of their own accord into the interest of the universal, and on the other, knowingly and willingly recognize this universal interest even as their own *substantial spirit*, and *actively pursue it* as their *ultimate end*. The effect of this is that the universal does not attain validity or fulfillment without the interest, knowledge, and volition of the

particular, and that individuals do not live as private persons merely for these particular interests without at the same time directing their will to a universal end and acting in conscious awareness of this end. (*PR* § 260)

With regard to individual interests, the state actualizes freedom in two different respects. First, it provides spheres in which particular, individual preferences can be expressed and exercised; the state leaves many choices up to the individual. Second, with regard to the most important interests, those that concern fundamental dimensions of freedom and the institutions necessary to support it, individual interests converge with the universal interests. The individual comes to value or have an interest in freedom, and comes to see this as united with the interest of the modern state. Subjective interests are thus satisfied because they have been raised to the universal; individuals recognize the state as their end because only in it can they fully become who they are. Only by unifying particular and universal interests in this manner can freedom as the coincidence of desire, society's expectations, and right be fully achieved.

This convergence of individual and universal interests is possible only and precisely because we all share the same essence and because this common essence determines our most fundamental interest or end: self-realization or freedom. While this end is concrete enough to provide ethical and political guidance—avoiding an empty formalism—it avoids totalitarianism in part because the anthropology that grounds it does not determine all particular interests but leaves room for subjective and even arbitrary preferences on many different issues. The great virtue of the modern state according to Hegel is its ability to give full range to individual subjectivity and yet to incorporate this into a more universal whole; it achieves its success not by suppressing individuals' subjective freedom but rather by providing for it (*PR* § 260).[40] The freedom involved in the "free" state, then, is not some abstract freedom but precisely the freedom of individual human beings, based in the anthropology: "[T]here is a single principle for both duty and right, namely the personal freedom of human beings" (*PR* § 261 A).

This unification of personal and universal interests is brought about most completely in the estate that occupies itself with the business of the state: the universal class. As the first estate finds its primary ethical orientation in the sphere of the family and the second estate in civil society, the third, universal estate has its ethical life in the state. This estate is made up principally of civil servants, those whose daily activity is directly concerned with the functioning of the state itself. Through such activity, Hegel thinks, they come to identify their particular interests with the ends of the state:

> [T]he service of the state requires those who perform it to sacrifice the independent and discretionary satisfaction of their subjective ends, and thereby gives them the right to find their satisfaction in the performance of their duties, and in this alone. It is here that, in the present context, that link is to be found between universal and particular interests which constitutes the concept of the state and its internal stability (see § 260). . . . The civil servant is not employed, like an agent, to perform a single contingent task, but makes this relationship [to his work] the main interest of his spiritual and particular existence. (*PR* § 294 A)

Hegel makes clear by his reference to paragraph 260 (cited at length above) that the universal class—made up of civil servants—is the group that identifies its own particular interests with the universal interest of the state. As he later argues, "It is integral to the determination [*Bestimmung*] of the *universal estate*—or more precisely, the estate which devotes itself to the *service of the government*—that the universal is the end of its essential activity" (*PR* § 303). To be sure, the interest of the state is not here conceived in terms of a narrow interest in the power, prestige, and wealth of the nation but in terms of the concept of the state as Hegel understands it, i.e., the actualization of freedom. The universal estate identifies its own ends with those of the state because the state's end is universal. In other words, it is essential to this ability to unify personal interests with those of the state that this represent a commitment to institutions that manifest our common essence, our potential for freedom. This is the concrete meaning to Hegel's claim that this group raises its interests to the universal. Only the group that has the opportunity to do this achieves complete freedom, and Hegel links this opportunity explicitly to the universal estate, not the other two.[41]

Because this freedom is based in the anthropology, only the universal class adequately responds to the demands for human self-realization elaborated there. Thus, it is in the account of the universal estate, and only here, that we finally see individuals who achieve the freedom prefigured in and called for by Hegel's theory of human beings. To the extent that others are not conscious of their interests (in the family) or conceive of these interests in opposition to the universal (in civil society), they are not fully free. In trying to justify the existence of groups whose lives are dominated by such perspectives,

Hegel's political thought falls short of the demands of his anthropology. Ultimately, even if we suspect that a perfect unity between individual and universal interests is unattainable, there are varying degrees of falling short of it. We can therefore aim toward it, even if we are doubtful of ever fully realizing the goal.

## Differentiation Revisited

This account of the universal estate returns us to the question of whether it is possible to provide differentiation within society without a hierarchy that necessarily leaves some members of society less than fully free. Each of the conceptions of differentiation emphasized by Taylor, Avineri, and Wood prove problematic for reasons internal to Hegel's thought. At the same time, Hegel's discussion of the state raises the political stakes of differentiation. As optimistic as Hegel can appear in his vision of a group that completely identifies its own interests with the universal good, he also emphasizes the need for power to be distributed. Politically, the estates mediate between the particular individual and the state in such a manner that neither is isolated from the other and the former is integrated into the latter (PR § 302). Giving political significance to "communities and corporations," not just civil servants, prevents the abuse of power (PR § 295; see also PR § 297). Having such legally recognized groups that are independent of the state bureaucracy is important for preventing corruption and the administration of the state to the favor of one group (see PR § 297 Z). Moreover, it is one key to preventing a totalitarian state and central to distinguishing Hegel's constitutional monarchy from an absolute monarchy. Finally, if one aspect of the need for differentiation concerns the need for a balance of power, another concerns the need to give external expression to the various moments of spirit's development.

To fulfill the demands of the anthropology, however, this differentiation cannot create a hierarchy among different members of society. Each member must somehow have the opportunity to express each dimension of his or her essence. While subjective spirit integrates these various dimensions within the individual, objective spirit does not (except within the universal estate). What the anthropology necessitates, then, is a vision of differentiation that is horizontal across society and allows all individuals to express these different dimensions of themselves—perhaps in different spheres of their lives, but without limiting any group to just one sphere. The family, for instance, might serve much of the role Hegel assigns it without limiting anyone's activity and consciousness exclusively to this sphere.[42]

At the same time, an adequate solution must provide for the kind of differentiation that distributes power so as to prevent a totalitarian state, while also linking or mediating between the individual and the state. To do so is to respond to the concerns that Avineri and Taylor make central without uncritically accepting Hegel's vision of civil society and the estates. Rejecting Hegel's particular conception of civil society seems particularly important in contemporary contexts where the danger of a civil society dominating—or masquerading as—the state seems as pressing as the danger of a totalitarian state eliminating civil society. Wood sees the power of multinational corporations to influence the "state" in order to promote their own interests as one of the deepest contemporary challenges to Hegel's vision.[43] An adequate solution must ensure that universal interests retain some control over particular interests, while providing for differentiation so as to prevent one group from taking over supposedly universal interests. This would be entailed by a vision of horizontal rather than vertical differentiation, a vision that aims to leave no one in society driven only by a self-interest that is understood to be opposed to the common interests of the polity.

While it may be possible to reconstruct an account of objective spirit that is adequate to these demands, doing so would require a reformulation of virtually the entire sphere and would extend far beyond the limits of the current project. The present treatment points in this direction and illuminates problems with Hegel's own response, but it does not in itself provide solutions to these problems. Ultimately, Hegel's account of what is required for freedom and thus of what we should aim for—which is grounded in the anthropology—is more compelling than many of the more concrete aspects of his political vision.

### Hegelian Ethics as Mid-level Norms

In light of the criticisms explored in this chapter, an alternative to attempting to rewrite objective spirit would be to express the ethico-political contributions of Hegel's anthropology in terms of what I would like to call mid-level norms.[44] Though they would not satisfy the demand for systematicity central to Hegel's own project, such norms would express at least part of the normative import of his anthropology. They would, therefore, be central to the criteria used to judge the rationality of inherited traditions.[45]

A Hegelian ethics must be fundamentally focused on human development toward a freedom that is self-conscious, self-determining, and in accord with our underlying essence.[46] If we are less confident than Hegel that the existing ethical life—our customs and institutions—manifest freedom as fully as they might, we could describe what the anthropology provides as mid-level norms that function between the most abstract commands, such as Kant's formal requirement of noncontradiction, and the most specific details of how individuals should act or societies should be ordered. We can accept these mid-level norms while rejecting aspects of Hegel's working out of the concrete details in the *Philosophy of Right*. A central norm generated by Hegel's thought is that all human beings should have opportunities to express or externalize each of the multiple elements essential to our being human. While we need spaces in which to express our immediate inclinations and to experience love and trust (the role Hegel assigns to the family), we also each need to have as a significant aspect of our lives an activity that brings to consciousness the convergence of our own deepest interests and the universal interests of the society.

Mid-level norms do not by themselves produce detailed instructions for how to behave or how to organize a society. Consequently, they cannot and do not seek to prescribe how to build a political order from the ground up (an undertaking which Hegel saw as a fundamental problem of the French Revolution). They do, however, provide a basis for both critiquing and justifying the traditions we have inherited. They also recognize that the best way to promote individual freedom may vary from one context to another. In one case, the right to private property may help to undermine unjust aristocratic privileges, while in another, it may intensify an unjust distribution of wealth that powerfully impedes most individuals' ability to realize their freedom.

At the same time, these norms have a more concrete content than Kant's categorical imperative—at least in minimalist interpretations thereof. Whereas the latter provides a criterion for testing an agent's maxims, the Hegelian norms provide an end that ethics should strive to realize. Whereas Kant's categorical imperative claims to draw its justification simply from what it means to be a rational agent, Hegel's claims attend to the specificity of what it means to be a human being. Hegel's discussion of morality indicates that he sees the Kantian requirements as largely valid though insufficient. The mid-level norms are in some sense still abstract, but they move beyond the formality of abstract principles.

The comparison with Kant's ethics returns us to Hegel's critique of a philosophy of "ought" (*Sollen*). The norms Hegel's thought produces are not simply claims for what we ought to do but might or might not do. Although in any given instance we may not move in this direction, the grounding of these claims in the anthropology signifies that they are human objectives, implicit in what it is to be a human being. They generate not simply claims about how society should be but also the claim that humans will—at least over time—push toward a society that satisfies these demands. Their dissatisfaction produces striving for change, sometimes consciously, sometimes unconsciously. This kind of ethics represents not simply an "ought" but also—if not an "is"—at least a becoming. The possibility of "backsliding" is not precluded, nor is it implied that this will be a steady, uninterrupted progress. History indicates that it will not be, and the conception of human beings does not require that it should. The need stands for reflective criticism of what we have inherited. But part of what it means to be human is that the drive for this realization of freedom will eventually reemerge.

# 8 Reconciling Tradition, Authority, and Freedom

## Anthropology in the Philosophy of Religion

The preceding chapters have demonstrated the central role of the anthropology in Hegel's ethical and political thought. The anthropology has proven crucial to Hegel's account of theory's critical potential as well as the process through which we initially appropriate the mores of our society through habituation, then subject them to critical scrutiny, and—where possible—reappropriate them on the basis of their rational justification. The anthropology has thereby been revealed as fundamental to Hegel's reconciliation of inherited tradition with reason and freedom. Because Hegel views religious traditions as the principal bearers of the most significant appropriated habits, this analysis has already demonstrated the relevance of his anthropology to his religious thought. The *Lectures on the Philosophy of Religion*, however, offer the most expansive account of the presence of the anthropology within the sphere of absolute spirit. Moreover, due to the attention it dedicates to the role of authority in the transmittal of tradition, to the relationship among modes of cognition of spirit, and to the conception of the cultus, Hegel's philosophy of religion provides the broadest perspective on his fundamental strategy for reconciling tradition and freedom.

The *Lectures on the Philosophy of Religion* describe a process that begins with an authoritative tradition and makes its way to a self-determining freedom that justifies the tradition with which it began. The authority of tradition is both necessary to begin the process and necessarily undermined by the further developments, which reveal the only entirely adequate justification to be that provided by thinking. As in the account of ethical life, insofar as we are dealing with the consummate religion that satisfies the demands of reason, the feelings, practices, and representations that this tradition conveys and inculcates are preserved with the new justification that thought provides. The culmination of the development therefore retrospectively justifies the ascent. This process is much more apparent in religion than in either of the other spheres of absolute spirit—art and philosophy—because of the function of the church as one of the principal institutions charged with instilling appropriate habits in children and because, as Hegel stresses, one cannot begin with the thinking that characterizes philosophy; the path toward thought must begin with more elementary forms of cognition. Consequently, in examining the *Lectures on the Philosophy of Religion*, the present chapter deepens the account of the process of appropriating and then critically reflecting upon tradition while revealing the continuing significance of anthropology as we move from objective to absolute spirit.[1]

To place the anthropological aspect of the *Lectures on the Philosophy of Religion* in relief requires approaching the material with a very different lens from the one that structures Hegel's presentation.[2] The latter begins with the abstract concept of the Absolute that Hegel claims has been generated by the earlier developments of the system and proceeds via the unfolding of this moment—first within "The Concept of Religion" and then through the historical manifestations of religion in history, in "Determinate Religion." The development is brought to a close in "The Consummate Religion" with (Lutheran) Christianity. Whereas the examination of objective spirit in chapter 6 required some rearrangement of Hegel's presentation of that material, an examination of the philosophy of religion from the perspective of the anthropology effects a more radical reconfiguration.[3]

Like the earlier treatment of objective spirit, the resulting perspective roughly tracks the development of individual human beings. Hegel's most explicit treatment of habituation appears in his discussion of the role of the cultus or church in transmitting the tradition. At this level, typically as children, we take on a religious tradition through habituation, which involves submission to authority. The second moment of the anthropology, relating to self-consciousness, remains largely implicit within the philosophy of religion itself, functioning principally to provide a basis for the third moment. The complex third moment, with both theoretical and practical aspects, appears prominently in "The Knowledge of God" as well as in the discussions of the cultus in both "The Concept of Religion" and "The Consummate Religion" (the first and third parts of the *Lectures*). While Hegel places representation—and therefore the intelligence—in the foreground, he conceives of the theoretical dimension as inseparable from the practical side of religion, which he treats most explicitly in terms of the cultus. Thus, in the philosophy of religion as well, we encounter a developmental process containing both theoretical and practical dimensions which begins with an unconscious appropriation of the norms of a tradition, moves through reflection upon this tradition, and finds reconciliation with this tradition by virtue of judging it rational.

### God, Spirit, and Human Beings

As a prelude to examining the anthropology's role in the philosophy of religion, Hegel's treatment of religion needs to be framed within the larger systemic context. Religion constitutes the second sphere of absolute spirit, following art and preceding philosophy. In turning from objective to absolute spirit, we enter the sphere in which spirit has itself for an object—in which spirit cognizes itself. As sketched in chapter 1, art, religion, and philosophy each portray spirit's attempts to grasp itself. While they share this common goal, however, they pursue it differently—and unequally. Art does so principally through intuition (*Anschauung*), while religion is characterized by representational thinking (*Vorstellung*). As Adriaan Peperzak has pointed out, however, art and religion both employ intuition and representation. The definitive difference is that whereas art's object is still finite, religion—like philosophy—deals with the infinite as its object (*Enz.* §§ 562–63).[4] Employing thought, rather than representation and intuition, philosophy overcomes the limitation or finitude intrinsic to the forms of art and religion. Although Christianity is the consummate religion because it recognizes spirit as spirit (*Enz.* § 384 A), the highest, most adequate recognition of this truth must move beyond the level of religious representational thinking into the realm of philosophy: "To know what God as spirit is— to apprehend this accurately and determinately in thought—requires thorough speculation" (*Enz.* § 564 A).[5] Hegel's account of this relationship thus builds directly upon the relation between representation and thought set out in theoretical spirit. This conception entails not an absolute conflict between religion and philosophy—Hegel rejects those interpretations of religion that posit faith in opposition to reason—but a recognition that philosophy does better what both art and religion seek to do: comprehend spirit.

This understanding of the relation between religion and philosophy thus entails that, for Hegel, "God" ultimately refers to spirit: "*The Absolute is spirit;*

this is the supreme definition of the Absolute" (*Enz.* § 384 A).[6] As Walter
Jaeschke argues, "there is little point in imputing to the Hegelian conception,
whether with positive or critical intent, another idea of God than that which it
develops in philosophical terms."[7] And as Hegel states while introducing the
"Concept of God" in the *Lectures*, "[o]ur starting point (namely, that what we
generally call 'God', or God in an indeterminate sense, is the truth of all things)
is the result of the whole of philosophy. . . . This One is the result of philosophy"
(*VPR* 1:266–67; see also *Enz.* §§ 30–31). The *Lectures* then proceed to explicate or
unfold this as yet indeterminate concept of God.

As we first saw in chapter 1, spirit is the essence of human beings. Hegel
expresses this point in religious language when he claims that "God is only
God insofar as he knows himself; his self-knowledge, further, is his self-
consciousness in humans and the knowledge of humans *of* God, which proceeds to humans' self-knowledge *in* God" (*Enz.* § 564 A). First, since God, or
spirit, only becomes itself through its development, through its becoming self-
knowing, it becomes fully spirit—implicitly and explicitly—only insofar as it
knows itself. Yet God's self-knowledge is nothing other than human beings'
consciousness of God, which is ultimately the same as our comprehension of
spirit, of our essence. Thus, knowledge of God is ultimately self-knowledge,
knowledge of ourselves as spirit, which is to say as "*in* God."

This understanding of religion as having as its ultimate object the Absolute,
spirit, that is our essence coincides precisely with the framing of the philosophy of religion necessitated by the interpretation of the logic sketched in chapter 1. There I argued that Hegel's logic attempts, not to overstep the limits of
reason established by Kant, but rather to undermine the presupposition of
"things-in-themselves" that exist beyond the limits of our thinking. The
resulting conception seeks to articulate the role of thinking in constituting the
object without construing this object as a metaphysical substance. Such a conception of thinking cannot support any conventional theism precisely because
it does not conceive of our thinking as referring to supersensible, metaphysical
substances. Accordingly, we neither should nor can interpret Hegel's use of
"God" as referring to some supersensible, metaphysical entity. While this
interpretation of Hegel's logic is incompatible with a more traditional theism,
it coheres smoothly with an interpretation of the philosophy of religion that
attends to Hegel's account of the relation between religion and philosophy.[8]
Framing the interpretation of Hegel's philosophy of religion in this manner
highlights its predominant concern with the process through which humans
attempt to relate to and grasp spirit through representation.[9] Consequently,

Hegel's broader conception of human beings deeply informs his account of the development of this relationship.

### Habituation and Religion

The first stage of this relationship is illuminated by Hegel's account of habituation. This model underlies the largely unconscious process through which individuals initially learn a tradition. Insofar as the sphere of religion is defined in terms of the relation of subjective *consciousness* to the absolute, habit falls outside the sphere of religion proper; religion as such only begins once a degree of consciousness has been achieved.[10] Nonetheless, at various points in the *Lectures*, Hegel indicates clearly both that religious traditions are initially learned through a process of habituation and that they are the principal bearers of the mores that constitute ethical life. In Hegel's view religion proper only develops on the basis of this tradition that has already been unconsciously appropriated.[11] The most developed analysis of this process occurs in Hegel's discussion of the cultus as the subsisting community or church, one of whose most important functions is to instill these habits in children.

Much as we saw in the discussion of education and ethical life, Hegel describes the assimilation of a tradition as "the concern of education, practice, cultivation. With such education and appropriation it is a question merely of becoming habituated to the good and the true" (*VPR* 3:259).[12] Feelings and intuitions are shaped to constitute habits. Despite the important differences between the habituation involved in walking upright and that involved in learning religious practices and beliefs, they both take place largely without conscious reflection. This process of education into the community includes not only "doctrines" in the sense of beliefs, but also practices. As Hegel describes earlier in the *Lectures*,

> Every individual is accustomed to live within these representations and sensations, and so a spiritual contagion spreads among the people; education plays its part, so that the individuals dwell within the atmosphere of their people. Thus the children, suitably attired and adorned, go along to worship; they share in the rites or have their own role to play in them; in any event they learn the prayers and attend to the representations of the community and of the people, taking their own place within these contexts and accepting them in the same immediate way in which

standardized styles of dress and the manners of everyday life are transmitted. (*VPR* 1:336 n.)

These practices both express doctrines and incorporate them into the individual to form our habits. Participation in the religious community is thus
more than sharing particular beliefs. Ritualized practices, including not only
sacraments but also such practices as "wearing your Sunday best," are integral
to the appropriation of tradition through habituation. Through this process, a
religious tradition comes to constitute our substance, just as Hegel argues in
other accounts of habituation. It is an association so immediate that it is not
actually a relation; it is the immediate unity out of which this relation emerges,
the foundation out of which faith proper develops.[13]

While this is fundamentally a process of education or *Bildung,* the emphasis
differs from that in the discussion of *Bildung* in *Reason in History.* As we saw in
chapter 6, there Hegel tends to describe the tradition as constituting the substance of the individual at such a fundamental level that it is misleading to see it
as something external.[14] In relating this process to the teaching of Christianity
in particular, however, Hegel presents this tradition as an external authority:

> Human beings are already born into this doctrine [*Lehre*]; they have their
> beginnings in this context of valid truth, already present [*vorhandenen*],
> and in the consciousness of it. . . . Since individuals are born into the
> church, they are destined straightaway, while they are still unconscious,
> to participate in this truth, to become partakers of it . . . . Initially, doc-
> trine is related to this individual as something external. The child is at
> first spirit only implicitly, it is not yet realized spirit, is not yet actual as
> spirit; it has only the capability, the potentiality to be spirit, to become
> actual as spirit. Thus the truth is something external to it, and comes to
> the subject initially as something presupposed, acknowledged, and valid.
> This means that the truth necessarily comes to humanity at first as
> authority. (*VPR* 3:257–258)

The doctrine initially appears as simply given and true, not as an object of critical scrutiny or as requiring justification by anything other than its existence. It is
in this sense something positive, something existing, to which individuals must
accustom themselves. Individuals have not chosen it, but it nonetheless exists as
authoritative (*VPR* 1:335 n.). This initial positivity of religion is the same as that
of laws: "[E]ven the ethical comes to us in an external mode, initially in the form

of education, instruction, doctrine: it is simply given to us as something valid as it stands" (*VPR* 3:180). Thus, even though at points in objective spirit—particularly in the philosophy of history—Hegel emphasizes such traditions as not external, whereas here he emphasizes their external aspect, both ultimately refer to the same process: Through habituation, we take on and make into our substance traditions that initially appear to us as something simply given. This tradition comes to constitute who I am. In both cases the process is preconscious, not justified by reflection.

The transmitting and teaching of this doctrine is a central function of the church, which Hegel describes as "essentially a teaching [*lehrende*] church" (*VPR* 3:257). The church preserves the doctrine and presents it as valid: "[I]t is acknowledged and immediately presupposed" (*VPR* 3:257). Through participating in the rites as well as receiving the explicit teaching of the church community, children take on the tradition: "Therefore it is the concern of the church that this habituating and educating of spirit should become ever more inward, that this truth should become ever more identical with the self . . ." (*VPR* 3:260). The church makes this tradition and its teaching part of the substance of individuals. This role for the church is particularly vital because neither art nor philosophy, the other two spheres of absolute spirit, have comparable institutions. The habits relevant to the Absolute must be passed on first and foremost by religion (*VPR* 1:298, 3:257).[15]

The object of the habits transmitted by the church, however, is not limited to the realm of absolute spirit. They provide not only representations of spirit in itself but also the foundations of ethical life. Thus, both religion and ethical life express an understanding of spirit, though they do so in different spheres: "Universally speaking, religion and the foundation of the state are one and the same—they are implicitly and explicitly identical. . . . The implicit and explicit unity is evident from what has been said; religion is knowledge of the highest truth, and this truth, defined more precisely, is free spirit. . . . The state is simply freedom in the world, in actuality. What essentially matters here is the concept of freedom that a people bears within its self-consciousness, for the concept of freedom is realized in the state . . ." (*VPR* 1:339–40).[16] The state objectifies or actualizes a people's concept of God. The state and religion therefore share a common foundation, and it is through the teaching of the church, as well as the transmission of religion in the family, that this foundation first comes to constitute the substance of individual members of a society. Religion is therefore "that moment which integrates the state at the deepest level of the disposition [of its citizens] [*Gesinnung*] . . ." (*PR* § 270 A).

The implications Hegel draws from this point for the relation between church and state are extremely complex and beyond the scope of present concerns. Nonetheless, it bears stressing that Hegel warns of the dangers of fanaticism associated with attempting to actualize religion immediately in the political realm. He also emphatically rejects the notion that this commonality at the core of religion and politics justifies a theocracy.[17] To the contrary, despite what can be considered a common foundation—a concept of spirit— religion and the state diverge by virtue of their belonging to different spheres. The modern state must allow for significant—though not unlimited—religious diversity: "[T]he state can have no say in the content [of religious belief] in so far as this relates to the internal dimension of representation. A state which is strong because its organization is fully developed can adopt a more liberal attitude in this respect, and may completely overlook individual matters which might affect it, or even tolerate communities whose religion does not recognize even their direct duties towards the state (although this naturally depends on the numbers concerned)" (PR § 270 A). The greatness of the modern state lies precisely in its ability to hold together groups with diverse religious views, even those who do not recognize their obligations to the state (Rph III 225). (Here Hegel has principally Mennonites and Quakers in mind.)[18]

As in the case of habit in other spheres, habituation here provides a necessary beginning but must be overcome. Hegel conceives of this habituated form of religion as merely a starting point, which is sublated as one achieves a greater degree of consciousness in one's relation to the Absolute. This initial appropriation provides the basis upon which a more conscious relation can develop, first in intuition and representation and ultimately in thought: "Accordingly, the doctrine of faith is essentially constituted in the church first of all, and then later it is thought, developed consciousness, which also asserts its rights in the matter, adducing the other [forms of truth] to which it has attained by way of the cultivation of thought, by way of philosophy" (VPR 3:257).[19] Hegel views this starting point as necessary in the sense that without it the higher levels do not develop. While it is a foundation in this sense, however, it is not justified from within itself. It is taken on unconsciously and as an authority that is not yet justified. The justification or validity can only be provided retrospectively, much later in the development, from the standpoint of thought. Thus, while Hegel portrays the individual as necessarily accepting this starting point uncritically, on the basis of authority, he explicitly rejects such authority as an adequate justification. Questioning of that authority—reflection—drives spirit forward toward more satisfying forms of cognition.

## The Hidden I in Religion

The second moment or level of the anthropology is considerably more complex than either the first or third moments. It does not constitute a distinct moment within the development of the philosophy of religion, as in the case of morality in objective spirit. Nonetheless—in addition to being an implicit presupposition of the developments in representation and thought—this moment plays an essential role in the account of the reconciliation achieved, specifically in Hegel's stress on the witness of spirit. Whereas within the sphere of objective spirit morality placed the moment of self-consciousness in relief, there is no comparable moment within the philosophy of religion; yet just as we saw self-consciousness incorporated as a necessary aspect of developed ethical life—in the subjective aspect of ethical life—so the I constitutes an essential, but here hidden, element of the reconciliation of the finite with the infinite attained in the sphere of absolute spirit. For this reason, it is most effectively examined as an aspect of this higher stage and analyzed in that context.[20]

## Reconciliation in Religion

Spirit's development beyond the immediacy in which a tradition's representations constitute the individual's substance to a stage of reflection and, ultimately, knowledge prominently displays the significance of Hegel's anthropology within the sphere of absolute spirit. Hegel's most explicit treatment of this development occurs in the account of the "Knowledge of God," the middle section of the first part of the *Lectures*, which tracks many of the developments that constituted theoretical spirit. Reflecting the inseparability of theoretical and practical spirit, however, Hegel's account of religion also gives an essential role to the cultus, which is presented as "practical" in the same sense that the will was in the "Psychology." And while self-consciousness always appears integrated within other moments, the reconciliation toward which this progress aims necessarily integrates self-consciousness as a basic dimension.

### The Theoretical Aspect

Hegel presents the "Knowledge of God" as tracing the development of consciousness out of the unity that characterized the "Concept of God" to the reconciliation between the finite and the infinite achieved in thought. While the individual initially takes on the tradition as a simply given authority, her relation to this content "should not remain in this form" (*VPR* 3:181). It should and—due to its immanent drive—does advance toward higher forms of cognition. In tracing this development in consciousness of the Absolute—through feeling, representation, and thought—Hegel analyzes how one achieves freedom in a tradition. This path recapitulates much of theoretical spirit. Moreover, because Hegel's analysis of the internal contradictions that make this development necessary is often more schematic than developed, reference back to theoretical spirit is particularly valuable for the interpretation of this material.[21] Especially significant for the philosophy of religion is the continuity and connection between the different levels of cognition. Hegel locates these within a hierarchy, but he also stresses what these different levels have in common: All constitute modes of consciousness of the Absolute.

In discussing the forms of knowledge of God, Hegel deals early on with feeling.[22] Like intuition, this mode of consciousness is defined by an immersion in particularity.[23] It is intrinsically connected with the body, and Hegel stresses this corporeal dimension: "The particularity of our own person is its corporeality so that feeling pertains also to this corporeal side. With feelings the blood becomes agitated and we become warm around the heart. That is the character of feeling" (*VPR* 1:286). This knowledge of the Absolute represents a kind of "bodily knowing" that marks our actions and responses. Although these responses are initially acquired through preconscious habit, here—as a form of cognition—these feelings have become a form of consciousness; we have become aware of them, such that they become an object for us. Despite this advance beyond habit, feeling is an "inadequate mode" of consciousness (*VPR* 1:290). The content of feeling can be either good or evil; passions can be ordered or disordered: "feeling is still nothing justificatory, for everything possible is capable of being in feeling" (*VPR* 1:298). Thus, consciousness must develop further; "we must look around for grounds of decision other than those of feeling" (*VPR* 1:290). Yet, as we saw earlier, this development does not leave feeling behind. Hegel's point is that feeling cannot justify actions or beliefs, not that we should seek to rid ourselves of feeling. Moreover, feeling and thought are not simply juxtaposed. They are distinct but related modes of cognition. What is true and valid in feeling can also be expressed in thought. Similarly, while feelings cannot justify themselves, they can and should be cultivated to carry much of the content that can be justified by thought.

The next mode of consciousness is representation, or *Vorstellung*, which is able to express more determinate content than is feeling. It partially overcomes the thoroughly particular character of feeling, as well as intuition, yet it is still characterized by images and metaphors and has not attained the self-transparency Hegel claims for philosophical thinking. This conception of representation—which implicitly draws upon the account in theoretical spirit—underlies Hegel's interpretative approach to religious teachings. He argues for allegorical rather than literal meanings of the myths concerning Prometheus, Pandora's box, and the tree of knowledge, for instance. Hegel's interpretation of much religious teaching in terms of representational allegories thus has a strongly demythologizing impact. History—or narrative—is a particularly common mode of representation: "For representation, history [*Geschichte*] exists in the mode in which it presents itself as story [*Geschichte*], or the way in which it exists in appearance. But all the same, even for those whose thoughts and concepts have not yet attained any determinate formation, that inner power is contained in a history of this kind. They feel it, and have an obscure consciousness of those powers" (*VPR* 1:295). Representations thus convey religious truths even to those who do not clearly "see through" the allegories. This is not only possible, it is the norm: "religion is the consciousness of absolute truth in the way that it occurs for all human beings" (*VPR* 1:292).[24] Moreover, while thought can surpass reflection, Hegel's developmental account entails that such thinking only emerges on the basis of what has already come to expression in representation.

Hegel makes apparent the limitations of a consciousness of spirit that remains at the level of representation when he contrasts representation with thinking. Whereas the former is characterized by particularity and contingency, the latter achieves a universality in which the developments and internal relations are necessary rather than contingent (*VPR* 1:299–301). As in theoretical spirit, thought takes what is essential in the content of the representations and expresses it in a more universal form. The distinction between the medium—the allegory—and the message or content is overcome. This process is the philosophizing of religion, the very task of the *Lectures on the Philosophy of Religion*. Hegel's entire philosophical project, in fact, can be described as thought's raising the content of representation into universality. This thinking provides the highest form of cognition of spirit. Here the immanent development driving the intelligence from feeling, through representation, comes to rest: "The highest need of the human spirit, however, is so to think that the witness of spirit is present not merely in that first resonating mode of sympathy, nor in the second way of providing firm foundations upon which views may be established and firm presuppositions from which conclusions can be drawn

and deductions made. The witness of spirit in its highest form is that of philosophy, according to which the concept develops the truth purely as such from
itself without presuppositions" (*VPR* 3:183; see also 3:211). Up until this point,
the cognition of spirit has been determined—to greater or lesser degrees—by
something other than spirit itself. In the imagery characteristic of representation, for instance, spirit appears as partly contingent, rather than as expressing
nothing other than itself. Even the revealed, consummate religion initially
appears as merely positive. Only in thought is the drive underlying cognition's
development satisfied: "[I]nsofar as thinking begins to posit an antithesis to the
concrete and places itself in opposition to the concrete, the process of thinking
consists in carrying through this opposition until it arrives at reconciliation"
(*VPR* 3: 268–69).

Philosophy thus validates, for the first time, the content that has been
expressed in religion; only thinking can provide a justification that is adequate
to spirit. It justifies religion on the basis of the latter's rationality. While this
culmination can only be reached through traversing a process that begins with
the "mere" authority of tradition, at the culmination of the process thinking
justifies all that was valid in the forms of cognition traversed up until this point.
Hegel describes this process as a whole in a single passage:

> The main ground, the one ground for faith in God [which Hegel uses
> here specifically to refer to the first mode of consciousness] is authority,
> the fact that others—those who matter to me, those whom I revere and in
> whom I have confidence that they know what is true—believe it, that
> they are in possession of this knowledge. Belief rests upon testimony and
> so has a ground. But the absolutely proper ground of belief, the absolute
> testimony to the content of a religion, is the witness of the spirit and not
> miracle or external, historical verification. The genuine content of a reli-
> gion has for its verification the witness of one's own spirit, that this con-
> tent conforms to the nature of my spirit and satisfies the needs of my
> spirit. (*VPR* 1:284–85; see also 3:181–82, 253)

If we human beings are—as Hegel argues—creatures defined by a potential to
become free, the only entirely satisfactory justification is one that corresponds
to our own highest potential, which in the realm of cognition is thought. For
Hegel, neither history nor a tradition on its own can provide this. Yet thinking
does justify the content of religion. The latter is not a mere means to the end of
philosophy but an expression—in the form of representation—of what spirit

is. Although this form is inadequate in relation to the thinking of spirit provided by philosophy, it is still justified as a representation.

Central to Hegel's account of the significance of thought in this development is that it provides the most adequate witness of spirit. As he states almost at the end of the lectures: "The witness of spirit is thought" (*VPR* 3:268). The importance of the witness of spirit throughout the lectures—even in the earlier forms of consciousness of God—expresses the necessary role of subjectivity within the sphere of absolute spirit. Just as developed ethical life incorporates the moment of self-consciousness in its subjective dimension, so religion must include a moment of self-conscious affirmation by the individual subject. It cannot remain merely habitual or taken for granted but must be brought to the level of consciousness. As in ethical life, the most adequate form is the one that endorses the relevant practices, commitments, and institutions on the basis of their rationality. For this reason, miracles cannot possibly provide adequate verification of the truth of religion (*VPR* 3:182). As Hegel expresses this point in the 1824 lectures, "The belief in miracles, however, is faith demanded for a content that is contingent, and hence is not true faith, for true faith has no contingent content" (*VPR* 1:239).

Paralleling Hegel's linkage of this point as it bears on ethical life to the modern ethical and political world, he here associates the demand for rational assent specifically with Protestantism: "Protestantism requires that human beings should believe only what they know—that their conscience, being something sacred, ought to be inviolable" (*VPR* 1:344). We can appreciate what Hegel here seeks to integrate into the account of religion without committing ourselves to his portrayals of either Protestantism or other traditions. While Hegel's philosophy of religion does not contain a separate moment corresponding to self-consciousness, a crucial feature of what makes Protestantism—as Hegel interprets it—the consummate religion is that it incorporates this moment of subjectivity by making the witness of spirit, not solely the objective content, essential to religion.

The Practical Aspect

In certain respects, Hegel's treatment of the practical side of religion bears greater similarity to the structure of the "Psychology" within subjective spirit than do sections of the *Philosophy of Right.* In the "Concept of Religion," the second section culminates in thought, which initially appears to have completed the development, since it appears to resolve the contradictions that have been driving the development up until this point. In the 1827 lectures, the subsequent discussion of the cultus then begins by contrasting the theoretical relationship considered in the previous section with the practical relationship to be considered in the cultus. Whereas the former begins with the subject immersed in the object, the latter begins with the subject: "I exist on my own account, I stand over against the object, and I now have to bring forth my own union with it" (*VPR* 1:330). Thus, as in the anthropology, the theoretical begins with determination provided by the object, the practical with determination provided by the subject.[25]

Hegel's framing of the account of the cultus in terms of the contrast between the theoretical and the practical (already set out in subjective spirit) suggests that the cultus will deal with the practices that express the consciousness of spirit that is expressed theoretically in representations and thinking.[26] It will therefore both reflect and further illuminate the complex interrelationship of the theoretical and practical in Hegel's thought. At the same time, not all of Hegel's discussion of the cultus concerns expressions of consciousness. As we saw above, the treatment of the cultus, especially the discussion of the subsisting community, is also the context in which Hegel provides some of his most explicit discussion of the process through which children are imbued with the relevant habits of their traditions. Thus, like his account of the "Knowledge of God," Hegel's analysis of the cultus moves between a largely preconscious level associated with habituation and a more conscious level in which actions express a particular understanding of spirit. Both perspectives deal with the same, often ritualized, practices, but the individual's relationship to them is very different in the two cases. The cultus therefore provides both the context in which habits are initially inculcated and the site of practices that express a consciousness of spirit. It is with the latter that we are concerned at this point in the analysis.

While each form of the cultus expresses some aspect of what spirit is, Hegel provides the most comprehensive account of the cultus's significance in claiming that "the community itself is the existing spirit, the spirit in its existence, God existing as community" (*VPR* 3:254). As expressed in Christian representations of the Holy Spirit present in the community of believers, the cultus as a whole concerns the union between the human and the Absolute. Of all religions, Christianity, Hegel argues, provides the ultimate account of the presence of the Absolute in the community, which has been elevated to God.

The cultus thus involves the practical overcoming of the separation between the subject and the Absolute—in more religious language, the actualization of the reconciliation of God with humanity (*VPR* 3:331). Hegel discusses different forms of the cultus as expressive of aspects of this union. The second form, for instance, contains "the external forms through which the feeling of reconciliation is brought forth in an external and sensible manner, as for instance the fact that in the sacraments reconciliation is brought into feeling, into the here and now of present and sensible consciousness; and all the manifold actions embraced under the heading of sacrifice. That very negation, about which our insight (in the case of the theoretical consciousness) was that the subject rises above the finite and consciousness of the finite, is now consciously accomplished in the cultus . . ." (*VPR* 1:333–34). Hegel's description of this second form presents the role of the practices of the cultus as expressing a particular consciousness of spirit. The practical side of the relationship gives this consciousness an "external form," which in turn further develops the consciousness expressed in the theoretical side as well. In the case of some types of sacrifice, for example, "the sensible enjoyment [of the sacrifice], for instance the eating and drinking, is itself the negation of external things. Thus from this negation or from the sacrifice one advances to enjoyment, to *consciousness of having posited oneself in unity with God by means of it.* The sensible enjoyment is linked directly with what is higher, with *consciousness of the linkage with God*" (*VPR* 1:334, emphasis added). In passages such as these, Hegel makes explicit that the practical contributes to the development of the theoretical within the realm of absolute spirit as well.

Paralleling the account of practical spirit—and the treatment of objective spirit as a whole—the practices of the cultus serve not only to contribute to the further development of cognition of spirit but also to actualize this theoretical moment. The reconciliation that is achieved inwardly must also be given expression: "In order that reconciliation may be real, it is required that it should be known in this development, in this totality; it should be present and brought forth" (*VPR* 3:262). An exclusively interior reconciliation is inadequate; "this reconciliation should also be accomplished in the worldly realm" (*VPR* 3:263). In the account of the consummate religion, Hegel first discusses two inadequate forms of this reconciliation: The first, "monkish withdrawal," renounces the world and therefore fails to actualize this reconciliation. In the second strategy for expressing this reconciliation, "worldliness and religiosity" relate to each other externally, by having the church dominate a world that is in itself unreconciled (*VPR* 3:263–64). Neither of these forms provides a genuine reconciliation.

The third, adequate form resolves the contradiction between the world and the divine by having the latter entirely permeate the former, so that "the worldly, because it has been thus conformed to the concept, reason, and eternal truth, is freedom that has become concrete and will that is rational" (*VPR* 3:264).[27] The practices of the cultus here express what spirit is. In doing so, however, they bring us explicitly into the realm of ethical life. We are not dealing only with practices pertaining to a religious community conceived of as distinct from the ethical and political realm: "[T]he ethical life is the most genuine cultus" (*VPR* 1:334). As Michael Theunissen argues, "the practical activity of the cultus must without exception take place in the medium of human intersubjectivity as well. . . . To be precise, the intersubjectivity inseparably bound to these activities is in essence not that of a private community in flight from the world but a public intersubjectivity of a society that is in principle worldwide . . . ."[28] Insofar as we understand the cultus in these terms, we understand the ethical mores and political institutions that constitute our society as expressions of spirit. In precisely this sense, Hegel can claim that "[t]he institutions of ethical life are divine institutions . . ." (*VPR* 3:264). They constitute a developed cultus to the extent that they are rational.

At the culmination of this development, the practices must not only be rational; they must be known as rational by the participants. Freedom requires that the objectively rational content be brought together with a subjective con-sciousness that knows the content as rational: "blind obedience is regarded as holy, whereas the ethical [*das Sittliche*] is an obedience in freedom, a free and rational will, an obedience of the subject toward the ethical" (*VPR* 3:264–65). When this is achieved, the theoretical and practical have been reconciled, such that we are at a level corresponding to the free spirit of the "Psychology." Hegel treats the final reconciliation as the third moment, uniting the theoretical and the practical, in the rich final pages of the 1827 lectures (*VPR* 3:267–70). This moment "consists in the fact that subjectivity develops the content from itself, to be sure, but in accord with necessity. It knows and acknowledges that a con-tent is necessary and that this necessary content is objective, having being in and for itself. This is the standpoint of philosophy, according to which the con-tent takes refuge in the concept and obtains its justification by thinking. . . . It is free reason, which has being on its own account, that develops the content in accord with its necessity, and justifies the content of truth. This is the stand-point of a knowledge that recognizes and cognizes a truth" (*VPR* 3:267). The positive content that is actual is known as expressing the essence of spirit itself. This complete knowledge, however, can be attained only by philosophy, not within religion itself. This standpoint therefore "is the justification of religion, especially of the Christian religion, the true religion; it knows the content [of religion] in accord with its necessity and reason. . . . The content is justified by the witness of spirit, insofar as it is thinking spirit. The witness of spirit is thought. Thought knows the form and determinacy of the appearance, and hence also the limits of the form. . . . Sustained by philosophy, religion receives its justification from thinking consciousness" (VPR 3:268). The culmination of this development therefore simultaneously surpasses religion, moving from religion as such to philosophy, and justifies religion in a way that was impossible from within religion itself. Only here is spirit satisfied and free. Like the other conclusions we have seen, however, this is not an exclusively cognitive one. Even in absolute spirit, the culmination incorporates the practical dimension as integral. Thus, "This reconciliation is philosophy. Philosophy is to this extent theology. It presents the reconciliation of God with himself and with nature, showing that nature, otherness, is implicitly divine, and that the raising of itself to reconciliation is on the one hand what finite spirit implicitly is, while on the other hand it arrives at this reconciliation, or brings it forth, in world history" (VPR 3:269; see also 3:212). Spirit is at once known as our essence and self-consciously actualized in the world.

This culmination rises from the sphere of religion to that of philosophy, yet in doing so it validates precisely the representations and associated practices of a religious tradition. That is, even when Hegel ultimately raises the cultus to the level of ethical life, he does not suggest that this renders practices of devotion, worship, sacrifice, and so forth irrelevant or obsolete. To the contrary, philosophy identifies what is rational in them and thereby validates them, defending their significance as expressions of the truth. Nonetheless, the transformation in consciousness achieved in the ascent to thought also transforms the understanding of those rituals. They must be understood as expressions of a representational understanding of the Absolute, much as Hegel interprets the representations that constitute much of the content of Christian doctrines.[29] They are thus retained yet understood differently than they are by the believer who has not attained this standpoint. Hegel could therefore still justify their performance as expressive of truth, yet adopt a distinct attitude toward them.[30]

A further—though merely instrumental—reason for their retention within Hegel's vision concerns their necessary role in launching individuals onto the path toward thinking in the first place. As discussed in the account of habituation, the cultus as the subsisting church plays an essential role in first habituating the child to specific representations of the absolute and corresponding practices. Hegel's underlying account of the relationship between feeling, representation, and thought entails that we must begin here and cannot start with thinking.[31] Within the realm of absolute spirit, only religion provides the institutions to perform this function. Although Hegel notes that "philosophy is a continual cultus" as well, he does not suggest that it could replace the cultus provided by religion (VPR 1:334). One must begin with religion, not philosophy. The cultus thus retains a necessary role for Hegel.[32]

In this cultus and with this knowledge of spirit—and only there—we are free. We know and actualize spirit as our own self-determining essence. We recognize the mores and institutions of our world as manifestations of this essence and know that we actualize ourselves through participation in these practices. Just as we saw in the account of developed ethical life, complete freedom is only possible in a society where the practices can be validated on the basis of thinking. Only there do we find ourselves entirely at home.

Within the context of religion in particular, this entails that we can find ourselves at home in a tradition only when its representations and the practices of its cultus express a conception of spirit that is justified by thought. Hegel's philosophy of religion thus builds upon the anthropology to develop a powerful but demanding strategy for reconciling authority and tradition with freedom. An inherited tradition provides the starting point for an ascending pathway through reflection and criticism to thought. Adequate justification for this path, however, can only be provided at its culmination—that is, retrospectively from the standpoint of free thought or reason. Through this combination, Hegel seeks to recuperate the content of tradition yet to justify this content with reason. Such a "philosophizing" of religion can only preserve the essential content of a religion if the religion's content is implicitly rational and capable of philosophical expression. Otherwise, the critical dimension of thought undermines, or at least significantly transforms, the content. It is therefore an extremely demanding vision.[33] In providing this reconciliation, however, the culmination of Hegel's philosophy of religion further explicates the conception of freedom central to Hegel's philosophy of spirit as a whole. It reveals a profound account of freedom that consistently seeks to incorporate both subjectivity and the opportunity for actualization in the world in the only manner appropriate to Hegel's complex vision of human beings.

# Postscript

*Tragedy or Liberation?*

In many respects, the vision of freedom that emerges from Hegel is deeply optimistic, verging on spectacular. It portrays a society, a life, in which we can and do reflect critically upon our inherited traditions and the institutions around us and find them rational and adequate expressions of who we are. Individual desires, social expectations, the good of society, and right all converge in the most extraordinary manner. Although we cannot claim to have achieved this freedom yet, it is at once inspiring and daunting. It can be admired for its ability to draw us ever onward, to outline an ideal so high that we should never be content to rest on our laurels.

Yet the glass can also be seen as half empty. Precisely its ideal nature can be seen as condemning us to self-alienation, to living in societies where our deepest habits are most likely at odds with rationality and our own reflective opinions. Because we are not at the end of history, we have grown up with habits that cannot be found entirely justifiable. Habits we acquire early run deep. They can theoretically be brought to consciousness and articulated, but—though progress is possible—Hegel is not optimistic about the practical possibilities for change. Unlike those who would allow expansive possibilities for self-transformation, Hegel thinks that we change slowly. We are historical creatures, deeply shaped by our traditions.

These tragic concerns are only strengthened if we take seriously the pluralism within our heritage. The habits we inherit do not comprise a whole. This is particularly the case in contemporary pluralistic societies, but it was the case in Hegel's day as well. We are heirs to multiple and frequently conflicting traditions. The conflicts that inevitably emerge between incompatible commitments may enhance our ability to develop critical distance from any of these particular traditions. They may enable us to forge a new synthesis or fusion; the glass is half full as well. But the power of habit also means that even in those cases where an individual is able to reflect and self-consciously choose a particular set of values, this new outlook will likely conflict with deeply ingrained habits that we will be unable to root out entirely. Perhaps we are ultimately not that different from Antigone as Hegel sees her, trapped by inescapable but irreconcilable claims.

This more tragic response is entirely compatible with the anthropology and the account of freedom that Hegel's thought yields. Freedom's grandeur and unattainability are inseparable. Even the tragic emphasis does not undermine the possibility of progress, however, and should not blind us to the profound difference between different degrees of freedom and oppression. The pervasive role of development in Hegel's thought makes this point. The unattainability of this freedom need not make us indifferent or incapacitate us. At its best, this tragic note reminds us that complete freedom is always beyond us and that we must always be suspicious of the intrinsically dangerous claim to have achieved it. Yet, if we add an element of hope, perhaps it need not prevent Hegel from inspiring us to borrow the words of Martin Luther King, Jr.: "I've seen the Promised Land. I may not get there with you. But I want you to know tonight, that we, as a people, will get to the Promised Land." Whenever we—as individuals—utter King's words, however, we must do so with the knowledge and conviction that, like King, we will not live to see this freedom realized.

# Notes

## Introduction

1. By contrast, a number of interpreters, such as Kolb (1986), have claimed to take Hegel's systematic claims seriously by applying the categories and analysis of the logic directly to the sphere of objective spirit. Although such a project can be fruitful, as an attempt to adhere to Hegel's own claims regarding the structure of his thought, the approach is inadequate.

2. Peperzak 1987b, 49, emphasis in original. Translations from this text are my own.

3. Regarding the relationship between anthropology and ethics in contemporary ethical debates, see Taylor 1995, especially 182.

4. 1975, 80.

5. 1990, 17. For another example, see Grégoire 1958, 10.

6. See the transition from the treatment of nature in chapter 13 to the treatment of objective spirit, beginning in chapter 14. Despite all that the *Phenomenology of Spirit*—to which Taylor assigns a central role—reveals about anthropology, it lacks the systematic focus on a theory of human beings that characterizes the philosophy of subjective spirit (Taylor 1975). Allen Wood's *Hegel's Ethical Thought* (1990) also claims the centrality of anthropology to Hegel's ethics yet dispenses with a serious engagement with subjective spirit. For a significant counterexample, see Peperzak 2001.

7. As Hegel states in the "Preface to the Second Edition" of the *Encyclopaedia* (1827), "the brevity and compression that an outline makes necessary, with materials that are in any case abstruse, will only permit this second edition to have the same vocation as the first: to serve as a textbook that has to receive the elaboration it needs through an oral commentary" (*Werke* 8:14/4; *GW* 19:5). Professors in German universities were at that time required to provide a text as the basis for their lectures. As Peter Hodgson notes, Hegel viewed the *Encyclopaedia* as well as the *Philosophy of Right* "as compendia for courses of lecture" (Hodgson 1988, 15).

8. These *Zusätze* were compiled by Hegel's students following his sudden death in 1831. They drew unsystematically on lecture notes from lectures given over several years. For this reason, although they can be quite helpful, they lack the authority of either Hegel's own publications or the recent publications of transcriptions of Hegel's lectures by the Hegel-Archiv in Bochum, Germany. On the problems with the *Zusätze* to the third part of the *Encyclopaedia* in particular, see Stederoth 2001, 9–11.

9. *Hegel's Philosophy of Subjective Spirit* (*PSS*), edited and translated by Michael Petry, includes transcriptions of part of Hegel's lectures on subjective spirit, though only on the second of the three sections, the "Phenomenology." These transcriptions are from Hegel's 1825 lectures, still based on the Heidelberg edition of the *Encyclopaedia* (1817). The *Vorlesungen über die Philosophie des Geistes*, however, are transcriptions of lectures based on the text of the 1827 *Encyclopaedia*. Although there are important differences between the 1827 and 1830 editions, such as in the concept of free spirit, these differences are far less significant than the immense differences between those of 1817 and 1827. Moreover, in his introduction to the *VPGst*, Tuschling has indicated the extent to which the 1827-28 lectures show Hegel moving beyond the 1827 *Encyclopaedia* formulation to make important steps toward the conception of subjective spirit expressed in the 1830 edition (Tuschling 1994). Consequently, the 1830 *Encyclopaedia* and the *VPGst* together can be seen as the most reliable account available of Hegel's mature conception of subjective spirit.

10. For a useful survey of the history of reflection on theory and practice in the West, see Lobkowicz 1967.

11. 1991, 121. Translations from this work are my own.

12. 1979, 203. Translations from this work are my own.

13. 2001, 149–50. See also Peperzak 1987b, 39.

14. For this reason, I discuss them both at greater length in chapter 5.

15. See Rawls (1971), Sandel (1982), Taylor (1985a, 1985b, and 1989), and MacIntyre (1984 and 1988). It bears repeating that most of those labeled "communitarians" in this and other contexts reject the term. Nonetheless, it provides a useful rubric for a series of related criticisms of the form of liberalism Rawls defends. For discussions of these and other central figures in this debate, see Stephen Mulhall and Adam Swift's *Liberals and Communitarians* (1992) and Elizabeth Frazer and Nicola Lacey's *The Politics of Community: A Feminist Critique of the Liberal-Communitarian Debate* (1993).

16. Different religious traditions will fare better or worse when judged by the standard of reason—the system is not neutral in this sense—but the traditions themselves do not provide criteria for judgment. Rather, they are judged by criteria found in reason that is independent of tradition. See Kant's *Groundwork of the Metaphysics of Morals* (1964). Rawls's *A Theory of Justice* (1971) is frequently considered the canonical recent work in this tradition. See also Susan Moller Okin's "Political Liberalism, Justice, and Gender" (1994).

17. In discussing communitarian critiques of liberalism, Seyla Benhabib has argued that "as a political theory, 'communitarianism' must primarily be identified *via negativa*, that is, less in terms of the positive social and political philosophy it offers than in light of the powerful critique of liberalism it has developed. It is on account of their shared critique of liberalism that thinkers like Alasdair MacIntyre, Charles Taylor, Michael Walzer and Michael Sandel have been called communitarians" (1992, 70).

18. Thinkers developing such criticisms of liberalism diverge in their views on these issues. Stanley Hauerwas (1981), for instance, focuses on Christian community, while

Charles Taylor (1989) conceives of the modern West in broader terms. Enrique Dussel, in turn, has criticized Taylor for his manner of circumscribing the "modern West" (1996, 129–59).

19. 1990, 214.

20. In chapter 6 I deal with this distinction at much greater length. Through a more detailed analysis of Hegel's anthropology, we can pursue the implications of this point much further than Wood does.

21. 1990, 218.

22. 1990, 222.

23. Wood 1990, 222 provides multiple examples. See also my discussion in chapter 6.

24. Other recent interpretations that stress the role of subjective freedom include Hardimon 1994; Knowles 2002; Neuhouser 2000; Patten 1999; and Tunick 1992, 1994, and 1998. I discuss their contributions in chapter 6.

25. See Taylor 1975, Avineri 1972, and Wood 1990. I examine each of their interpretations in detail at the beginning of chapter 7.

26. See Taylor 1975, 374.

27. See *VPR* 2:415–16.

28. I do not seek to evaluate Hegel's analysis of Protestantism—or other religions—in this work. That task belongs to a more comprehensive examination of his philosophy of religion than is possible in the present context.

29. 1970, viii. Translations from this work are my own.

30. For a detailed commentary that draws upon Hegel's unpublished early lectures as well as later materials in order to study the evolution of his treatment of subjective spirit, see Stederoth, 2001.

31. Framing an examination of the philosophy of religion in this manner highlights Hegel's response to a fundamental issue in modern religious thought: whether tradition and reason can be reconciled. Nonetheless, it does not in itself direct us to many of the other major issues and problems addressed in the philosophy of religion. For this and other reasons, chapter 8 does not pretend to provide a comprehensive account of Hegel's philosophy of religion.

### 1. Developing toward Spirit: Logic, Nature, and Human Beings

1. This context has been extensively examined in a number of works. For a useful discussion of this cultural context, see Taylor 1975, chapter 1. Though Taylor makes a powerful case regarding what Hegel shares with the Romantics of his generation, he overstates Hegel's concern with a reconciliation with nature. For a discussion of Hegel's confrontation with religious questions and challenges in his early work, see Crites 1998. On the immediate philosophical background, see Pippin 1989, chapters 1 through 3. For broad discussions of Hegel's background, see Dickey 1987 and Pinkard 2000.

2. 1990, 5–6.

3. See, for instance, Taylor 1975, 80 and 351.

4. Wood 1990, 6.

5. Wood 1990, 6.

6. See Pippin 1989, 1991, and 1997. See also Brandom 2002, chapters 6 and 7; Kolb 1986; Pinkard 1985 and 1994; and Redding 1996.

7. Pippin 1989, 5.

8. At the same time, they have also provoked adamant opposition; see Peperzak 2001. For important alternative interpretations of the logic, see Klaus Düsing 1976 and Horstmann 1984.

9. Peperzak 2001, 79–80 is very helpful on these issues.

10. The Idea, which is a result of the developments of the logic itself and can therefore only be presented provisionally at this point in Hegel's argument, is the unity of the concept and its objectivity [*Objektivität*] (*Enz.* § 213).

11. See also *WL* 1:44/50 and *PR* § 1.

12. See, for instance, Westphal 2000 and Peperzak 2001.

13. My interpretation here is greatly indebted to Robert Pippin's *Hegel's Idealism: The Satisfactions of Self-Consciousness* (1989). Neither my argument nor the opposing one can be made on the basis of appeals to particular passages alone. An adequate defense of either reading requires a much more extensive discussion of the logic and its development than is possible in the present context.

14. Pippin 1989, 176.

15. See also *WL* 1:25–26/36.

16. 1989, 248.

17. Pippin (1989) is particularly effective in identifying the tasks and goals of Hegel's argument at particular points and identifying the precise sense in which terms are used.

18. Hegel also addresses this issue in the preliminary sections of the *Encyclopaedia Logic*, in the discussion of empiricism.

19. Regarding the difficulty of definitions within the Hegelian dialectic, Nicolai Hartmann states: "Here, all definition is merely that of a moment, a stage in the stream that runs—in unity and without limit—through the whole" (1957, 224, my translation).

20. Ernst Bloch is particularly eloquent on this point (1962, 34).

21. Michael Theunissen highlights the centrality of manifestation to the concept of spirit by maintaining that Hegel's entire system can be characterized, without qualification, as a philosophy of history (1970, 61).

22. Regarding this parallel between Hegel and Aristotle, see Hartmann 1957, esp. 235–36. On the specific connection between Hegel's conception of "*an sich*" and Aristotle's "*potentia*," see *VG* 157/131. For a more comprehensive examination of Hegel's relation to Aristotle, see Ferrarin 2001.

23. In the introduction to the *Phenomenology of Spirit*, Hegel uses the example of the oak tree as a metaphor for spirit's development. My point here is the limit of this metaphor, which lies in the distinction between the spheres of nature and spirit.

24. For two excellent recent works that make Hegel's debt to Rousseau and Kant central, see Franco 1999 and Neuhouser 2000. In Hegel's understanding of spirit's development in freedom, one sees his effort to bring together contemporary conceptions of freedom with a classical teleology, revealing an important sense in which he is a modern attempt to appropriate Aristotle. It is for this reason that Hegel merits special notice in the context of today's efforts to revive Aristotle. This is not to say that Aristotle precludes this level of reflection or consciousness, but it does not play the central role for Aristotle that it does for Hegel.

25. See Kant 1964, 95. Hegel's distinction between *Willkür* and the rational will will be discussed in chapter 4.

26. Similarly, Richard Schacht defines Hegel's conception of freedom as rational, self-conscious self-determination (1972). Because of the rational character of spirit, discussed in chapter 4, I take rational to be already entailed by the concept of self-determination.

27. Peter Steinberger, by contrast, contends that Hegel provides categories that are "supplemental or attendant to the categories of metaphysics strictly understood" (1988, 63). These constitute a method that is distinct from the "content of thought" in the various branches of philosophy, which is then applied in these branches (63). This un-Hegelian distinction between form and content reflects an interpretation of Hegel's logic as metaphysics rather than an account of thinking.

28. 1987b, 47. It is essential to keep in mind, however, that that with which spirit is filled only initially appears as something external but eventually reveals itself as spirit's essence.

29. "Wenn gefragt wird, was der Geist ist, so ist der eigentliche Sinn dieser Frage: was ist das Wahrhafte des Geistes, und das ist gleichbedeutend damit: was ist die Bestimmung des Menschen?—Bestimmung sagt einen Unterschied aus, ein Ziel, einen Zweck, der erreicht werden soll, zu was soll der Mensch sich machen, was *soll* er sein, was in sich durch seine Freiheit hervorbringen? Bestimmung heißt aber auch auf der anderen Seite ebenso das Ursprüngliche, was der Mensch an sich ist. Der Mensch soll sich hervorbringen, aber er kann sich zu nichts anderem machen, kann keinen anderen Zweck haben, als was er ursprünglich an sich ist. Das, was er an sich ist, ist, was man Anlage heißt. Die Natur des Geistes ist, was er ist, hervorzubringen, zur Manifestation, Offenbarung, zum Bewußtsein zu bringen. So ist seine Bestimmung sich zu dem zu machen, was er an sich ist" (*VPGst* 6–7).

30. On spirit as the essence of human beings, see also *Rph III*, 49.

31. See *PSS* 2:85, 223, 295, 397. Although Hegel at times identifies *Anlage* with what we are by nature in contrast to what we become through realizing our essence as spirit, in this case Hegel seems to use it in a broader sense to refer to the underlying structure of spirit, what spirit implicitly—but not yet explicitly—is. This is also suggested by the identification of *Anlage* with what we are implicitly in *Enz.* § 410 A (*PSS* 2:396–97). *PR* § 22 A also contrasts *Anlage*, as potential, with actualization.

32. See *VGP* 2:222/204.

33. Michael Hardimon is particularly clear on these issues (1994, 48–49).

34. See *PR* 26/22 and § 130.

35. See *VPR* 2:424: "The human being as he is by nature is not what he ought to be; he ought to be what he is through spirit, to which end he molds himself by inner illumination, by knowing and willing what is right." On this process of self-creation, see also *Rph II*, 231.

36. Peperzak 1987b, 37. Although Peperzak sees this translation of "become what you are" into "know thyself" as Hegel succumbing to his intellectualizing tendencies, this is not necessarily the case, simply because of all that is involved in the development of this knowledge, i.e., the whole of world history (see Peperzak 1987b, 37).

37. Peperzak 1987b, 49, emphasis in original. I stress this point because some have objected to the idea that Hegel's system even has an ethics; for a discussion, see Wood 1990, 8-10.

38. "[P]erhaps we shall find the best good if we first find the function of a human being. For just as the good, i.e., [doing] well, for a flautist, a sculptor, and every craftsman, and, in general, for whatever has a function and [characteristic] action, seems to depend on its function, the same seems to be true for a human being, if a human being has some function" (Aristotle, *Nicomachean Ethics* 1097b).

39. *Nicomachean Ethics* 1098a. They also share the view that human excellence must be developed through teaching, experience, and habituation; human potential must be manifested or actualized (*Nicomachean Ethics* 1103a–b).

40. Hegel uses the term "Anthropology" (*Anthropologie*) to refer to the first of the three stages of subjective spirit. Used in this manner, it has a much more limited reference than my general use of the term.

41. See, for instance, the reference to religious and ethical aspects of habit in *Enz.* § 410 A and the comments regarding the healthy individual's relation to actuality in § 406 A.

42. Moreover, Tuschling argues that the conception of free spirit (which first appears in the 1827/28 lectures transcribed in the *Vorlesungen über die Philosophie des Geistes* and was then incorporated into the 1830 edition of the *Encyclopaedia*—both of which I will be using extensively here) provides the first adequate basis or grounding for Hegel's final understanding of objective spirit (see Tuschling 1994, xxix–xxxi).

## 2. Habit: The First Overcoming of Natural Determination

1. Fetscher has suggested that Hegel's discussion of the relation between the geography of continents and the populations that occupy them is so ridiculous that it raises the question whether Hegel was playing with the categories of the system (1970, 40–41; see *Enz.* § 393 Z). Similarly, in the *VPGst* Hegel states that "the earth is partitioned, and in general there are four continents. The fifth is an aggregate of scattered islands that show a great immaturity. These differences are what matter, and these terrestrial differences

are connected with differences in the natural determination of human beings. We fully admit that America constitutes another world compared to the old" (39). He then goes on to discuss the three parts of the "old" world—Africa, Asia, and Europe—in terms of the usual three moments of the system. That Hegel so quickly writes off the Americas and other parts of the world and then forces the geographies and races of Africa, Asia, and Europe into his system does suggest that he is playing with possibilities, rather than convinced. Hegel's treatment of Africa, however, is by no means innocent. Robert Bernasconi has argued that Hegel's pejorative attitudes regarding Africa cannot simply be attributed to the poor quality of the information he received and that Hegel himself was guilty of sensationalism (1998, 45).

2. Indigenous people of the Americas are for Hegel so insignificant as to be left entirely outside the system.

3. I assume here that physiological characteristics associated with "race" are in some sense given. Another strategy would be to suggest that these physiological characteristics change with spirit's development. This strategy is hinted at in transcriptions of Hegel's 1825 lectures, included in PSS (2:46).

4. "Spirit is the existing truth of matter, [which is] that matter itself has no truth" (Enz. § 389 A).

5. See VPGst 31.

6. In an article on Hegel's critique of phrenology in the Phenomenology of Spirit, alasdair MacIntyre argues that Hegel's point entails the impossibility of explaining human actions purely in terms of physical characteristics: "Hegel wants to say that if we regard the traits of a rational agent as belonging to the type of item that can stand in a genuinely causal relation to anatomical or physiological or chemical states, then we are misconceiving the traits of a rational agent" (1972a, 227). Thus, MacIntyre sees fundamental motifs in Hegel's thought that stand in tension with any conception of human freedom as constrained by fixed physical features.

7. Nonetheless, in the case of local spirits, Hegel seems to interpret these differences as innate to people from particular countries rather than specifically cultural. In the addition in particular, he suggests that the ethical achievements of any given nation are "the highest development reached by the original disposition of the national character, the spiritual form to which the natural spirit residing in the nation raises itself"; they are the actualization of innate characteristics. He also contends that "national differences are just as fixed as racial diversity," though he links the former to geography and climate (Enz. § 394 Z).

8. See also PR § 187. Bildung is one way of framing central elements of Hegel's project. For two valuable treatments of it, see Neuhouser 2000, 148–65 and Hardimon 1994, 155. On the relation to Greek conceptions of paideia, see Smith 1989, 43 and 175–76.

9. It is worth noting that the details regarding the further subdivisions of natural dispositions, talents, and character which are in the addition are not repeated in the VPGst, suggesting that Hegel either questioned this earlier categorization or at least came to see it as less important.

10. See also Benhabib 1992, 145–50.

11. Benhabib 1992, 254.

12. On this issue, see Hösle 1987, 362–63.

13. See also *VPGst* 129 and Fetscher 1970, 89.

14. See also *VPGst* 128.

15. Hegel's account at this level shows significant parallels to Martin Heidegger's conception of "thrownness." In explicating this concept, Heidegger states, "This characteristic of Dasein's Being—this 'that it is'—is veiled in its 'whence' and 'whither', yet disclosed in itself all the more unveiledly; we call it the *'thrownness'* of this entity into its 'there'; indeed, it is thrown in such a way that, as Being-in-the-world, it is the 'there'. The expression 'thrownness' is meant to suggest the *facticity of its being delivered over"* (1962, § 29). Dasein is thrown into a situation in such a way that it not simply "is there," in a locational sense, but that it "is the 'there.'" Dasein is not some thing distinct from or independent of this "there" into which it has been thrown. Similarly, Hegel's account of habit emphasizes that these modes of behavior are not chosen, since they are primarily a function of the society in which one lives—aspects which become particularly apparent in the sphere of objective spirit. More important, these habits are not external to the subject; they make up our substance, constitute who we are.

### 3. The I and the Individual

1. Following Inwood (1992) and Nisbet (*PR*), I translate "*das Ich*" as "the I" rather than "the ego"—as Petry (*PSS*) and Wallace (*Enz.*, part. 3) do—in order to maintain the connection with the everyday use of "*Ich*" or "I."

2. As Fetscher indicates, "The essence of the I is that *'being-for-self,' that 'reflection,'* that reflecting back [*Rück-spiegelung*], that as a process is identical with (and is effected simultaneously with) the process of consciousness" (1970, 100).

3. Several commentators have rightly emphasized that in its substantive sections the "Phenomenology" is centrally concerned with the guiding themes of Kant's treatment of theoretical reason. See de Vries 1988, 88–89; Fetscher 1970, 100; and Petry 1981, xii. Petry also emphasizes Fichte's and Schelling's roles in this background to this discussion. Given my focus on anthropology, however, these aspects of the section are not central to my treatment.

4. See *Enz.* §§ 413 Z, 423, 423 Z, 437 and *VPGst* 138.

5. 1987, 365

6. See also *Enz.* § 432 Z.

7. Hegel believes that modern European society most fully develops this recognition of the universal I, which is the perspective developed philosophically in the thought of Kant and Fichte.

8. See Hardimon 1994, 160 and 169. Although Hegel's analysis of the I shares much with Kierkegaard's conception of the self—especially as developed in *The Sickness Unto*

*Death*—it is in this dependence of Hegelian "transcendence" on particular social conditions that we see the contrast with the wider accessibility of conceptions of authenticity or faith developed in thinkers such as Kierkegaard, Martin Heidegger, and Rudolf Bultmann.

9. See my discussion of the contrast between potentiality and possibility in chapter 1.

10. 1988, 99.

11. 1970, 99.

12. ". . . daß der Gegenstand vielmehr *Erscheinung* und seine Reflexion-in-sich ein dagegen für sich seiendes *Inneres* und Allgemeines ist."

13. As should be apparent, Hegel here revisits themes also addressed in the logic (and prior to that in the *Phenomenology of Spirit*).

14. Hegel also points out that one is limited in such expressions of desire in that there are some objects that I cannot transform, such as the sun (*VPGst* 165). This limitation constitutes a further reason why self-consciousness cannot achieve satisfaction through desire.

15. Although I will not be treating the 1807 version of the master-slave dialectic, it is worth noting that the centrality of overcoming immediacy in the presentation of the master-slave dialectic in the *Encyclopaedia* and *Vorlesungen über die Philosophie des Geistes* contrasts substantially with the 1807 *Phenomenology,* where this kind of overcoming of particularity plays little role. The difference highlights how central this overcoming is to the development of subjective spirit—and thus Hegel's conception of human beings—in his Berlin period. See *PhG* 145ff./111ff. Whereas the *Encyclopaedia* version of the master-slave dialectic has received little treatment by commentators, the earlier version has been one of the central themes of twentieth-century Hegel scholarship. For perhaps the most influential treatment, see Kojève 1969. Whereas Kojève emphasizes the role of the slave's work for the advancement of the dialectic, Gadamer (1976) emphasizes the slave's fear of death, and Kelly (1972) emphasizes the contribution of the master. In none of these is the overcoming of immediacy central. See also Taylor 1975, 152–57. Wood discusses the *PhG* and *Encyclopaedia* versions together, without identifying contrasts between them; he does, however, refer briefly to the overcoming of particularity (1990, 88). For the most extensive recent treatments of Hegel on recognition, see Siep 1979 and Williams 1992 and 1997.

16. See also *PSS* 3:330–31/*BP* 74–75.

17. While self-consciousness as a concept transcends particular human beings, Hegel is not here positing a superhuman self-consciousness belonging to another being. To interpret this passage in this manner is to import uncritically a non-Hegelian understanding of "self-consciousness." Universal self-consciousness is one self-consciousness insofar as it is abstract and not particular (i.e., not self-interested), a pure moment of the anthropology. It is in this sense that all self-consciousness is the same.

18. Even acknowledging these caveats in Hegel's claims for the widespread recognition afforded by modern Western societies, one can well argue that it is not nearly as widespread or comprehensive as he often suggests.

19. See, for example, Stuart Hampshire 1989, 115.

### 4. Pursuing Reconciliation: Theoretical and Practical Spirit

1. See Tuschling 1994, xviii. For the contrast with the 1827 *Encyclopaedia*, in which the culmination of the subjective spirit in freedom is treated only summarily and without clearly uniting will and intelligence, see *GW* 19, § 351. While free spirit only emerges as a distinct level at this relatively late stage, Hegel is explicit already in the 1817/1818 *Lectures on Natural Right and Political Science* that at the culmination of its development the will is also thinking: "The will's drive is to realize itself in such a way that the will and the intelligence are identical" (*Rph I*, § 7 A). Hegel's emphasis on this unity generally grows through the early 1820s. See *PR* § 21 A; *Rph V*, 150; and *Rph VI*, 107–8.

2. See *PR* §§ 5–24 and corresponding sections of *Rph I, II, III, V*, and *VI*. The discussion in *Rph VI* does, however, advance beyond previous treatments of the relationship between theoretical and practical spirit (102–9).

3. I take up this issue at length in the next chapter.

4. Further, "What, then, is the purpose, the aim, of this production? The knowledge of rationality . . ." (*VPGst* 182).

5. 1991, 121. Translations from this work are my own.

6. 1987b, 46. At the same time, he maintains that another tendency in Hegel's work emphasizes cognition over practical activity (39).

7. See also *VPGst* 185: "The true [rather than one-sided existence] is that there is no *truly* more highly cultivated intelligence without good will, just as there is no cultivated heart without spirit. . . . This drive, to cognize reason, is a drive toward it [reason] and is thus at the same time good will." See also *Enz.* § 443 Z and *Rph VI*, 107–8.

8. Moreover, this sentence comes from the same paragraph cited above in which Hegel sets out knowing as the end of spirit's development. Its placement there emphasizes that it is integral to the conception of knowing under discussion.

9. 1970, 192 and 193, emphasis in original.

10. See also *VPGst* 184.

11. See also *Enz.* § 443. For a concise and very useful outline of this development, see *Rph VI*, 102–4.

12. *Enz.* § 445 A.

13. Thus, as in the section on consciousness, Hegel is confronting problems central to Kant's *Critique of Pure Reason*.

14. With regard to the inadequacy of this form, see *Enz.* § 447 A: "Yet the form of selfish singularity, which spirit has in feeling, is the lowest and worst . . . ."

15. See *VPGst* 188. Goethe represents such a person for Hegel.

16. For an example of a contemporary ethics which gives a central role to the emotions, see Martha Nussbaum's *Love's Knowledge* (1990). As a paradigmatic statement of the emphasis on duty rather than feeling, I have in mind Kant's *Groundwork of the Metaphysics of Morals*.

17. Here, it is important to keep in mind that the German term *allgemein* that is often translated as universal is also the everyday term for "general"; thus, when Hegel

speaks of "*allgemeine*" categories in this context, the claim is not as strong as the English term "universal" suggests.

18. As we will see below, this transformation is not of the same order as that effected by practical spirit.

19. Cf. *VPGst* 219.

20. See *VPGst* 217. A more significant potential objection arises from recent work in cognitive science suggesting that even more abstract concepts are highly dependent on bodily experience of precisely the kind Hegel wants to overcome for the universality of thought. See Lakoff 1987.

21. See *VPGst* 222.

22. Reading the account of mechanical memory, one easily suspects it would be better presented as an account of the potential distortion of one of the stages, which fails by overemphasizing one aspect to the detriment of another, much as Hegel describes various psychological disorders in the "Anthropology." See, for instance, *Enz.* § 408, including the addition.

23. Cf. *VPGst* 225.

24. *Enz.* § 467 Z and *VPGst* 234.

25. See also *Rph VI*, 104.

26. See *VPGst* 224, 225, and 227.

27. This allows Klaus Düsing to argue that "the concept of subjective spirit" is attained "already at the conclusion of the examination of 'theoretical spirit' in the concept of thought" (1979, 203).

28. On this tendency, see Peperzak 1987b, 39.

29. This passage from the *Encyclopaedia* also demonstrates that the transition to practical spirit set out in the *Vorlesungen* does not introduce an argument foreign to the *Encyclopaedia* account. Rather, the relationship is systematically there in the *Encyclopaedia*, though it is incorporated without being made explicit.

30. *Enz.* §§ 443–44; *VPGst* 185–86; *Rph V*, 108–9; and *Rph VI*, 105–6.

31. See also *VPGst* 243.

32. See also *VPGst* 245.

33. This passage comes from the same sentence quoted above, which reads in whole: "Inclinations and passions have as their content the same determinations as practical feeling and likewise, on one hand, have the rational nature of spirit as their basis; and, on the other hand, they are, as belonging to the still subjective and single will, tainted with contingency and appear to the individual as particular and to each other as external and therefore to be related to as unfree necessity" (*Enz.* § 474). The two parts of this sentence, linked by "on the other hand," exemplify Hegel's distinction of the development toward externalization and the development of the content of the internal determination itself. See also *VPGst* 255, where Hegel makes the same transition.

34. Hegel's claim that given impulses are acted upon or made actual only by virtue of being adopted—not simply by virtue of their existence—is a significant aspect of his conception of human freedom. Because impulses or inclinations must be appropriated

in order to become effective, they cannot remove the agent from responsibility for action: "It is a higher honor for a human being to regard himself as guilty than to be innocent. . . . When a man says with regard to an act he has committed that he is not responsible for it, he declares himself to be out of possession of his freedom. What he is responsible for is that what drove or provoked him was related only to the particular, and that he willed what he did, that it was only his in that he made it that" (*VPGst* 257). To remove responsibility would remove freedom. It is a higher estimation of an individual to hold him or her responsible. At the same time, it is essential to keep in mind that although human beings as such have this freedom as their telos, many have not actualized it. Thus, while one may be guilty in light of her highest potential, translating this into a penal philosophy, for instance, requires substantial further analysis.

35. Although Hegel might appear to presuppose this momentary unity—seemingly introducing a unified subject out of nowhere—it is precisely such unity that has been developed in the account of self-consciousness in the "Phenomenology of Spirit."

36. Hegel's conception of arbitrary will receives extensive treatment in his *Philosophy of Right*, the related lectures, and secondary literature on these materials. As in the *Encyclopaedia* and *Vorlesungen*, the fundamental problem with arbitrary will is that "it does not yet have itself as its content and end, so that the subjective side is still something other than the objective . . ." (*PR* § 15 A). The broader anthropological context for this claim places this fundamental issue in the foreground for our discussion. Paul Franco is very precise on the arbitrary will's inadequacy (1999, 165); see also Tunick 1992, 56–60.

37. Since Hegel explicitly bases his concept of *Glückseligkeit* on the concept of eudaemonia and this term has regained currency in recent ethical discussions, I use it rather than the potentially misleading "happiness."

38. *VPGst* 259.

39. The 1827 edition of the *Encyclopaedia* provides further evidence that *Willkür* characterizes the sphere of eudaemonia as well. There, the second moment of practical spirit is labeled "Impulse" and the third "Eudaemonia and Arbitrary Will [*Willkür*]." See *GW* 19.

40. See *PR* §§ 20–21 and Wood 1990, 64.

### 5. From Anthropology to Ethics (1): Theory and Practice

1. Virtually every discussion of Hegel's ethical and political thought addresses them. For important recent analyses that challenge conservative readings of the preface, see Hardimon 1994, 52–83; Wood 1990, 10–11 (and his footnotes in the English translation of *PR*); Neuhouser 2000, 257–60; Knowles 2002, 67–82; Tunick 1992, 152–67, and 1998; and especially Franco 1999, 123–39. Though less recent, Avineri's discussion is also noteworthy (1972, 123–31). For additional secondary discussions rejecting the conservative interpretation, see Franco 1999, 364 n. 10. Sayers provides a more ambivalent recent interpretation (1987). For additional examples of the conservative interpretation, see Tunick 1998, 532 n. 11. See also Adorno 1993, 82–83. In their discussions, Tunick,

Neuhouser, and Smith (1989) stress the possibility of immanent criticism; I return to this issue in chapter 6.

2. Herbert Marcuse, for instance, emphasizes the centrality of the connection between reason and actuality for a leftist appropriation of Hegel's political thought (1960, 11ff.). See also Avineri 1972, 123–31 and Tunick 1992, 153–54.

3. *PR* 389 n. 18 in the English translation. Karl-Heinz Ilting (1973 and 1974) has argued that Hegel's efforts to disguise his true views in his published writings were so substantial that one can distinguish an apparently conservative exoteric Hegel from an esoteric Hegel that comes through in several of his lectures on the same topics. Nonetheless, Dieter Henrich (1983) and Rolf-Peter Horstmann (1974 and 1976) have responded that Ilting overstates the contrast. For a very useful discussion of the debates regarding the significance of the immediate political context, see Tunick 1992, 9–10. On this issue, see also Peperzak 1987a, 15–31.

4. Moreover, while the introduction to the 1819/20 lectures on the *Rechtsphilosophie* does stress the distance between the science of right and any positivist account of the existing state in a way that the *PR* preface does not (*Rph III*, 47–48), it simultaneously articulates the conception of philosophy as recognizing the actualization of reason in the present and maintains that "[p]hilosophy should not overfly its time; it stands within its time, it cognizes the present. The eternally true is not some past or future" (48). Such statements indicate that the claims that raise concern about the preface are not radically different from what Hegel claimed in less public contexts.

5. Hardimon 1994, 52; Henrich 1983, 13–17.

6. See *PR* 25/21, § 1; *VG* 76/66. For the distinction between contingency and actuality in the logic, see *Enz.* § 145. Wood emphasizes the distinction in his note to the English translation of the *Philosophy of Right* (389–90 n. 22). See also Avineri 1972, 127 and Franco 1999, 135–38.

7. Hardimon 1994, 55.

8. In *VG*, see especially section B, "The Actualization of Spirit in History."

9. Both Tunick (1992, 154) and Wood, in his footnotes to the English translation of the *Philosophy of Right* (390), stress the importance of this version to the interpretation of the *Doppelsatz*.

10. Though Hegel's prefaces and introductions are almost always rich in content, he tended to dismiss them as unimportant insofar as they were merely "external and subjective comments" rather than a scientific exposition (*PR* 28/23).

11. 1987, 143.

12. According to Lobkowicz, the conception of "theoria" as a type of life can be traced back to Pythagoras (1967, 5), whereas Aristotle seems to have been the first to use "praxis" in a technical sense (1967, 9).

13. Nicholas Lobkowicz's *Theory and Practice: History of a Concept from Aristotle to Marx* (1967) provides a very helpful account of the development of the discussion in the Western tradition. For a concise treatment of Aristotle's treatment of theory, praxis, and poiesis, see Planty-Bonjour 1983, 20.

14. Lobkowicz points out that in addition to praxis and poiesis, there was another notion: *poros,* "an expression which meant not only hard labor and toil but also, and by no means incidentally, distress, suffering, and even sickness" (Lobkowicz 1967, 17). The contrast between praxis and *poros* highlights that praxis is not concerned or preoccupied with life's basic needs. For Aristotle, when humans are occupied with the satisfaction of basic needs, they are living a largely animal existence and are only marginally human.

15. Lobkowicz 1967, 8. See also his chapter 3, "Thinking and Acting." Moreover, "when Aristotle distinguishes three 'theoretical sciences,' he in fact is speaking about three objects of contemplation: the universal and therefore unperishable features of nature, the mathematical realm which Plato had placed among the Ideas and which Aristotle himself sometimes seems to identify with the heavenly bodies . . . , and the First Causes, which of all things divine obviously are the most eternal ones" (Lobkowicz 1967, 8). Although sciences such as mathematics are today seen as having substantial application for practical tasks, such technological use of science was, according to Lobkowicz, quite foreign to the ancient Greek world.

16. Translations between English and German are difficult on this point. Hegel writes of *praktischer* spirit, but there is no corresponding noun. Generally, the closest term within his writing would be *Handlung,* for action or act. Discussions on this theme in the German secondary literature generally use the term "*Praxis,*" though the term is not as technical or specific in German as it is in English. Hegel uses "*Praxis*" only rarely, and it seems to be synonymous with practical activity (*Rph V,* 109). Nonetheless, "praxis" risks obscuring the distinction between a specifically Aristotelian meaning to the term and the broader sense of "practice." Because the German *Praxis* has a broader meaning than specifically Aristotelian praxis, I translate *Praxis* in passages below as "practice."

17. See Franco 1999, 124–25.

18. Regarding the capitalization of "One" (*Ein*), see *GW* 20, § 2.

19. 1982, 39–40, emphasis in original.

20. See also *VPR* 2:415.

21. 1994, 348.

22. Cf. Hardimon 1994, 28–29.

23. Hans Friedrich Fulda in his *Das Recht der Philosophie in Hegels Philosophie des Rechts* (1968) is one of the few to raise this question directly with regard to the relation of theory and practice in Hegel. In discussing Hegel's sanctioning of critique, he states that "Hegel dealt with the powerless [*machtlose*] practice required by philosophy in relation to political actuality in connection with two world-historical paradigms. Of these, one must ask whether Hegel considered them still unmodified for his own present" (48). Although this manner of asking the question effectively probes the significance of historical development for the relation of theory and practice, Fulda frames his investigation as a whole in terms of the questions, "What right and which corresponding duties does philosophy—as an institution of the society and state—acquire within an actuality determined by the concepts of right? And how are conflicts between this institution and

others to be judged?" (12). To ask what role philosophy should be allowed to have, however, is fundamentally different from a broader consideration of theory that is concerned with what it should do when not *given* the role it should have in an ideal society.
In inquiring about the role of philosophy within the sphere of objective spirit, Fulda
localizes his question far more than a broader analysis of the relation of theory and practice should. As much as Fulda's question might reveal, it is not well suited to asking
about philosophy's role in the unjust state. Translations from this text are my own.

24.  Habermas 1973, 133.

25.  See Bloch 1962, 235.

26.  1973, 133.

27.  Hegel can thereby endorse much of the world brought about by the French
Revolution, particularly the transformations forced by Napoleon upon Germany, without endorsing a revolutionary consciousness (Habermas 1973, 138–39).

28.  Prior to these two, Theunissen also discusses another form of their unity, namely
that "Hegel's philosophy is theory of a practice" (1970, 390). As Theunissen acknowledges, however, theory's having practice as an object is not the same as its being practice
(392). Thus, this point does not entail a unity of theory and practice in any strong sense.
Translations from this text are my own.

29.  1970, 393.

30.  1970, 403.

31.  1970, 403.

32.  1970, 405–6.

33.  1970, 407–8.

34.  1970, 413.

35.  See 1973, 136–39.

36.  As Avineri states, "*The crux of Hegel's argument is that a mere reform of the fran-
chise cannot by itself cure the social problems of English society.* Hegel's essay is one of the
most scathing indictments of English social conditions to come from a continental
writer. Yet his critique is aimed not only at existing conditions in early industrial Britain,
but also at the liberal attempts to overcome through a purely electral reform of parlia-
ment. . . . Hegel believed that English conditions could not be changed unless Britain
underwent a social, as well as political, transformation . . ." (1972, 208–9). See also 1972, 219.

37.  1983, 24.

38.  1983, 21. While Planty-Bonjour does not make this point, this central role for
labor in Hegel's thought means that *poros*, too, transforms the agent and is also an aspect
of practical activity.

39.  Regarding work as transforming the agent, Manfred Riedel traces the development of Hegel's understanding of this issue from his early writings (1984, 10–22, especially 20).

40.  Ritter 1982, 39–40.

41.  1994, 168.

42.  *Nicomachean Ethics* 1094b.

### 6. From Anthropology to Ethics (2): Tradition, Criticism, and Freedom

1. Tunick 1992, 98–99. See also 1992, 72–73, 171. These two dimensions of freedom are also central to Frederick Neuhouser's excellent account (2000, 53, 81, 82–113, 229–32). See also Hardimon 1994, 166; Patten 1999, 44, 59, 191; Steinberger 1988, 153–60, 209; and Wood 1990, 196–98. For a recent interpretation maintaining that freedom does not require moving beyond habit, see Franco 1999, 229–32. Allen Wood (1990) seems to take both sides in this debate without reconciling them; compare 214–18 with 219–23.

2. Frederick Neuhouser, for instance, is forced to interpret Hegel's claims about the identity of institutions with individuals' "essence" in terms of "practical identities," thereby lessening the scope of Hegel's claim (2000, 93–94). Neuhouser also weakens the significance of self-determination by construing it "in the sense that it is determined in accord with their understanding of their [individuals'] own practical identities," rather than as expressing the underlying *Anlage* of human beings (109). Tunick fails to identify the role of the underlying anthropology in providing the criteria according to which one judges inherited norms (1992, 104–7); as a result, to avoid a strongly metaphysical account of Hegelian ethics, he opts for an overly historicized "existentialist" appropriation of Hegel on this issue (104). Very few treatments of Hegel's ethical thought give a significant role to subjective spirit. For important exceptions to the tendency, see Williams 1997 and Peperzak 2001. John McCumber also addresses the existence of habit in higher spheres of spirit; whereas he approaches the issue from the perspective of what it reveals about the downfall of societies—when habits cannot be justified by reason—I focus on the implications for Hegel's conception of freedom: what is necessary for habits to be justified by reason (1990).

3. Cf. Patten 1999, 77. While I find much of Patten's reading excellent, he relies too exclusively upon the concept of recognition—rather than the anthropology as a whole—to ground the account of freedom. The result is a tendency to make the principal justification of the institutions considered in the *PR* simply the promotion of personality—rather than a more complex process of self-actualization—and for abstract right to assume an inordinately central role in the account of Hegel's political thought (134–35, 144–45, 177–78).

4. Thus, interpreting this anthropology together with the reading of the logic set forth in chapter 1 allows us to do justice to Hegel's own claims about the basis for his ethical and political thought in the earlier stages of the system without appealing to the metaphysical claims that so many have attributed to him yet found absurd.

5. This is one of the reasons that Hegel's conception of human beings is both so elusive and so omnipresent. In order to understand the broader significance of subjective spirit for Hegel's overall conception of human beings *and* to provide the proper context for understanding Hegel's comments on human beings that appear in other parts of the system, it is necessary to relate these accounts to each other. I suspect that a principal reason why so many interpreters, even those who have looked seriously at his understanding of human beings, have given so little attention to subjective spirit is that it is quite abstract and often appears only indirectly relevant to ethics. Charles Taylor 1975 and Wood 1990 are significant examples. At the same time, the few commentaries

focused on subjective spirit have left relatively unexamined the connection to Hegel's other comments on human beings. The essays from the 1973 Hegel-Tage on Hegel's philosophical psychology, published in Henrich 1979, on the whole demonstrate this tendency. See also Drüe 1976 and deVries 1988, though neither of these intend a comprehensive treatment of Hegel's theory of human beings.

6. On the centrality of the free will to Hegel's conception of right, see in particular Riedel 1984. See also Neuhouser 2000, 55.

7. This correlation derives from the rough correlation between the moments of the anthropology and the development of individual human beings. (See also *Rph V*, 169 on the order in which ethical institutions emerged in history.) By contrast, Hegel stresses that his ordering of the *Philosophy of Right* does not in any way correspond to historical developments. Whereas the conceptual structures of other spheres of spirit have a loose correspondence to history, objective spirit does not have even this (*PR* § 32).

8. Neuhouser makes the same distinction in his discussion of *Rph II* § 74: "*Sittlichkeit* is [1] objective, real freedom that [2] has an existence in self-consciousness befitting of freedom." Translation and numbering by Neuhouser 2000, 53.

9. The introduction to ethical life in the *Encyclopaedia* presentation of objective spirit also emphasizes the element of consciousness (*Enz.* §§ 513–17). See also *Rph VI*, 406 and *VPG* 134–38/104–7, 540/456. For a discussion of these issues that draws extensively on the *Lectures on the Philosophy of History*, see Patten 1999, 43–44.

10. Hegel characterizes the ethical life of the ancient Greek polis largely in these terms. Its limitation corresponds to the failure to move beyond this habitual stage of ethical life. See *PR* § 185 A; *Rph VI*, 407; *VPG* 308–9/252–53; Patten 1999, 59.

11. "*Subjekt* αα) *ist* sittlich—steht in der Einheit—*ist* gemäß—ββ Bewußtsein des α) Verhältnisses zu Pflichten, sie *sind*, fest—γγ) gibt Zeugnis—hat sich darin—Wille—Geist . . . ."

12. See also *Rph III*, 123–24, 144; Neuhouser 2000, 112.

13. "*Sitte*," the root for *Sittlichkeit*, refers to both distinctly ethical behavior and customs or traditions more broadly. Hegel makes deliberate use of the breadth of the term. For him, ethics is ultimately embedded in the customs and traditions of a good society.

14. Although learning customs generally requires a degree of what we call consciousness, the process is often not conscious in the sense of deliberately reflecting on the norm being learned, and it is in this sense that I use "consciousness" here.

15. See Tunick 1998, 521. While Hegel discusses this process largely in the context of the family, civil society also plays an important role; see Anderson 2001, 199.

16. Thus, although the full justification for Hegel's conception that we are free in living in accord with these customs only becomes apparent in the more developed conception of ethical life, one aspect of their being free is precisely the liberation from natural drives that they entail: "Pedagogy is the art of making human beings ethical: It considers them as natural beings and shows them how they can be reborn, and how their original nature can be transformed into a second, spiritual nature so that this spirituality becomes *habitual* to them" (*PR* § 151 Z).

17. I am grateful to Merold Westphal for his suggestions on this issue.

18. The norms necessary to realize freedom, however, can be at least partially determined on the basis of the general anthropology. The point here is simply that not all, if any, societies possess such norms, and the particular norms they do have—because they are particular—do not constitute part of the general anthropology.

19. See also *PR* §§ 153, 155 N.

20. See also *PR* § 155 N, *Enz.* § 514.

21. It is because these social customs constitute us that Hegel repeatedly emphasizes that the best way to raise good individuals is to raise them in good states. See, for example, *PR* § 153. Dudley Knowles demonstrates the extent to which Hegel's account of patriotism elaborates upon this trusting, habitual relationship to society's mores. As he writes, "The patriotic citizen *habitually* complies with the state's demands, he *trusts* the state as he goes about his business. But there is nothing in this that precludes the citizen asking . . . the philosophical question of what is the basis of this trust . . ." (2002, 318). On patriotism, see *PR* § 268 and Patten 1999, 185–88.

22. For Hegel's critique of theories of human nature so conceived, see *VG* 51/44–45.

23. See subdivision A, "Its [the philosophy of history's] general concept," *VG* 28–49/27–43, especially 28–29/27–28.

24. See also *VG* 44/39.

25. Although Hegel does speak at times of "taking over" these norms, this is largely a preconscious process. It is something we can observe, from an external perspective, about the individual; but during the process the individual generally lacks the consciousness necessary to say this about her own life. Consequently, we already are those norms before we raise questions about being true to ourselves.

26. I am grateful to Sally Sedgwick for suggestions on this point.

27. On the I in abstract right, see *PR* § 35; *Enz.* § 490; *Rph I* § 12 A. See also Riedel 1984, 172; Tunick 1994, 327; Williams 1997, 119, 120, and 135.

28. Charles Taylor, for instance, focuses on morality primarily in this hypostatized mode and therefore treats it quite briefly. See 1975, 376–77; 1979, 83–84.

29. See also *PR* § 106 A.

30. See also *PR* § 132 A.

31. Patten most explicitly discusses these two aspects of subjective freedom (1999, 44). Although the first is important, to reduce subjective freedom to it is to identify subjective freedom with *Willkür* rather than to view it as an intrinsic dimension of the highest form of freedom (see *PR* § 260). Regarding the space for "petty passions and imaginings . . . [to] indulge themselves," see *PR* § 289 A.

32. See *PR* § 137.

33. 1992, 91. Michael Hardimon's discussion is also very useful (1994, 166).

34. "[B]ut *the objective* will, inasmuch as it *lacks the infinite form* of self-consciousness, is the will immersed in its object or condition, whatever the content of the latter may be—it is the will of the child, the ethical [*sittliche*] will, or the slavish will, the superstitious will, etc." (*PR* § 26). In his notes to this paragraph, Hegel explicitly links this moment to a lack of subjective freedom, to heteronomy, and the significance of Kant (*PR* § 26 N). By contrast, Paul Franco maintains that in an ethical world that

incorporates a moment of reflectivity, freedom does not require that all individuals move beyond habit to a reflective consciousness (1999, 226–33). Hegel certainly acknowledges that many people lack this degree of self-consciousness, and at times he seems—unjustifiably—content with that situation. Nonetheless, if we take Hegel's anthropology seriously, it is impossible to view such a habitual or nonreflective acceptance of norms as constituting freedom. On this issue and its consequences for Franco's interpretation, see my review of Paul Franco, *Hegel's Philosophy of Freedom* (2002, 273–74).

35. As discussed below, at least in significant instances Hegel does indicate that freedom is capable of a satisfactory expression in the objective sphere. Cf. Wood 1990, 222.

36. See *PR* §§ 152 A, 257, 258.

37. See *Rph VI*, 89–90.

38. See also *Rph VI*, 398, 400.

39. Peter Steinberger is excellent on the extent to which Hegel preserves Kant's moral insight (1988, 153–60).

40. Cf. *PR* § 258 A.

41. 1987b, 76; see 65–78.

42. If we are to do justice to the centrality of practical spirit to Hegel's anthropology, the degree of perfection of the existing, objective world cannot be a matter of indifference. That is, it is not that there is never a more adequate possible manifestation. If that were the case, history would not have developed; there would have been no drive for the ever more adequate manifestation of reason in the world.

43. As several interpreters have noted, Hegel's assessments of his present were often more sober and even pessimistic than the one presented in the *Philosophy of Right*. See Taylor 1975, 509 and Fackenheim 1967, 234.

44. The closest Hegel comes to providing such a guarantee that the existing customs and norms will be found rational is in his claim that philosophy "is *its own time comprehended in thoughts*" (*PR* 26/21). When taken as the complete account of the relation between theory and practice, this element in Hegel's thought—which entails that theory proceeds from and follows practice and actuality—implies that freedom can only be understood or adequately theorized when it is actual in the world. If this were the case, then whenever we were capable of understanding freedom sufficiently to judge whether a particular political order is rational, we would necessarily live in a rational, free political order. The complex, dialectical relationship between theoretical and practical spirit, however, undermines such an interpretation as a one-sided, inadequate account of the relation between theory and practice. Because theory can also be critical of practice, informing and altering it, Hegel's conception does not entail that we necessarily will or should find the mores of our society rational.

### 7. Equality, Differentiation, and the Universal Estate

1. Similarly, Frederick Neuhouser briefly notes the tension between "the demands of moral subjectivity," which I base within the anthropology, and Hegel's view of women's role in the family as well as his account of a market economy (2000, 273).

2. Thus, Michael Hardimon's formulation of Hegel's position as allowing for a "full human life" even for those who do not achieve self-actualization captures just that aspect of Hegel's political thought that ultimately proves incompatible with his anthropology (1994, 187–88).

3. See *PR* § 142, discussed in the previous chapter.

4. Objective spirit, particularly the *Philosophy of Right* version, has already been extensively discussed in the secondary literature. For extended treatments—in addition to Avineri, Taylor, and Wood—see in particular Franco 1999, Hardimon 1994, Marcuse 1960, Peperzak 1991 and 2001, and Reyburn 1929.

5. See Hardimon 1994, 99; Neuhouser 2000, 37–52; Taylor 1979, 94; and Wood 1990, 197, 238.

6. 1982, 175. See also Riedel 1984, 173.

7. "Hegel's dilemma for modern democracy, put at its simplest, is this: The modern ideology of equality and of total participation leads to a homogenization of society. This shakes men loose from their traditional communities, but cannot replace them as a focus of identity" (1975, 414).

8. 1975, 384.

9. 1975, 415.

10. 1975, 410.

11. 1972, 134.

12. 1972, 134.

13. 1972, 145.

14. 1972, 150.

15. 1972, 151.

16. To be sure, Wood discusses other forms of differentiation as well. See in particular his discussion of the role of corporations in integrating the individual into the larger society (1990, 239–41).

17. 1990, 243–44.

18. 1990, 244.

19. 1990, 244.

20. 1990, 245.

21. 1990, 246.

22. See Wood 1990, 243–44.

23. See Hardimon 1994, 181.

24. As discussed in chapter 8, Hegel assigns the church an essential role in this process as well.

25. Wood 1990, 245.

26. Neuhouser also addresses concerns about the inegalitarian aspects of Hegel's account of estates but argues that "a comparison of early with later sources reveals that Hegel's thought underwent an unmistakable development from the more strongly holistic position described earlier to the view that a defining aim of the rational social order is to allow for all (male) individuals to incorporate, as fully as possible, each of the

types of identities associated with membership in the three basic social spheres" (2000, 141). He then contrasts a passage from the 1818–19 lectures with the discussion at the same point in the *Philosophy of Right*. Even in the latter text, however, sections such as § 203, quoted above, reveal clearly that Hegel still envisions some members of society devoting themselves principally to one mode of activity, such as agricultural labor, correlating with what Hegel sees as a less developed self-consciousness. To give that up would entail abandoning Hegel's conception of the estates. Admittedly, Hegel acknowledges at points that freedom cannot be achieved through participation in only one sphere, as in *PR* § 264 and *Rph III*, 127–28: "[T]he human being fails to achieve his determination [*Bestimmung*] if he is only a father, only a member of civil society, etc." (Both passages are cited in Neuhouser 2000, 141–42.) This admission supports my larger point. Yet Hegel never reconceives the estates in a manner that makes such freedom possible for members of either of the first two estates. In the footnote in which he qualifies the passage from *Rph III*, Neuhouser seems to concede that this inequality remains (2000, 311–12 n. 28).

27. See Wood 1990, 27.

28. See Wood 1990, 282 n. 6.

29. In an interesting discussion of corporations, Joel Anderson stresses their role in educating particular interests to the universal (2001, 197). In doing so, he reveals the extent to which corporations constitute a transition to the state. My point is that precisely when the convergence of the universal and the particular becomes transparent to the actors, we have passed from civil society to the state.

30. See Taylor 1979, 131.

31. Michael Hardimon provides perhaps the most developed argument that Hegel's conception allows for individuals to be both bourgeois and leading a universal life: "[T]he most distinctive thing [Hegel] has in mind by 'leading a general life' is carrying out one's everyday activities within the family and civil society with a certain frame of mind. One views these activities not only as one's private pursuits but also as ways in which the politically organized community of which one is a member actualizes *its* shared form of life. And one engages in these activities not merely for one's own sake or the sake of one's family but also for the sake of the politically organized community itself" (1994, 226; see 218–27). Hardimon's description accurately captures the convergence of individual and universal interests in the universal estate. Hegel is explicit, however, that as long as one remains within the sphere of civil society, the universal interest *appears* divided from the individual's. Hegel describes the resulting consciousness clearly in *PR* §§ 204 and 207, where the bourgeoisie fails to grasp adequately the relationship between the individual and universal interests. See also *PR* § 289.

32. As many have emphasized, this perspective has been particularly apparent in the United States. See, for instance, Avineri 1972, 135 n. 6.

33. See Avineri 1972, 146.

34. Based on the related discussion in *Rph III*, Dieter Henrich argues that Hegel there justifies the right of the poor to rebel (1983, 20). Even if we do read the passages from *Rph III* in this manner, Hegel still never develops this point or allows it to inform

his larger political vision. Thus, while it may expose, it certainly does not resolve the problems that I see in Hegel's conception.

35. See Avineri 1972, 151.

36. Thus, Norbert Waszek points out that Hegel's recommendation of the Scottish policy of licensing "beggars" illustrates not the callousness that it appears to but rather Hegel's understanding of the practice as lessening the shame of poverty and increasing the self-esteem of the poor (1984, 313–14; see also *PR* § 245 A).

37. Joel Anderson suggests that another solution to poverty is implicit in Hegel: the cultivation by the corporations of the "educated consumer." He "believe[s] that Hegel thought that, as members of *Korporationen*, individual consumers can promote the common good—they 'will the universal'—by *spending their money in ways that increase the general resources . . . , thereby alleviating poverty*" (2001, 195). While this may be an important means of lessening poverty, however, Hegel is explicit that no measures he proposes will be sufficient to solve the problem. Moreover, while the corporations are crucial to the transition from civil society to the state—as Anderson clearly demonstrates—their essential role is to advance the interests of their members, where these are understood as distinct from those of the society as a whole. Their interest is thus more general [*allgemein*] than any individual's, yet still not genuinely universal.

38. 1990, 238.

39. On the many misunderstandings associated with Hegel's claim that "es ist der Gang Gottes in der Welt, daß der Staat ist" (*PR* § 258 Z), see Avineri 1972, 176–77.

40. This emphasis on individual subjectivity is one more reason that an adequate conception of freedom must be manifest in individuals, not simply at the level of a society. In other words, every individual must be free; otherwise, such subjectivity is severely limited.

41. Thus, despite the different emphasis, my criticism corresponds to Hardimon's point that "[t]he real power in the Hegelian state lies in the hands of a professional class of civil servants. This—and not the fact that it is a monarchy—is the profoundly anti-republican and disturbing aspect of Hegel's account of the modern state" (1994, 255).

42. Hardimon provides a compelling account of the manner in which the different spheres of ethical life provide outlets for different dimensions of ourselves (1994, 180–83). For precisely this reason, apportioning these opportunities to different members of society is comparable to allowing some members of society to eat and some to drink but none to do both.

43. See Wood 1990, 30.

44. I use the term "norms" to encompass both rule-based ethical guides—associated with Kantianism, for instance—and those guides defined in terms of ends rather than rules—frequently associated with Aristotelianism.

45. This is not to say that they would be the only criteria. As Mark Tunick stresses, Hegel is also concerned with the coherence of our practices to constitute a system (1994, 334–35).

46. On these three elements as defining freedom for Hegel, see Schacht 1972.

### 8. Reconciling Tradition, Authority, and Freedom: Anthropology in the Philosophy of Religion

1. Hegel lectured on the philosophy of religion four times in Berlin, in 1821, 1824, 1827, and 1831 (the last series was not completed due to his death). In the course of these series, Hegel significantly restructured the material. Because they were delivered immediately before the *Vorlesungen über die Philosophie des Geistes* and because they seem to provide Hegel's most developed conception of the philosophy of religion (at least excluding the incomplete 1831 lectures), I focus principally on the 1827 lectures.

2. Moreover, in focusing on the anthropological dimensions of the *Lectures on the Philosophy of Religion*, I necessarily leave unaddressed many of the other issues raised by Hegel's philosophy of religion. This approach does not examine Hegel's interpretation of Protestant Christianity as expressing his vision of spirit, a central task for a more extensive examination of the philosophy of religion. Nor do I address the very significant problems raised by his account of the history of religions in part two of the *Lectures*. I hope to take up these issues in a future project. My purpose here is not a comprehensive treatment of this sphere of Hegel's system but an analysis of the presence of the anthropology within this sphere.

3. A principal reason for this is that in Hegel's analyses of the "Knowledge of God" and the cultus, he moves back and forth between conscious and predominantly preconscious levels.

4. Peperzak 1987b, 87–88.

5. As Jaeschke states, "the manuscript [for the lectures on the philosophy of religion] too deems adequate knowledge of the truth to be achieved only when I have in the absolute content 'the consciousness of the concept.' Only then do I have truth '*as* truth *in the form* of truth—in the form of the absolutely concrete and of that which harmonizes within itself purely and simply.' And according to the manuscript too, this knowledge belongs no longer to religion but to philosophy [*VPR* 1:159]" (1990, 228; see also 231–33). For a bibliographical overview of the debates about the relation between religion and philosophy in Hegel, which began almost immediately following his death, see Hodgson 1985, 118–21.

6. "God is essentially spirit, is [God] as knowing [spirit]" (*VPR* 1:279 n.). See also *VPR* 3:179.

7. 1990, 302.

8. The consequences of this approach to the logic—largely influenced by interpreters such as Robert Pippin and Terry Pinkard—for the reading of Hegel's philosophy of religion exceed what can be examined in the present context. I hope to return to this project in the near future.

9. This is simultaneously an examination of spirit itself, precisely because it examines spirit seeking to grasp itself.

10. See *VPR* 1:86, 277.

11. See also Hegel's focus on the subsisting rather than the emerging church (*VPR* 3:256).

12. In another of the transcriptions of the lecture, the final phrase reads "the good and the rational."

13. Passages such as *PR* § 147 make particularly evident the crucial role of religion in inculcating ethical habits.

14. See *VG* 59–60/52, 122/103, discussed in chapter 6. By contrast, *VG* 67/58 uses language more closely resembling that of the *VPR*.

15. This role for the church neither competes with nor replaces the family in this process. Rather, the two work together, as when parents bring their children into a religious tradition by bringing them up in a church.

16. Hegel also discusses this point extensively in the *Philosophy of Right* and the corresponding lectures. See in particular *PR* § 270 A; *Rph II* § 76; *Rph III*, 216.

17. See *PR* § 270 A.

18. Notwithstanding the power and contemporary relevance of Hegel's treatment of the relation between the church and state, to examine adequately Hegel's treatment of this point would take us well beyond the scope of the present discussion.

19. See also *PR* §§ 247, 247 A; *Rph V*, 487–88.

20. This moment of the anthropology is also expressed by the consummate religion itself in the account of "Knowledge, Estrangement, and Evil" (*VPR* 3:228–33). This is the moment immediately before reconciliation, in which the cleavage within the self is raised to its extreme: "These are the highest, most abstract moments of all; here the antithesis is at its height, and both sides embrace the antithesis in its most complete universality" (*VPR* 3:232). This is the absolutizing of the internal differentiation effected by self-consciousness. It is defined precisely by the overcoming of one's naturalness. Thus, "One can say: Since I am a natural human being I have, on the one hand, consciousness of myself. But on the other hand my natural being [*Natürlichkeit*] consists rather in a lack of consciousness with regard to myself, in being without a will. I am the sort of being that acts according to nature, and in this respect I am innocent, it is often said, having no consciousness of what I do, being without a will of my own, acting without inclination, allowing myself to be surprised by instinct." This is a precise description of a stage that precedes consciousness, precisely the stage that Hegel treats in his "Anthropology." Hegel continues: "But here, in the antithesis that we have observed, the innocence disappears, for precisely the natural being of humanity, lacking in consciousness and will, is what ought not to be" (*VPR* 3:230). I am now aware that I am more than an animal immersed in nature, and this is what makes evil possible. This moment of evil and estrangement parallels the absolutizing of subjectivity or self-consciousness and consequent rejection of duty portrayed at the end of morality in objective spirit (*PR* §§ 140, 140 A).

21. See, for instance, Hegel's discussion of the relationship between thought and representation in *VPR* 1:299–301.

22. Hegel begins with what he calls immediate knowledge. Here, the individual possesses an apparently immediate certainty of the existence of God. While Hegel takes Friedrich Jacobi as the preeminent exemplar of this conception of religion, much that

Hegel here argues applies to virtually any religious conception that appeals to immediacy as the defining quality of religion. He does not so much challenge this knowledge as wrong but rather undermines its claim to immediacy and to providing justification. Linking this mode to the term "faith," he maintains that it comes about only on the basis of "authority, the fact that others—those who matter to me, those whom I revere and in whom I have confidence that they know what is true—believe it, that they are in possession of this knowledge" (*VPR* 1:285). Such faith therefore constitutes a kind of habit that is taken on preconsciously, typically in the context of being raised in a community. While this mode of consciousness is limited and can appear to be in tension with thinking, it is not a dead end. Rather, it develops into what Hegel sees as the higher levels of consciousness that lead to thinking.

23. See *VPR* 1:286. Although Hegel does not here, as in theoretical spirit and as in the 1821 manuscript for lectures on religion, begin with intuition, the analysis of feeling shares defining features with intuition. Further, although Hegel portrays the entire development as a development of consciousness (*VPR* 1:277–78), his treatment of this development in "The Knowledge of God" differs somewhat from that provided in theoretical spirit, in part because his analysis here actually moves back and forth between forms of cognition that incorporate consciousness and thus belong to theoretical spirit and preconscious relations that correspond more closely to a habitual relationship than to theoretical spirit itself. This preconscious level appears most significantly in the discussion of feeling; see *VPR* 1:286–87, especially the variant reading in the note on 286, which makes explicit reference to habit [*Gewohnheit*]. (The English translation by Brown, Hodgson, and Stewart here renders "*Sitte, Gewohnheit*" as "custom and usage.")

24. In this and similar passages, Hegel seems satisfied for the majority of humanity to remain at this level of cognition. (See also *VPR* 1:88, 3:268.) Insofar as complete freedom requires the attainment of thinking—since this is integral to the complete self-actualization intrinsic to Hegel's account of freedom—he appears again to settle for a situation that falls short of the requirements of his conception of freedom. Nonetheless, whereas the *Philosophy of Right* incorporated this inequality into the institutions of the state, this inequality is not integral to the larger conception of the philosophy of religion.

25. Moreover, nowhere in the 1827 lectures does Hegel make explicit what drives the transition from the theoretical to the cultus; the practical simply appears as another aspect of the relation that has not yet been considered, but it does not develop immanently from the analysis up until this point. The situation therefore appears similar to the culmination of theoretical spirit in the *Encyclopaedia*, which in turn suggests the relevance of the analysis in the *Vorlesungen über die Philosophie des Geistes*.

26. See "Concluding Reflections on the Relation of Theoretical and Practical Spirit" in chapter 4.

27. These three stages of reconciliation seem roughly to reflect Hegel's understanding of the dominant Christian strategies from Jesus' death until Constantine, from Constantine until Luther, and from Luther to the present. Since Hegel views Lutheran Protestantism as the consummate religion, he is here less concerned with

other developments in Christianity since Luther's time. For a concise summary of the three stages, see *VPR* 3:265.

28. 1970, 403.

29. See, for instance, *VPR* 1:293–96, 3:224–28.

30. Whether this strategy would ultimately undermine these practices and/or transform them beyond recognition is an important question that I leave open at this point.

31. See *VPR* 3:256, 258, cited above. See also Fackenheim 1967, 21.

32. See *PR* § 270 A.

33. Further exploration of Hegel's philosophy of religion thus requires, among other tasks, investigating and judging the success of Hegel's attempt to interpret Protestantism in these terms in "The Consummate Religion."

# Selected Bibliography

Adorno, Theodor W. 1993. *Hegel: Three Studies*. Translated by Shierry Weber Nicholsen. Cambridge, MA: MIT Press.

Anderson, Joel. 2001. "Hegel's Implicit View on How to Solve the Problem of Poverty: The Responsible Consumer and the Return of the Ethical to Civil Society." In *Beyond Liberalism and Communitarianism: Studies in Hegel's "Philosophy of Right,"* edited by R. R. Williams, 185–205. Albany: State University of New York Press.

Aristotle. 1985. *Nicomachean Ethics*. Translated by Terence Irwin. Indianapolis: Hackett. Cited in text as *NE*.

Avineri, Shlomo. 1972. *Hegel's Theory of the Modern State*. Cambridge: Cambridge University Press.

Beiser, Frederick C., ed. 1993. *The Cambridge Companion to Hegel*. Cambridge: Cambridge University Press.

Benhabib, Seyla. 1992. *Situating the Self: Gender, Community, and Postmodernism in Contemporary Ethics*. New York: Routledge.

Bernasconi, Robert. 1998. "Hegel at the Court of Ashanti." In *Hegel After Derrida*, edited by S. Barnett, 41–63. New York: Routledge.

Bernstein, Richard J. 1971. *Praxis and Action: Contemporary Philosophies of Human Activity*. Philadelphia: University of Pennsylvania Press.

Bloch, Ernst. 1962. *Subjekt–Objekt: Erläuterungen zu Hegel*. Enlarged ed. Frankfurt am Main: Suhrkamp.

Brandom, Robert B. 2002. *Tales of the Mighty Dead: Historical Essays in the Metaphysics of Intentionality*. Cambridge, MA: Harvard University Press.

Burbidge, John W. 1981. *On Hegel's Logic: Fragments of a Commentary*. Atlantic Highlands, NJ: Humanities Press.

Crites, Stephen. 1998. *Dialectic and Gospel in the Development of Hegel's Thinking*. University Park: Pennsylvania State University Press.

Dallmayr, Fred R. 1993. *G. W. F. Hegel: Modernity and Politics*. Newbury Park and London: Sage Publications.

deVries, Willem A. 1988. *Hegel's Theory of Mental Activity: An Introduction to Theoretical Spirit*. Ithaca, NY: Cornell University Press.

Dickey, Laurence. 1987. *Hegel: Religion, Economics, and the Politics of Spirit, 1770–1807*. Cambridge: Cambridge University Press.

Drüe, Hermann. 1976. *Psychologie aus dem Begriff: Hegels Persönlichkeitstheorie.* Berlin and New York: Walter de Gruyter.

Düsing, Edith. 1991. "Zum Verhältnis von Intelligenz und Wille bei Fichte und Hegel." In *Psychologie und Anthropologie, oder Philosophie des Geistes: Beiträge zu einer Hegel-Tagung in Marburg 1989,* edited by F. Hespe and B. Tuschling, 107–33. Stuttgart-Bad Cannstatt: Frommann-Holzboog.

Düsing, Klaus. 1976. *Das Problem der Subjektivität in Hegels Logik: Systematische und entwicklungsgeschichtliche Untersuchungen zum Prinzip des Idealismus und zur Dialektik.* Beiheft 15, *Hegel-Studien.* Bonn: Bouvier.

———. 1979. "Hegels Begriff der Subjektivität in der Logik und in der Philosophie des subjektiven Geistes." *Hegel-Studien* 19:201–14.

Dussel, Enrique. 1996. *The Underside of Modernity: Apel, Ricoeur, Rorty, Taylor, and the Philosophy of Liberation.* Translated by Eduardo Mendieta. Atlantic Highlands, NJ: Humanities Press.

Eley, Lothar, ed. 1990. *Hegels Theorie des subjektiven Geistes.* Stuttgart-Bad Cannstatt: Frommann-Holzboog.

Ellacuría, Ignacio. 1976. "La historización del concepto de propiedad como principio de desideologización." *Estudios Centroamericanos* 335/336 (September–October): 425–50.

Erdmann, J. E. 1840. *Grundriss der Psychologie.* Leipzig.

Fackenheim, Emil L. 1967. *The Religious Dimension in Hegel's Thought.* Bloomington: Indiana University Press.

Ferrarin, Alfredo. 2001. *Hegel and Aristotle.* Cambridge: Cambridge University Press.

Fetscher, Iring. 1970. *Hegels Lehre vom Menschen: Kommentar zu den §§ 387 bis 482 der "Enzyklopädie der philosophischen Wissenschaften."* Stuttgart-Bad Cannstatt: Friedrich Frommann Verlag.

Franco, Paul. 1999. *Hegel's Philosophy of Freedom.* New Haven, CT: Yale University Press.

Frazer, Elizabeth, and Nicola Lacey. 1993. *The Politics of Community: A Feminist Critique of the Liberal-Communitarian Debate.* Toronto: University of Toronto.

Fulda, Hans Friedrich. 1968. *Das Recht der Philosophie in Hegels Philosophie des Rechts.* Frankfurt am Main: Vittorio Klostermann.

Gadamer, Hans-Georg. 1976. *Hegel's Dialectic: Five Hermeneutical Studies.* Translated by P. Christopher Smith. New Haven, CT: Yale University Press.

Grégoire, Franz. 1958. *Études hégéliennes: Les points capitaux du système.* Louvain: Publications Universitaires de Louvain.

Habermas, Jürgen. 1973. *Theory and Practice.* Translated by John Viertel. Boston: Beacon Press.

Hampshire, Stuart. 1989. *Innocence and Experience.* Cambridge, MA: Harvard University Press.

Hardimon, Michael O. 1994. *Hegel's Social Philosophy: The Project of Reconciliation.* Cambridge: Cambridge University Press.

Hartmann, Nicolai. 1957. "Aristoteles und Hegel." In *Kleinere Schriften,* vol. 2, 214–52. Berlin: Walter de Gruyter.

Hauerwas, Stanley. 1981. *A Community of Character: Toward a Constructive Christian Social Ethic.* Notre Dame, IN: University of Notre Dame Press.

Heidegger, Martin. 1962. *Being and Time.* Translated by John Macquarrie and Edward Robinson. New York: Harper and Row.

Henrich, Dieter, ed. 1979. *Hegels philosophische Psychologie.* Beiheft 19, *Hegel-Studien.* Bonn: Bouvier.

———. 1983. "Einleitung des Herausgebers: Vernunft in Verwirklichung." In *Philosophie des Rechts: Die Vorlesung von 1819/20 in einer Nachschrift,* edited by D. Henrich. Frankfurt am Main: Suhrkamp.

Hespe, Franz, and Burkhard Tuschling, eds. 1991. *Psychologie und Anthropologie, oder Philosophie des Geistes: Beiträge zu einer Hegel-Tagung in Marburg 1989.* Stuttgart-Bad Cannstatt: Frommann-Holzboog.

Hodgson, Peter C. 1985. "Georg Wilhelm Friedrich Hegel." In *Nineteenth Century Religious Thought in the West,* edited by N. Smart, J. Clayton, S. Katz, and P. Sherry, vol. 1, 81–121. Cambridge: Cambridge University Press.

———. 1987. Editorial introduction to *Hegel's Lectures on the Philosophy of Religion.* Vol. 2, *Determinate Religion,* edited by P. C. Hodgson. Berkeley and Los Angeles: University of California Press.

———. 1988. Editorial introduction to *Hegel's Lectures on the Philosophy of Religion: One-Volume Edition, The Lectures of 1827,* edited by P. C. Hodgson. Berkeley and Los Angeles: University of California Press.

Horstmann, Rolf-Peter. 1974. "Ist Hegels Rechtsphilosophie das Produkt der politischen Anpassung eines Liberalen?" *Hegel-Studien* 9:241–52.

———. 1976. Review of *G. W. F. Hegel: Vorlesungen über Rechtsphilosophie 1818–1831,* vols. 2–4, edited by Karl-Heinz Ilting. *Hegel-Studien* 11:273–77.

———. 1984. *Ontologie und Relationen: Hegel, Bradley, Russell und die Kontroverse über interne und externe Beziehungen.* Königstein/Tg.: Athenäum.

Hösle, Vittorio. 1987. *Hegels System.* Vol. 2, *Philosophie der Natur und des Geistes.* Hamburg: Felix Meiner Verlag.

Ilting, Karl-Heinz. 1973. "Einleitung: Die 'Rechtsphilosophie' von 1820 und Hegels Vorlesungen über Rechtsphilosophie." In *G. W. F. Hegel: Vorlesungen über Rechtsphilosophie: 1818–1831,* edited by K.-H. Ilting, vol. 1, 23–126. Stuttgart-Bad Cannstatt: Frommann-Holzboog.

———. 1974. "Einleitung des Herausgebers: Der exoterische und der esoterische Hegel (1824–1831)." In *G. W. F. Hegel: Vorlesungen über Rechtsphilosophie: 1818–1831,* edited by K.-H. Ilting, vol. 4, 45–66. Stuttgart-Bad Cannstatt: Frommann-Holzboog,

Inwood, Michael, ed. 1985. *Hegel.* Oxford: Oxford University Press.

Inwood, Michael. 1992. *A Hegel Dictionary.* Oxford; Cambridge, MA: Blackwell.

Jaeschke, Walter. 1990. *Reason in Religion: The Foundations of Hegel's Philosophy of Religion.* Translated by Michael J. Stewart and Peter C. Hodgson. Berkeley and Los Angeles: University of California Press.

Kant, Immanuel. 1964. *Groundwork of the Metaphysics of Morals*. Translated by H. J. Paton. New York: Harper Torchbooks.

Kelly, George Armstrong. 1972. "Notes on Hegel's 'Lordship and Bondage.'" In *Hegel: A Collection of Critical Essays*, edited by A. MacIntyre, 189–217. Garden City, NY: Doubleday, Anchor Books.

Kierkegaard, Søren. 1980. *The Sickness Unto Death: A Christian Psychological Exposition for Upbuilding and Awakening*. Translated by Howard V. Hong and Edna H. Hong. Princeton, NJ: Princeton University Press.

———. 1983. *Fear and Trembling, Repetition*. Translated by Howard V. Hong and Edna H. Hong. Princeton, NJ: Princeton University Press.

Knowles, Dudley. 2002. *Hegel and the "Philosophy of Right."* London: Routledge.

Kojève, Alexandre. 1969. *Introduction to the Reading of Hegel*. Translated by James H. Nichols, Jr. New York: Basic Books.

Kolb, David. 1986. *The Critique of Pure Modernity: Hegel, Heidegger, and After*. Chicago: University of Chicago Press.

Lakoff, George. 1987. *Women, Fire, and Dangerous Things: What Categories Reveal about the Mind*. Chicago: University of Chicago Press.

Lamb, David, ed. 1987. *Hegel and Modern Philosophy*. London: Croom Helm.

Lewis, Thomas A. 2002. Review of *Hegel's Philosophy of Freedom*, by Paul Franco. *Hegel-Studien* 37:269–74.

Lobkowicz, Nicholas. 1967. *Theory and Practice: History of a Concept from Aristotle to Marx*. Notre Dame, IN: University of Notre Dame Press.

MacIntyre, Alasdair, ed. 1972a. *Hegel: A Collection of Critical Essays*. Garden City, NY: Doubleday, Anchor Books.

———. 1972b. "Hegel on Faces and Skulls." In MacIntyre 1972a, 219–36.

———. 1984. *After Virtue: A Study in Moral Theory*. 2d ed. Notre Dame, IN: University of Notre Dame Press.

———. 1988. *Whose Justice? Which Rationality?* Notre Dame, IN: University of Notre Dame Press.

Marcuse, Herbert. 1960. *Reason and Revolution: Hegel and the Rise of Social Theory*. Boston: Beacon Press.

Marx, Karl. 1978. "Economic and Philosophic Manuscripts of 1844." In *The Marx-Engels Reader*, edited by R. C. Tucker, 66–125. New York: W. W. Norton.

McCumber, John. 1990. "Hegel on Habit." *Owl of Minerva* 21 (2):155–65.

Min, Anselm Kyongsuk. 1989. *Dialectic of Salvation: Issues in Theology of Liberation*. Albany: State University of New York Press.

Mulhall, Stephen, and Adam Swift. 1992. *Liberals and Communitarians*. Oxford: Blackwell.

Neuhouser, Frederick. 2000. *Foundations of Hegel's Social Theory: Actualizing Freedom*. Cambridge, MA: Harvard University Press.

Nussbaum, Martha C. 1990. *Love's Knowledge: Essays on Philosophy and Literature*. Oxford: Oxford University Press.

Okin, Susan Moller. 1994. "Political Liberalism, Justice, and Gender." *Ethics* 105 (1): 23–43.

O'Regan, Cyril. 1992. "Hegelian Philosophy of Religion and Eckhartian Mysticism." In *New Perspectives on Hegel's Philosophy of Religion*, edited by D. Kolb, 109–29. Albany: State University of New York Press.

———. 1994. *The Heterodox Hegel*. Albany: State University of New York Press.

Patten, Alan. 1999. *Hegel's Idea of Freedom*. Oxford: Oxford University Press.

Pelczynski, Z. A. 1971a. "The Hegelian Conception of the State." In *Hegel's Political Philosophy: Problems and Perspectives*, edited by Z. A. Pelczynski, 1–29. Cambridge: Cambridge University Press.

———, ed. 1971b. *Hegel's Political Philosophy: Problems and Perspectives*. Cambridge: Cambridge University Press.

Peperzak, Adriaan. 1987a. *Philosophy and Politics: A Commentary on the Preface to Hegel's "Philosophy of Right."* Dordrecht: Martinus Nijhoff.

———. 1987b. *Selbsterkenntnis des Absoluten: Grundlinien der Hegelschen Philosophie des Geistes*. Stuttgart-Bad Cannstatt: Frommann-Holzboog.

———. 1991. *Hegels praktische Philosophie: Ein Kommentar zur enzyklopädischen Darstellung der menschlichen Freiheit und ihrer objektiven Verwirklichung*. Stuttgart-Bad Cannstatt: Frommann-Holzboog.

———. 2001. *Modern Freedom: Hegel's Legal, Moral, and Political Philosophy*. Boston: Kluwer.

Petry, Michael J. 1981. Introduction to *The Berlin Phenomenology*, by G. W. F. Hegel. Translated by Michael J. Petry. Bilingual ed. Dordrecht: Reidel.

Pinkard, Terry. 1985. "The Logic of Hegel's *Logic*." In *Hegel*, edited by M. Inwood, 85–109. Oxford: Oxford University Press.

———. 1994. *Hegel's Phenomenology: The Sociality of Reason*. Cambridge: Cambridge University Press.

———. 2000. *Hegel: A Biography*. Cambridge: Cambridge University Press.

Pippin, Robert B. 1989. *Hegel's Idealism: The Satisfactions of Self-Consciousness*. Cambridge: Cambridge University Press.

———. 1991. *Modernism as a Philosophical Problem: On the Dissatisfactions of European High Culture*. Cambridge, MA: Basil Blackwell.

———. 1997. *Idealism as Modernism: Hegelian Variations*. Cambridge: Cambridge University Press.

Planty-Bonjour, Guy. 1983. "Hegel's Concept of Action as Unity of Poiesis and Praxis." In *Hegel's Philosophy of Action*, edited by L. S. Stepelvich and D. Lamb, 19–29. Atlantic Highlands, NJ: Humanities Press.

Popper, Karl. 1966. *The Open Society and Its Enemies*. Vol. 2, *The Hightide of Prophecy: Hegel, Marx, and the Aftermath*. London: Routledge, Kegan & Paul.

Rawls, John. 1971. *A Theory of Justice*. Cambridge, MA: Harvard University Press.

———. 1993. *Political Liberalism*. New York: Columbia University Press.

Redding, Paul. 1996. *Hegel's Hermeneutics*. Ithaca, NY: Cornell University Press.

Reyburn, Hugh A. 1921. *The Ethical Theory of Hegel: A Study of the Philosophy of Right.* Oxford: Clarendon Press.

Riedel, Manfred. 1984. *Between Tradition and Revolution: The Hegelian Transformation of Political Philosophy.* Translated by Walter Wright. Cambridge: Cambridge University Press.

Ritter, Joachim. 1965. *Hegel und die französische Revolution.* Frankfurt am Main: Suhrkamp.

———. 1982. *Hegel and the French Revolution: Essays on the Philosophy of Right.* Translated by Richard Dien Winfield. Cambridge, MA: MIT Press.

Rorty, Richard. 1991. "The Priority of Democracy to Philosophy." In *Objectivity, Relativism, and Truth: Philosophical Papers Volume 1*, 175–96. Cambridge: Cambridge University Press.

Rosenkranz, Karl. 1837. *Psychologie oder Wissenschaft vom subjektiven Geist.* Königsberg.

Sandel, Michael J. 1982. *Liberalism and the Limits of Justice.* Cambridge: Cambridge University Press.

Sayers, Sean. 1987. "The Actual and the Rational." In *Hegel and Modern Philosophy*, edited by D. Lamb, 143–60. London: Croom Helm.

Schacht, Richard. 1972. "Hegel on Freedom." In *Hegel: A Collection of Critical Essays*, edited by A. MacIntyre, 289–328. Garden City, NY: Doubleday, Anchor Books.

Shanks, Andrew. 1991. *Hegel's Political Theology.* Cambridge: Cambridge University Press.

Siep, Ludwig. 1979. *Anerkennung als Prinzip der praktischen Philosophie: Untersuchung zu Hegels Jenaer Philosophie des Geistes.* Freiburg: Alber Verlag.

Smith, Steven B. 1989. *Hegel's Critique of Liberalism: Rights in Context.* Chicago: University of Chicago Press.

Stederoth, Dirk. 2001. *Hegels Philosophie des subjektiven Geistes: Ein komparatorischer Kommentar.* Berlin: Akademie Verlag.

Steinberger, Peter J. 1988. *Logic and Politics: Hegel's Philosophy of Right.* New Haven, CT: Yale University Press.

Stepelvich, Lawrence S., and David Lamb, eds. 1983. *Hegel's Philosophy of Action.* Atlantic Highlands, NJ: Humanities Press.

Stout, Jeffrey. 1994. "The Rhetoric of Revolution: Comparative Ethics after Kuhn and Gunnemann." In *Religion and Practical Reason: New Essays in the Comparative Philosophy of Religions*, edited by F. E. Reynolds and D. Tracy, 329–62. Albany: State University of New York Press.

Taylor, Charles. 1975. *Hegel.* Cambridge: Cambridge University Press.

———. 1979. *Hegel and Modern Society.* Cambridge: Cambridge University Press.

———. 1985a. *Human Agency and Language: Philosophical Papers 1.* Cambridge: Cambridge University Press.

———. 1985b. *Philosophy and the Human Sciences: Philosophical Papers 2.* Cambridge: Cambridge University Press.

———. 1989. *Sources of the Self: The Making of the Modern Identity.* Cambridge, MA: Harvard University Press.

———. 1995. "Cross-Purposes: The Liberal-Communitarian Debate." In *Philosophical Arguments*, 181–203. Cambridge, MA: Harvard University Press.

Taylor, Mark C. 1980. *Journeys to Selfhood: Hegel and Kierkegaard*. Berkeley and Los Angeles: University of California Press.

Theunissen, Michael. 1970. *Hegels Lehre vom absoluten Geist als theologisch-politischer Traktat*. Berlin: Walter de Gruyter.

———. 1978. *Sein und Schein: Die kritische Funktion der Hegelschen Logik*. Frankfurt am Main: Suhrkamp.

Toews, John Edward. 1980. *Hegelianism: The Path toward Dialectical Humanism, 1805–1841*. Cambridge: Cambridge University Press.

Tunick, Mark. 1992. *Hegel's Political Philosophy: Interpreting the Practice of Legal Punishment*. Princeton, NJ: Princeton University Press.

———. 1994. "Hegel's Nonfoundationalism: A Phenomenological Account of the Structure of the Philosophy of Right." *History of Philosophy Quarterly* 11 (3):317–37.

———. 1998. "Hegel on Justified Disobedience." *Political Theory* 26 (4):514–35.

Tuschling, Burkhard. 1994. Editorial introduction to *Vorlesungen über die Philosophie des Geistes*. Edited by F. Hespe and B. Tuschling. Vorlesungen, vol. 13. Hamburg: Felix Meiner Verlag.

Waszek, Norbert. 1984. "Hegels Schottische Bettler." *Hegel-Studien* 19:311–16.

Westphal, Merold. 1992. *Hegel, Freedom, and Modernity*. Albany: State University of New York Press.

———. 2000. "Hegel and Onto-Theology." *Bulletin of the Hegel Society of Great Britain* 41/42:142–65.

Williams, Robert R. 1992. *Recognition: Fichte and Hegel on the Other*. Albany: State University of New York Press.

———. 1997. *Hegel's Ethics of Recognition*. Berkeley and Los Angeles: University of California Press.

Williams, Robert R., ed. 2001. *Beyond Liberalism and Communitarianism: Studies in Hegel's "Philosophy of Right."* Albany: State University of New York Press.

Wood, Allen W. 1990. *Hegel's Ethical Thought*. Cambridge: Cambridge University Press.

Yearley, Lee H. 1990. *Mencius and Aquinas: Theories of Virtue and Conceptions of Courage*. Albany: State University of New York Press.

# Index

Aristotle (*cont.*)
    on praxis, 121–22, 130–31, 219nn.12, 13,
        220nn.14, 16
    on theoria, 121–22, 219nn.12, 13, 15
art, 4, 5, 22, 37, 39, 89, 143
    and intuition (*Anschauung*), 83, 189
    vs. religion, 188, 189, 193
authority of tradition, 17, 20, 21, 187–88,
    192–94, 196, 198, 230n.22
Avineri, Shlomo, 7, 209n.25, 218n.1, 219n.6,
    221n.36, 226n.4
    on civil society, 14, 15, 167–68, 173, 176,
        183
    on differentiation, 14, 15, 167–68, 182,
        183

Benhabib, Seyla, 53, 208n.17
Bernasconi, Robert, 212n.1
Bloch, Ernst, 210n.20
body, the, 62, 67
Bultmann, Rudolf, 214n.8

choice. *See* arbitrary will (*Willkür*); free
    will
Christianity
    as consummate religion, 188, 189, 199,
        200, 202–3, 231n.27, 232n.33
    and the cultus, 125, 132
    and freedom, 110–11, 125–26
    Lutheranism, 143, 188, 231n.27
    Mennonites, 194
    monasticism in, 6, 201
    Protestantism, 17, 143, 188, 199,
        209n.28, 229n.2, 231n.27, 232n.33
    Quakers, 194
    reconciliation of infinite and finite in,
        195–206, 231n.27
    *See also* religion
civil rights movement, 132–33
civil servants. *See* universal estate
civil society, 10, 12, 109, 134, 173–78
    Avineri on, 14, 15, 167–68, 173, 176, 183

collaboration in, 174–76
conformism in, 174
corporations in, 175, 182, 226n.16,
    227n.29, 228n.37
economic life in, 168–69, 177–78,
    225n.1
egoism in, 167–68, 174, 175–76, 181,
    227n.31, 228n.37
vs. the family, 14, 171, 172, 173, 179, 180,
    223n.15
poverty in, 14, 15, 73, 168–69, 176–78,
    184, 227n.34, 228nn.36, 37
and reflective principle, 169
relationship to self-consciousness,
    64–65, 67, 71, 73–74, 164, 173–74,
    181–82, 195, 204, 214nn.7, 8, 215n.18
relationship to the state, 14–15, 19, 164,
    167–69, 175, 179, 182, 183, 227n.29,
    228n.37
*See also* differentiation; estates; ethical
    life (*Sittlichkeit*); family; state, the
cognition (*Erkenntnis*), 83
communitarianism, 10–11, 208nn.15, 17
consciousness
    consciousness as such, 62, 66–67, 76,
        84
    of freedom, 1, 12, 39, 48, 56–57, 72–73,
        107–8, 109, 110, 137–38, 180, 184
    *See also* self-consciousness
contingency, 31–33, 117, 118, 119, 170, 197,
    199, 219n.6

death, 33
desire, satisfaction of, 100–105, 122, 133,
    149–50, 153, 168, 174
    and self-consciousness, 67–68, 69, 71,
        215n.14
determination
    by habit, 47–48, 54–59, 137–46, 171
    by natural forces, 2, 47–56, 58, 71,
        139–40, 142, 143–44, 168, 170, 171,
        172–73, 212n.1, 223n.16, 230n.20

## THOMAS A. LEWIS

is assistant professor in the Committee on the Study of Religion and the Divinity School at Harvard University.